The Sisterhood

The Sisterhood

Inside the Lives of Mormon Women

Dorothy Allred Solomon

THE SISTERHOOD
Copyright © Dorothy Allred Solomon, 2007.
All rights reserved.

First published in hardcover in 2007 by PALGRAVE MACMILLAN® in the
US–a division of St. Martin's Press LLC, 175 Fifth Avenue, New York, NY
10010.

Where this book is distributed in the UK, Europe and the rest of the world,
this is by Palgrave Macmillan, a division of Macmillan Publishers Limited,
registered in England, company number 785998, of Houndmills, Basingstoke,
Hampshire RG21 6XS.

Palgrave Macmillan is the global academic imprint of the above companies
and has companies and representatives throughout the world.

Palgrave® and Macmillan® are registered trademarks in the United States,
the United Kingdom, Europe and other countries.

ISBN-13: 978-0-230-60786-6
ISBN-10: 0-230-60786-1

Library of Congress Cataloging-in-Publication Data
Solomon, Dorothy Allred.
    The sisterhood : inside the lives of Mormon women / by Dorothy Allred
Solomon.
        p.   cm.
    Includes bibliographical references and index.
    ISBN 1-4039-8278-3 (alk. paper)
    ISBN 0-230-60786-1 (paperback)
    1. Mormon women.   2. Marriage—Religious aspects—Mormon Church.
I. Title.
BX8641.S64   2007
289.3082—dc22

2007005359

A catalogue record of the book is available from the British Library.

Design by Letra Libre

First PALGRAVE MACMILLAN paperback edition: October 2008
10 9 8 7 6 5 4 3 2 1
Printed in the United States of America.

I dedicate this book to the women in my life: my own dear mother, Mabel Finlayson Allred, her twin and sister-wife, my Aunt Melba, and my father's other plural wives who were the "mothers" in my family. I make tribute to my grandmothers, Etta Josephine Hanson Finlayson and Mary Evelyn Clark Allred. I have written this as a letter to my daughters, Denise Andreianne Solomon Gibson Sanchez, Layla Janelle Solomon Hardy, Laurissa Jeanne Solomon Reese, and Jennifer Leavitt Solomon and for my granddaughters, Jenna Christine Gibson and Cassaundra Justine Gibson. I have written with love for the many sisters and sisters-in-law in my family, and for my "girlfriends" who keep me thinking, smiling, daring and dancing—all of them my sisters in Zion.

Contents

Acknowledgments   ix
Note to the Reader   xi

Chapter 1.   Introduction: As Sisters in Zion   1
Chapter 2.   For Time and All Eternity   17
Chapter 3.   A Righteous Seed   51
Chapter 4.   Call the Man   75
Chapter 5.   Love at Home   97
Chapter 6.   Charity Never Faileth   123
Chapter 7.   What Would Jesus Do?   161
Chapter 8.   The Sisterhood   193

Glossary   219
For Further Reading   227
Other Reading and Viewing   229
Notes   231
Index   239

Acknowledgments

A great outpouring of gratitude goes to Amanda Johnson Moon, the wonderful editor who initiated the idea of this book and then midwifed it into being. Thanks also to Luba Ostashervsky for her enthusiasm, editorial skill, and support. Thanks to Yasmin Mathew for carefully overseeing production. Thanks to Wendy Weil for believing in me and representing my work. I offer much gratitude to Carol Houck Smith who has consistently fed the flame of literary inspiration. Thanks also to the many women whose insight, research, and commitment to truth contributed hugely to my enlightenment and to this book. I am especially grateful to Layla Hardy for reading every word, for taking on the arduous task of indexing, and for reassuring me each time I trembled before the blank screen. I am grateful to Denise Sanchez for her stabilizing presence and her assistance with notes. Thanks also to Laurie Reese for her close reading and generous feedback. I would also like to thank Renon Hulet and Reuben Bradley for their help in compiling the glossary and Ellis Levine.

I am also grateful to the men whose lives have provided me with examples, especially my husband, Bruce Solomon, my son, Jeff Solomon, and my son-in-law, Todd Hardy, for sharing their insights and knowledge regarding men in the LDS Church. Thank you to the many women of the sisterhood who have shared their stories, their dreams, and their lives with me, especially Trudy Tracy, Jamie Blum, and my sister of the heart, Sally Smith.

Note to the Reader

It seems only fair to warn the reader that I am the twenty-eighth of forty-eight children born into a polygamous household and that my life includes experiences not typical of other Latter-day Saint women. Although I am monogamous and a member in good standing of The Church of Jesus Christ of Latter-day Saints, my parents were excommunicated from the church for living the outlawed Principle of Plural Marriage. I hope that my unusual background will bring some perspective, create some clarity, and serve the highest good of all concerned.

I have changed some names and details to protect people's privacy, while others have given me permission to use their names.

Introduction: As Sisters in Zion

As sisters in Zion we'll all work together;
The blessings of God on our labors we'll seek.
We'll build up his kingdom with earnest endeavor;
We'll comfort the weary and strengthen the weak.

The errand of angels is given to women;
And this is a gift that, as sisters, we claim:
To do whatsoever is gentle and human,
To cheer and to bless in humanity's name.

How vast is our purpose, how broad is our mission
If we but fulfill it in spirit and deed.
Oh, naught but the Spirit's divinest tuition
Can give us the wisdom to truly succeed.[1]

The Church of Jesus Christ of Latter-day Saints has been called a cult, a sham, a miracle, and the hope of a new millennium. It is also the fastest-growing American-born church in the world, with a membership of 12 million and climbing. Founded on new Scripture, it claims to be the restored Church of Jesus Christ, reestablishing lost elements of Christianity as well as truths of the Gospel that have been missing or pending since the foundation of the world. These include living prophets, the priesthood as held by Peter, James, and John, new Scriptures and religious knowledge, a bevy of spiritual gifts, and certainty about the divine nature of man and woman. The elements claimed by The Church of Jesus Christ of Latter-day Saints (whose members are officially called LDS or Latter-day Saints, and unofficially, called Mormons) create effulgence in a dark world: the light of personal revelation, the promise of eternal togetherness for family, and the full redemption of mankind, including Eve restored to her glory and wholeness, the curse of the Garden of Eden lifted.

Many outsiders regard LDS women as atavistic and pitiable, progeny of a throwback consciousness that would invalidate a century of women's rights. But long before the term "sisterhood" was yoked to women's liberation, LDS women were calling each other "sister." In fact, the poem "As Sisters in Zion" which was written in the late 1800s and has become an anthem for the sisterhood of the Latter-day Saints. Although most people believe that the women's movement passed over Utah, sisters in the nascent Church of Jesus Christ of Latter-day Saints spoke for women's rights alongside Susan B. Anthony and Elizabeth Cady Stanton. They were the second group of women in America to win the right to vote and the first group ever to cast their ballots.[2] The concept of sisterhood defined the LDS women's auxiliary known as Relief Society, which championed suffrage and sent emissaries to Washington, D.C. Just as men in the LDS Church were "Brothers in Christ," women were "Sisters in Christ" dedicated to one another's growth and well-being and to serving the community and the world.

The early practice of polygamy underscored sisterhood among women, who referred to their husbands' plural wives as "sister-wives." The political climate surrounding the early church jeopardized the holdings of Mormon patriarchs, especially polygamists, an environment requiring pioneer women to become proprietors of homes and farms and businesses and to use their talents to make a living. Sometimes the women lived in the same house or compound, and they often worked together, delivering each other's babies and raising each other's children. They started enterprises together and shared service projects and taught each other what they knew. One of the first women in Utah Territory to become a doctor, Ellis Shipp, having been advised by LDS Church President Brigham Young to leave her frontier home and family to procure a medical education in the east, was able to entrust her children to her sister-wives who raised them as if they were their own. Dr. Shipp returned to Utah to teach classes in midwifery and nursing, supporting other women in gaining an education.

The support available in plural marriages may have some appeal but the problems with that way of life outweighed the advantages. The Church of Jesus Christ abolished the practice of the Principle of Plural Marriage in 1890, and began excommunicating polygamists. Over the years all guise of legitimacy has vanished and surviving polygamous cultures are susceptible to the abuses of any outlaw community. Women and children suffer from the secrecy of the lifestyle and from the proprietary relationship polygamous patriarchs tend to have with their families. But whenever they make the most of their sisterhood, women can find unity, support, and cheer that some present-day nuclear families do not enjoy.

In the modern LDS Church where monogamy is the way of life, sisterhood remains strong. In most instances, women work together to insure each other's well-being, meeting the challenge of Lucy Mack Smith, mother of the LDS Prophet Joseph Smith, when she spoke at one of the first Relief Society meetings, urging the sisterhood to "cherish one another, watch over one another, comfort one another and gain instruction that we may all sit down in heaven together."[3] Church leaders emphasize family harmony over personal desire while at the same time encouraging women to progress. Women can regard their situation as liberation or suppression or both. LDS women who stay at home with their children often have college diplomas and prodigious talent, but they usually postpone the exercise of their worldly contributions until the children are grown. Within their culture, these stay-at-home LDS wives don't get dismissed as "just homemakers" but stand as honored mothers and goddesses of the hearth, freed of many cares in this materialistic world. The biggest risks of the arrangement are that the homemaker's life can be confining, and that modern LDS women tend to define themselves through their husbands. But it wasn't always so: In the early church, women organized a

Theosophists Society, exercised spiritual gifts, and asserted their rights before the United States Congress. This shift in women's empowerment raises questions for some: Why don't modern LDS women consistently determine their own lives? Why do we sometimes feel that our decisions are overlooked in our homes and our voices hushed in our ward houses? Answering and remedying these questions while being true to the ways of the sisterhood promises to strike a healthier balance for all of us, including our husbands and children.

The conflict between individuality and plurality makes the LDS culture peculiar in itself, for Christian religions promote the development of the individual soul, while the group consciousness implicit in "sisterhood" and church doctrines such as the United Order and the Law of Consecration introduce a pluralistic mentality into a Christian religion. This poses a contradiction for some Christians and others steeped in western traditions of thought. LDS sisters postpone personal dreams and often sacrifice their well-being to serve others: family first, then the church and the surrounding community. Yet we sisters are generally well-grounded and happy with our lives. Personal dedication to the greater good brings the restoration full circle, combining Western and Eastern spirituality into one and introducing greater possibilities for wholeness. As we integrate the disparate parts of ourselves (right- and left-brain ways of thinking, individualism and pluralism) we find that something similar can happen between man and woman and in the larger world as well. In LDS Scripture, the Lord commands the sons and daughters of Adam and Eve: "I say unto you, be one; and if ye are not one ye are not mine."(Doctrine and Covenants 38:27)[4]

Despite its unifying influence, loyalty that is extracted under pressure can override individual worth, create imbalance, and generate hypocrisy. When we prize obedience above all else, individual capacities for decision-making, self-reliance, and personal development can suffer. However, most LDS women realize the importance of their unique contribution to the greater good, learning in their teen years that some of their most important values include divine nature, accountability, choice and individual worth. Using these values, they can complete the integration necessary to personal and universal restoration if they honor their heritage as creative beings and daughters of God.

Salt Lake City, the Zion of the Latter-day Saints, gleams with clear western sunlight in a beautiful bowl of purple-tinged mountains, the Wasatch Range of the Rockies. In the summer the mountains cool the dry heat of the desert. In the winter, their snowy caps offer mystery, adventure, and a chill reminder of eternity. At the center of the Salt Lake valley the LDS temple reaches six spires to the heavens, a golden angel trumpeting the Gospel of Jesus Christ to the world. As Wallace Stegner, who spent his teen years in Salt Lake City observes:

> "From its founding, Salt Lake City has been sanctuary: that has been its justification and its function. And it is as sanctuary that it persists even in my Gentile mind and insinuates itself as my veritable hometown."[5]

The valley continually reminds us that we are here at the Lord's discretion, that as Latter-day Saints, we must be as humble in our opinions of ourselves as the valley floor, a slate as blank as the Salt Flats on which God may inscribe His purpose. And yet the mountains speak of stature, reminding us that we can cultivate "men to match my mountains,"[6] that we can provide, as Stegner said, "a society to match the scenery."[7]

Indeed, lofty standards can complicate the lives of women, who take major responsibility for teaching life skills to their families. The sky literally is the limit, for we take to heart Jesus' admonition in Matthew 5:48: "Be ye therefore perfect, even as your Father which is in heaven is perfect." Men and women are promised that through faithfulness to the Gospel, they can become creators in their own right. LDS doctrine promotes the belief that "as man is, God once was, and as God is, man [and woman] may become."[8] In believing that we are fashioned from the genetic blueprint of divine parents, we also believe that perfection can be attained. This guarantees frustration, given that we are all at one stage or another of learning. Church authorities apply the standard of perfection in various ways. A bishop or stake president, while interviewing a member to determine if they are worthy to enter the LDS temple can deny an individual a temple "recommend" (recommendation) for such misdemeanors as drinking champagne at a celebration or skipping church meetings. A bishop can also see a couple struggling, a family striving to stay together, and support the individuals with forgiveness, faith, and tenderness.

LDS women in every situation—married or not, with or without children—are more likely to remain faithful to their religious beliefs than are LDS men. The values upheld by the church often coincide with what matters to us: We want a forum for men to empower each other in upstanding behavior; we want family to be of central importance; we want respect for physical health (as represented by the Law of Chastity and the Word of Wisdom); and we love the idea of eternal marriage.

Ironically, given that the church once practiced and then outlawed polygamy, monogamy enjoys greatest health among LDS people. Compared to other couples in the United States, LDS couples who marry in the temple have a very low divorce rate.[9] Although even highly committed, eternal marriages sag beneath the weight of contradictions and attendant miseries, eternal commitment seems to serve women well. Whether our men stand beside us or have divorced or died on us, most LDS women continue to participate obediently in the patriarchal design. We remain good homemakers, avid community members, and faithful daughters of God doing our best to "raise up a righteous seed unto the Lord."[10]

Whence this pure devotion, this rare dedication in our modern, cynical world? Whence this American-born religion inspiring personal revelation and harmonious congregation, reflecting the values of democratic union and personal freedom? The revered and powerful *Book of Mormon,* translated from golden plates found in the Hill Cumorah in upstate New York established Christ in ancient America and stands as foundational Scripture for The Church of Jesus Christ of Latter-day Saints, along with the Bible, the *Doctrine and Covenants,* and the *Pearl of Great Price.* Each of the new Scriptures offers additional testament to the divinity of Jesus Christ as Son of God, Messiah, and Savior of the World, supporting rather than replacing the *Holy Bible.* Because of this new Scripture, we are popularly known as Mormons and our church is inaccurately called "the Mormon Church." But in fact, The Church of Jesus Christ of Latter-day Saints bears the Savior's name and we consider ourselves earnest Christians. In fact, we believe that Jesus Christ stands at the head of His church and governs it through the Living Prophet.

The golden plates were delivered into the hands of Joseph Smith, Jr. by an angel named Moroni, who had abridged the record of his father,

Mormon, a leader among the ancient Americans. Shortly after the publication of the *Book of Mormon,* the translator, 24-year-old Joseph Smith, Jr., and five others established the Church of Jesus Christ of Latter-day Saints on April 6, 1830, in New York State. After the Prophet Joseph Smith Jr. was assassinated in 1844, chaos tore through the young church, the biggest split coming from Smith's first wife, Emma, who resisted plural marriage, and their son, Joseph Smith III, who claimed patrilineal authority.

During the regimes of Joseph Smith, Jr. and Brigham Young, the second LDS Church president, the early church adamantly defended the practice of plural marriage as a religious right protected by the U.S. Constitution. But the primarily Christian and monogamous population of America saw polygamy as immoral and plural wives as harems in a satrapy. After the U.S. legislature passed several laws to criminalize the practice of plural marriage, the government began to seize church properties and assets as well as personal property of members, and incarcerated leading church authorities. After decades of trials, imprisonment, and loss, the church relinquished the Principle of Plural Marriage, passing the Manifesto of 1890 to outlaw the practice for its members. Some people emigrated to Canada or Mexico where they could live the principle without breaking the laws of the land. In 1903 my grandfather traveled with his first wife and family to Colonia Juarez in the state of Chihuahua, Mexico, and arranged for my grandmother to meet him there, where he took her as his second wife. My father was born in nearby Colonia Dublan, the oldest living son of my grandfather's second wife. Because clandestine plural marriages were still being performed, the church passed another manifesto in 1904 to reinforce the first.

Although the Principle of Plural Marriage continues to affect LDS culture, abolishing polygamy made way for international growth of the church. The missionary program had always been strong, with LDS elders leaving homes and families (including plural families) for England and Europe or traveling throughout the United States to proselytize as directed in Doctrine and Covenants 24:18, carrying "no purse nor scrip," relying on the Holy Spirit to guide them and the goodwill of others to sustain them. As the shadow of polygamy retreated, the missionary program created exponential growth, baptizing new members in every state and from all the nations of the earth. The Church of Jesus Christ of Latter-day Saints has since influenced the moral orientation of the United States and the world.

Being a positive force in the community and the world aligns with the church's purpose to reunite the children of God. Concern for the well-being of people at home and in the far reaches of the world has motivated the LDS Church to cultivate initiatives for public welfare. Hospitals, businesses, and academies count as a few of the amazing results created by LDS people, particularly the sisterhood, in their great desire to serve their fellow beings.

In the early years of the twenty-first century, these community inclinations grow as we grow. The concern about community and world fits the doctrinal scope of The Church of Jesus Christ of Latter-day Saints, for the prophet or president of the LDS Church stands as mouthpiece and intermediary for God, speaking to all His children and watchfully caring for them. The aim of the church—to bring the Gospel of Jesus Christ to all members of the human family—involves giving people the "good news" that they have been granted salvation through the Atonement of Jesus Christ. Having taken on Christ's name through baptism, all members, male and female, child and adult, feel responsible to act as agents of Christ in serving God's purpose "to bring to pass the immortality and eternal life of man" (Moses 1:39) and to remind their brothers and sisters that we have been given the gift of life so that, as LDS Scripture tells us, "[we] might have joy" (2 Nephi 2:25).

Everyone in the church, women included, listens to the prophet and president of The Church of Jesus Christ of Latter-day Saints, who speaks on behalf of the Lord. His counselors assist him, along with twelve apostles, as in the original church founded by Jesus Christ. One of the most powerful experiences a person can have involves being in the presence of these loving and enlightened men. Even from a distance, they emanate palpable radiance.

The church is divided into regions supervised by directors, none of them women, who belong to the Council of the Seventy, counted among the general authorities of the church. The church also has a presiding bishopric to see to the members' needs, and a general Relief Society presidency, Young Men's and Young Women's general presidencies, and the general presidency for Primary, the organization for children. All these organizations, including those guided by the sisterhood, are accountable to the Twelve Apostles and the First Presidency of the LDS Church.

From there, the church is divided into stakes and branches, and wards, also governed by male hierarchy. Several wards make up a stake, and several stakes make up a region. Stakes are supervised by the stake president and his counselors and the stake high council, with auxiliary presidencies for organizations pertaining to women, young men and young women, and children. Women leaders may be invited to share in the authority of the men in charge, but they do not hold the priesthood, so they don't have ultimate decision-making power. The same is true at the ward level. Wards are governed through the bishop and his counselors. The ward Relief Society presidency, the Young Men's and Young Women's presidency, and the Primary presidency report to the bishop and are dependent on his vision and goodwill. Most bishops draw on the wisdom and knowledge of the female leaders, including the Relief Society president, who often works hand in hand with the bishopric to answer members' needs.

Some important doctrinal issues distinguish The Church of Jesus Christ of Latter-day Saints from other Christian churches. Unlike the usual doctrine of Trinity, the LDS belief purports that Father in Heaven and His Son, Jesus Christ, and the Holy Ghost are three distinct beings. The three members of the Godhead play different roles: Father in Heaven fathered all spirits of all people who have been or ever will be born on the earth, and He physically fathered His Son, Jesus Christ, through his celestialized body of flesh and bone. Lord Jesus came to fulfill the Gospel Plan and to create atonement, so He acts "at one with" or in complete accord with Heavenly Father. The Holy Ghost attends us on behalf of Heavenly Father and Jesus Christ, guiding and directing us from within. (In their desire to insinuate the presence of feminine divine into this trinity, some LDS women have suggested that the Holy Ghost might be female, but ecclesiastical authority has quashed this idea. Although Latter-day Saints acknowledge that Mother in Heaven exists, She remains a mystery.)

Another doctrinal difference has to do with perceptions of Heaven and Hell. LDS people believe that all beings are granted immortality through the Atonement of Jesus Christ. From there, we are assigned to the level of exaltation we earn through good works and obedience to the commandments and the ordinances of the Gospel. According to LDS doctrine, Heaven is made up of three degrees of glory. The Celestial Kingdom, or highest degree, allows us to live with God and our loved ones. Only through belief in Jesus Christ, repentance, and righteousness can we reach this highest level of exaltation. The second degree, the Terrestrial Kingdom, holds good people who are not valiant in following Christ, who hear the Gospel but do not testify to it. This kingdom far surpasses our earthly experience but lacks the presence of God and family in celestial glory. The third degree, the Telestial Kingdom, includes murderers, adulterers, and others who refuse redemption and reject the Gospel of Jesus Christ until they suffer for their sins and finally accept His atonement. Those who enter this lowest degree of glory, which is still superior to earthly life, have not openly fought against Christ.

According to Doctrine and Covenants 101:90–91, the "wicked, unfaithful and unjust stewards" are candidates for "outer darkness" a place of "weeping and wailing and gnashing of teeth" where they will receive "their portion among hypocrites and unbelievers." There are few candidates for the Hell known as Perdition, where those with full knowledge of the Gospel willfully contend with the Holy Spirit and are banished to become "sons of Perdition." Due to their continuous rebellion, like Lucifer, they deliberately place themselves beyond forgiveness. But like everyone, they are resurrected and the knowledge of their damnation contributes to their experience of Hell.

There is plenty of room in this religion for all sorts of people who are committed to life and light to manifest their individual souls and to pursue excellence, happiness, and fulfillment in an infinite system of eternal progression. But the parameters of life require that we struggle with discord, oppression, and misunderstanding and that we ask ourselves to prevail against the darkness.

With this in mind, modern LDS women face a threefold problem. The first difficulty emanates from basic misunderstandings with the larger world, where people make a number of assumptions based on the church's history, their own standards and expectations, and rumor, some of it spun by religious sects that regard The Church of Jesus Christ of

Latter-day Saints as a serious competitor for members in the Christian congregation or from misguided but popular interpretations of the life of Mormon women based on shows like HBO's *Big Love.*

The second difficulty involves pressure within the church. Pressure to conform, various judgments and criticisms born of "herd mentality," and occasional power struggles create a large share of heartache and alienation. Since human beings make up the body of the church, such challenges are predictable.

The third problem comes from inside, from women's perfectionism and unrelenting expectations of themselves. Some of what lives inside each woman—the DNA as well as the doctrine—comes from her mother and her grandmothers and her great-grandmothers. Some of what lives inside her is all her own—her soul or spirit calling her to act on behalf of her own purpose regardless of the milieu that surrounds her. Some of what goes on has to do with what she expects of herself or believes others expect of her. Sometimes an LDS woman feels at odds with herself, an experience we share with most of humanity.

But the doctrines of the church can counteract this internal conflict. Often, sisters or friends or mothers and daughters will join each other in genealogical pursuits, and they will attend the temple together. The LDS belief in the Second Coming of Christ and in the sealing of families through temple ordinances places emphasis on genealogy and on "work for the dead," which involves proxy baptisms, endowments, and sealings which can only be performed in the temple. The opportunity to redeem departed loved ones by performing ordinances brings comfort and establishes family unity. Since family stands prominent in the LDS version of the Gospel, members watch for any type of adversarial influence on the family. As caretakers of family, LDS women shore each other up against onslaughts on motherhood and marriage. In addition, women as well as men are called to transform adversarial energies that threaten the family in the larger world.

In every culture, the lives of women reflect the quality of life in the culture as a whole. The way we treat women often mirrors the way we treat our own bodies, our children, and our elderly parents. Most people call our beautiful blue planet "Mother Earth" and how we treat her reveals how we feel toward mother and woman. In cultures where women are respected, the earth and her life-forms tend to be respected, so natural health and beauty thrive. The LDS culture was established with this kind of respect for the vessel of life: "Among the great and mighty ones who were assembled in this vast congregation of the righteous were . . . our glorious Mother Eve, with many of her faithful daughters who had lived through the ages and worshiped the true and living God" (Doctrine and Covenants 138:38–39). According to LDS doctrine, we are accountable for our treatment of all forms of life and for our stewardship of the earth, which belongs to God: "For it is expedient that I, the Lord, should make every man accountable, as a steward over earthly blessings, which I have made and prepared for my creatures. I, the Lord, stretched out the heavens, and built the earth, my very handiwork; and all things therein are mine" (Doctrine and Covenants 104:13, 14).

We women carry irrefutable knowledge in our bodies that we are subject to the laws of nature, the laws of creation. Men know these laws too, but they are not subject to monthly reminders of the ebb and flow of life, nor do they experience the immediacy of co-creating life within one's own body. Through the enormous power of sisterhood, women can use this knowledge to command the attention of those attuned to our local or our global situation. We can inspire and empower good stewardship.

At the same time, LDS women are faced with contradictions in our own religion. So much of our history has been buried, and it rises up to haunt us in modern times. The golden plates of Mormon were hidden in the Hill Cumorah. The Principle of Plural Marriage was hidden for a decade from many Mormons, including Emma, first wife of the Prophet Joseph Smith. The secrecy continued after the saints had made their exodus to the Promised Land, with patriarchs running and hiding from federal agents. As a child of polygamy, I was taught to lie to protect my family, to keep our secrets from the authorities and especially from members of the official church who were embarrassed by the skeletons in historical closets, who worked against us. During the last century, LDS Church archives have been carefully guarded and filtered, information hoarded to protect belief and tradition and to maintain a shroud of secrecy that troubles some within the church and many on the outside. Secrecy surrounding sacred temple ceremonies has generated speculation and doubt, and attracted unfounded accusations that the church engages in cultish practices. Fundamentalists who continue banned practices such as the Principle of Plural Marriage and "Blood Atonement" (exacting an Old Testament price for shedding innocent blood) have generated animosity and misunderstanding for the mainstream church. Despite extensive media coverage and advertising to clear away the confusion, people still have a range of intriguing and inaccurate ideas about the LDS Church.

Controversies regarding Mormon women contribute to the confusion. Back in 1870, when Utah women vied for suffrage, success of the franchise seemed a matter of survival—of their way of life, of their religious beliefs and of themselves as a people. When they gained the right to vote, the women celebrated on behalf of all members of their sex and for all members of their church. Their jubilant words reveal their wholehearted intensity: Emmeline Wells, who became the longtime editor of the first LDS women's publication, *Woman's Exponent,* pronounced, "That greater liberty has been given to women in our church than elsewhere is indeed true; that now equality of sex prevails is undeniable." "The yoke on women is removed," rejoiced Phebe Woodruff, president of the Fourteenth Ward Relief Society. Presendia Kimball, plural wife to the Prophet Joseph Smith and then to Apostle Heber C. Kimball, said "I am glad to see our daughters elevated with man and the time come when our votes will assist our leaders and redeem ourselves." Bathsheba Smith, who would one day lead Relief Society, defended the capacity of women to wisely exercise their new freedom, saying, "there is nothing required of us we that cannot perform."[11]

These women believed that the time had come for a new relationship between the sexes, a harmonious partnership reminiscent of the Garden of Eden. A new culture, a new land, a new church—a church that promised to restore all truth that had been taken from the earth since the beginning of time. Since the time of the goddess worshipped by Rebecca of Old. Since the time when we knew and spoke of and worshipped our Eternal Mother, our Heavenly Mother who assisted our Heavenly Father in the creation of our spirits. As Eliza R. Snow wrote in the third verse of her lovely hymn, written in the early 1840s, "O My Father":

I had learned to call thee Father,
Thru thy Spirit from on high,
But until the key of knowledge
Was restored, I knew not why.
In the heavens are parents single?
No, the thought makes reason stare!
Truth is reason; truth eternal
Tells me I've a mother there.[12]

Indeed, Joseph Smith taught the early saints this doctrine and freely encouraged women to exercise their power. Yet in later years, the Church of Jesus Christ of Latter-day Saints mounted a massive campaign to keep the Equal Rights Amendment from passing. Although this trend of liberalism toward women in nascent religions to conservatism in established religions may be predictable, the contradiction disturbs many LDS women today as we struggle to be faithful to the church we love.[13] The quiet dialogues of LDS women echo the opaque worlds of Old Testament women in *The Red Tent,* and the clandestine study group of Iranian women in *Reading Lolita in Tehran,* and the foot-bound women confined to their upstairs rooms with their *nu shu,* secret writing which they used to keep their feelings, their memories, and their identities alive as depicted in *Snow Flower and the Secret Fan.* One discovery made by the protagonist in *Snow Flower* is that *nu shu* is not really secret; it is just that men place no serious value on it. Our husbands and fathers and ecclesiastical leaders know about our meetings in book groups and chat rooms and retreats where we find the courage to value ourselves and one another and thus can fulfill our responsibilities in a world that puts us in difficult positions. The sisterhood consistently grows stronger through mutual support, communication, and enlightenment.

In the ranks of the Church of Jesus Christ of Latter-day Saints, where the patriarchy exercises authority with benevolence, confinement and appropriation do not seem so menacing. In comparison with the many dangerous patriarchal systems in the world, the patriarchs in LDS communities practice kindness, protection, respect for womanhood, and reverence for life. But not all LDS men are benevolent. Despite their claim to sainthood, some use their power to pillage the earth and others use their patriarchal privilege to diminish women and children. According to Oscar McConkie, author of *She Shall be Called Woman,* "Many of the brethren, who are otherwise disciplined Christians, exercise unrighteous dominion over women."[14] Those who try to commandeer others' lives must be reminded that an appropriated life is a life stolen, whether male or female, child or adult.

But women always have the ability and the right to counter such unfairness. When a woman stands firm in her true character, as a daughter of God, the tyrant bows his head. When we give way to tyranny, we disable and distort everything around us. We women have the power of life within us, the power to create balance and order. We can conceive new life and, as with Mother Eve, who risked biting into the fruit of knowledge so that mankind could be, we can establish new paradigms of being. In the restored church of these latter days, men and women have equal significance in the eyes of God and in one another's eyes. The brethren who hold leadership positions recognize that partnership is truly aligned with Heaven and they have said, essentially, that men and women are different, but they are equally important, and together they create wholeness.

The LDS people are rich in guidance. We can tune into General Conference twice a year and hear the voice of the Living Prophet. We can hear messages of ecclesiastical leaders every Sunday and by reading our church publications. We can hear the words of God as spoken in Scripture. Yet no voice can guide us moment by moment or speak more specifically and appropriately than the voice of the Holy Spirit within us. Our interaction with the Holy Spirit assists us in determining how to live our lives. When we listen to the voice of Spirit, we are no longer confined by roles; instead we can honor callings. When we have studied Scripture and sought the guidance of "the still, small voice" we have the right and the responsibility to bring our creative inspiration to our interactions with life. But when people believe that every occasion has a preestablished response, or when they consult someone else at every turn, or when they think that everything in life must be done in a certain way, sheer predictability stifles people's capacity to hear the voice of the Holy Spirit. "When nothing is left to the imagination, people forget that they can show up in the moment," says Sally Smith, who grew up in Utah and opened A Woman's Place Bookstores to provide women with a place to shore up identity, create mutually supportive relationships, and free imaginations. Or as journalist Robert Kirby indicates in his *Salt Lake Tribune* column, if LDS people seem to shun you, it's not that they mean to be rude; they're just busy and preoccupied with doing what's right. Our convivial concern for our fellow beings suffers when we we're obsessed with perfectionism rather than being who we are: creators fully interacting in each moment. The LDS doctrines of divine nature and individual worth indicate that people can be trusted to design the quotidian of their own lives with the help of personal revelation.

Perceptual distortions and contradictions create discord, unrest, and chaos. Clarity creates order, allowing us to align with the ascending organization of life. When we work together, man and woman, woman and woman, human being and God, our personal contributions synergize with the whole, creating something much more powerful through harmony and unity. In the spirit of partnership, I offer these pages to share some stories, celebrate our mutual vision, and explore who we are as sisters in Zion.

2

For Time and All Eternity

If you are a young Latter-day Saint woman, the words "eternal companion" and "celestial marriage" fall readily from your lips, part of your native tongue. Staying single doesn't even occur to you, for Scripture commands that you "multiply and replenish the earth," and you wouldn't consider doing that outside of wedlock. Since earliest childhood, you've understood that the entire purpose of your creation focuses on being a "help-mate" for a young man who is committed to teach the Gospel and build up the kingdom of Heaven. You have been taught that those who don't marry cannot attain the highest degree of glory in the hereafter. So you spend your adolescence preparing to meet your "eternal companion"—the one boy or man through whom you will claim queenhood. You want someone who shares your ideals, who believes, as you have been taught to believe, that the highest degree of glory requires celestial marriage, a marriage "sealed . . . by the Holy Spirit of promise, by him who is anointed . . . in time and through all eternity" (Doctrine and Covenants 132:19).

During your first year of college, you fall in love while on your first extended stay away from home, a love-at-first-sight encounter. A ripple of déjà vu passes through you, a sense that you have met him before or that you have always known him. You find that he comes from an LDS home, with parents who trace their ancestry to powerful and upstanding members of the LDS Church, and they pride themselves in this heritage. At times their ancestral pride has prompted their son's rebellion. But this maverick streak only makes him more charming. Besides, you like his smile, his broad shoulders, and that he's obviously nuts about you.

A year passes before his mission call comes. During this time, you have dated, broken up, and struggled to keep yourselves chaste. You have been to your bishop; he has been to his bishop. Then he receives a letter from the office of the president of The Church of Jesus Christ of Latter-day Saints, summoning him to begin a mission in a far-off land. You promise not to marry anyone until he returns. The two years drag on. While he is converting and baptizing members into the church, you are going to college, working, and dating other men. The two of you talked beforehand about the importance of you being free to date so he could be free to focus on his mission—all this upon the advice of parents, siblings, friends, and ecclesiastical leaders who warn you not to put your life on hold. He knew when he left that most young women don't wait for their missionaries; no wonder tears filled his eyes as he said good-bye, being careful not to hug you too closely, for he had been "set apart" to teach the Gospel.

During his absence, you meet some fun and exciting guys, and you realize that there may be other candidates for eternal companion, but you aren't accepting resumes. The mission completed, the two of you undergo a frayed and confused reconnection before you break up one more time. Then he does all the right things: asks your father, buys the ring you want, and takes you to Temple Square in Salt Lake City, the site of the Tabernacle (where the Mormon Tabernacle Choir practices), the first Assembly Hall, and most important, the Salt Lake City Temple with the Angel Moroni gleaming at the top. At the temple personal endowments are received, celestial marriages performed, baptisms, endowments, and sealings completed by proxy for people who have died before receiving the Gospel. Here dwells the Lord; the temple was built to be His resting place. With the temple as backdrop, your sweetheart drops to one knee and asks for your hand in marriage. You know that he proposes temple marriage, for time and all eternity, which will require that you keep all the covenants you've made so far and that you will make as you take out your endowments, which involves additional covenants. The commitment you declare as you say yes boggles your mind and stirs your heart with anticipation and terror and joy. The fact that you "shopped around" and that you kept your promise to marry no one else until he returned, that you have already been through a kind of refining fire together, makes your engagement especially wonderful. You wholeheartedly approach your eternal happiness.

~⤵

Now you stand before a mirror in the Bridal Room of the Salt Lake Temple. It is almost 8:00 A.M. You have spent the earliest hours of the morning—from 4:30 to 6:00—having your hair and makeup done by a cosmetologist. Sparkling, carefully lined and shadowed eyes look back at you from the beveled three-way mirror. Your white-slippered feet stand on the fabled rose rug that has been in the temple since it opened in 1893. Adorned in white—your beautiful lace wedding gown and your new underwear, the "temple garments" in which you were clothed after receiving certain blessings and promises—you feel innocent and pure, and that you are truly beginning a new life. Today you will be married for time and all eternity. But not before you receive your endowments, a two-hour process of making commitments to God, a necessary preparation for celestial marriage. Already you are enervated to the point of exhaustion: thrilled, excited, terrified.

Think of yourself as the daughter of an LDS couple: that is, both your parents are members of The Church of Jesus Christ of Latter-day Saints, and both sincerely want you to live your life with this religious protection. Neither of them are fanatics, and despite a strong family history in the church, they sustain a simple and sincere belief that this path leads to eternal happiness. Your family was sealed when you were a child, and your eyes still mist with the memory of the day your parents were married in the temple, how you waited and napped and watched church videos until a matron dressed in white brought you into the sealing room, and you were bonded to them, sealed so that you can be together in this life and the next, an eternal family. Unlike your parents, who started out with a civil marriage and entered the temple to be sealed in marriage after you were born, your children will be "born under the covenant"—sealed to you and your husband as long as you keep the promises you are making today. This knowledge that you get to keep your paternal family and your new family forever floods your heart with happiness. One thing that has set your religious life apart from that of your friends who are Lutheran or Methodist or Jewish or nondenominational can be found in the phrase, "eternal family." Most religions teach that marriage bonds couples only until death—"till Death do us part"—but LDS people believe that couples can be married and have their children sealed to them forever, progressing together, for even death cannot part an eternal family.

You earned the right to be here. Even though you enjoy wild and crazy fun as much as any young woman, you know that creating a foundation for eternal life matters more than a few good times. You met with your bishop to report that you have refrained from typical college wildness, such as drinking, having sex, or doing drugs. You have turned over 10 percent of your hard-earned dollars to the bishop every month. You spend Sundays in church or studying Scripture instead of water-skiing or hiking. You do your best to treat people with love and respect—including members of your own family. You lead a Christian life, for that is the true character of a member of The Church of Jesus Christ of Latter-day Saints. Once the bishop filled out and signed your "temple recommend" you testified of your worthiness to the stake president, who also signed it.

The temple matron escorts you and your mother into a small room where you receive instructions to wear your temple garments day and night. These sacred garments represent your relationship with Heaven, and they are to be treated with respect. Don't drop them on the floor, don't let them fall into disrepair, don't hang them outside where people can make a mockery of God. When they wear out, dispose of them carefully, the way you would the nation's flag.

Now you follow the matron into a beautiful, lavishly muraled room to begin the two-hour process of receiving endowments. Other people, most of them taking out endowments for the dead and many of them

friends and family members, accompany you as you take out your endowments for yourself. You see your fiancé across the room, his countenance
serene. He is taking out endowments for someone who has died, having
previously made his own covenants in preparation for his mission: promising to obey commandments, to live the Gospel, to be chaste, and to
dedicate his life to building the kingdom of God in order to gain special
blessings, including the right to exaltation and eternal progression. You
journey through the creation of the earth and the "three degrees of
glory"—different levels of experience and consciousness represented in
four separate rooms. You experience the Creation Room where you learn
about the creation of the world and mankind. Then you go to the Garden
Room, where you are reminded about the fall of mankind, and you realize
that without a Savior, we are doomed. Eve seems to be responsible for
this fall from grace, which to some degree explains the patriarchal hierarchy of the church and the belief that it parallels the organization of
Heaven. This troubles you some: Does this mean that you no longer
make your own decisions? Does this mean you can blame your husband
for what you do or don't do? Does this mean that God will no longer hear
your prayers if you and your husband disagree? You murmur your concerns, and your mother, who sits beside you as your escort, reminds you
that you have the right to your own relationship with God and that you
are entitled to personal revelation. The structure of the church and
priesthood authority establishes order, not domination.

The company moves to the Telestial Room—a wilderness both
splendid in its beauty and heartbreaking in its trials, where good people
live, many of them misguided by those who exploit and corrupt the
teachings of God with the teachings of men.

Then you move into the Terrestrial Room, where you are prepared
to enter God's presence. This room sparkles with chandeliers and gold
leaf. You observe that each "degree of glory" is beautiful in its own right.
But the promises you are making are staggering, the words rich in
metaphor, and the processes anagogical. You will need to experience
these sessions again and again in order to discern their meaning.

You move to the Celestial Room, realizing that you have spent no
time in Hell or any corollary of it while in the temple. In this breathtak-
ingly beautiful room, you find friends and family who have also proven

their worthiness in a metaphorical sense, having completed the endowment process for someone who has already died. This work for the dead adds a special aura to the process and to the temple itself, giving you the sense that truly committed human beings can build a sustainable future and transform the past as well, that devoted Latter-day Saints can live well on the earthly plane and also reach beyond the Veil to progress throughout eternity. Your fiancé greets you there, and the two of you stand in this glorious room surrounded by loved ones and you believe that Heaven shimmers with this kind of light and beauty, that this moment of happiness can be an eternal experience.

The celestial marriage or sealing ceremony takes place in a chamber off the Celestial Room. The guests seat themselves while you and your fiancé meet with the man who will perform the sealing, an ordinance that will bond the two of you "for time and all eternity." The sealer (a lay person, like all who are called to serve in the LDS Church, who has been set apart and given special authority by the highest priesthood-holders to perform this ceremony) happens to be someone your father knows, a man gifted with clairvoyant wisdom, and he gives you some kinds words, then invites you to fill out the necessary paperwork. You enter the Sealing Room, which is already filled to capacity. Many loved ones are present, and many are not. Your grandparents, for instance, are not here. They are excluded from the temple for different reasons, but in any case, they do not have "temple recommends," which means that they do not get to attend this wedding ceremony. You miss them especially, as well as your siblings who, either due to youth or the condition of their faith, are not allowed to enter the deep recesses of the temple. They are impatiently passing time in the marriage waiting area, just beyond the temple's foyer. You have always been an inclusive person, and this exclusion bothers you more than you want to admit.

Once, while working at your part-time job during your college years, you overheard an older woman confide to a colleague about her daughter's impending temple marriage. She confessed that she'd been going to church, "going through all the motions," so that she wouldn't have to wait outside when her daughter was married in the temple. She had said, with a wry laugh, "If they don't get to you in your own right, they get to you through your children." You understood that she faced a difficult choice: Should she hold out for her peculiar brand of autonomy, refuse to give up her morning coffee and her 10 percent of income and forgo her daughter's marriage ceremony, or should she give up her idiosyncrasies and small rebellions so that she could be there? You suspect that there's more at stake for this woman than small rebellions, but you don't want to think that you may be entering a way of life that could threaten your independence. You are about to be married! You are grateful to be there with both of your parents. And with your sweetheart, of course.

The Sealing Room bears the same sort of exquisite appointment as the Celestial Room, pale green damask chairs and brocade-covered marriage altar. One hundred twenty-five LDS temples grace the globe, architecture and style differing according to place and time of construction, but always distinguished by ethereal beauty. And always with mirrors on either side of the Sealing Room, reflecting bride and groom from their respective positions, a symbolic rendering of the relationship. The sealer points this out and your two infinitely reflected selves provide an apt metaphor for the nature of eternal marriage. The experience evokes amazement at the endless journey on which you've embarked.

The sealer's talk aims specifically at the two of you, as if he has known both of you all your lives. Surprise washes over you, then the realization that this man has been called by the Lord to this position; he is informed by the Holy Spirit. Of course he knows you. Your sweetheart takes your hand. You make your vows, responding affirmatively to the questions. You are married for time and all eternity.

After changing into street clothes, you leave Temple Square and cross the street to the legendary Lion House, where Brigham Young once lived and housed some of his plural wives. The home gets its name from the lion over the front entrance, a reminder that the owner was often called "Lion of the Lord" as he served as second president of The Church of Jesus Christ of Latter-day Saints. There you partake of lunch with your family members and wedding party, savoring the cheese rolls and chicken pot pie that the Lion House has been making for decades. One of the easier hours spent this day, you relish the time to laugh and chatter, to feed your body and sustain your spirit.

Typical of many brides and weddings, you and your parents have invested more money, time, and energy on the reception than any other part of the wedding. You have chosen bridesmaids' gowns and grooms-men's tuxedoes, mothers' dresses and fathers' boutonnières. With the help of the women in both families, you have decorated the rooms and foyers, selected tablecloths and flowers and food. Despite a general feeling of cooperation, a disagreement has marred the preparations.

Because so many of your loved ones could not attend the temple ceremony (which happens more often these days in a world of shifting faith), you have made many of the reception arrangements with them in mind. You feel a little pang, thinking of more solidly LDS families, where most of the adult family members are eligible to attend, and for the briefest moment, you wonder if your marriage will make it. Will there be a context of devotion around you sufficient to sustain this eternal commitment? But you love them; for their sake as much as your own, you have dressed up your closest friends and family members, ordered all this food and all these flowers. You wanted a little bit of ceremony to justify all the trappings of the reception and to preserve the sense that they, too, have a part in upholding and sustaining your marriage. Your boss, who serves as a bishop, suggested that a ring ceremony might be appropriate, since the exchanging of rings is secular and material, therefore out of place in the temple ceremony. But your fiancé's father objected to this plan, saying that the only ceremony should be the temple wedding. Your mother reacted passionately, asking the purpose of the dresses and flowers, the food and music: Was it all about taking pictures, or was it meant to include your loved ones? The opinions went round and round, throwing a few wrenches into your budding relationship. Finally, understanding reached, you chose to create your own little ceremony and the members of both families returned to sanity. Your heart swells with gratitude that goodwill buzzes through the company as you pose for pictures before the ivy-twined wrought-iron heart.

The groomsmen seat people. Then you follow your bridesmaids down an aisle, hanging on your father's arm, and he gives you away, a poignant moment for everyone who knows how close you are to your dad. You stand beside your husband, trying to absorb every word as your boss talks about how you have already been married in the temple and how the exchange of rings will allow those who could not be at the sealing to participate in supporting your marriage. He talks some about the nature of marriage and gives a little advice. Then you light a taper from a burning wax pillar, whose light represents God, and your husband does the same, and the two of you look into one another's eyes shining bright with candlelight, and you identify the gifts you see in each other.

After the traditional wedding dances and making your getaway through thrown birdseed to a whitewashed, can-festooned car, your new husband carries you over the threshold. You are better prepared than some Mormon brides. *The Family: A Proclamation to the World,* a document drawn up by the First Presidency and Twelve Apostles of The Church of Jesus Christ of Latter-day Saints and read by President Gordon B. Hinckley as part of his message to Relief Society on September 23, 1995, states: "We declare the means by which mortal life is created to be divinely appointed." This sets a context for LDS attitudes toward sex and procreation. Since at least half the LDS parents seem to regard sex as too sacrosanct to speak about, the schools in predominantly Mormon Utah do not offer much sex education. (Ironically, the religious right attempts to dismiss the LDS Church as a non-Christian cult, yet they stand with the LDS people on this and other conservative points.) You happen to have parents who speak frankly about sex and a big sister who tells you what to expect. Still, you struggle to understand the implications of agreeing to share your body with a man. At the end of the big event, weary beyond belief, you can't figure out what all the fuss is about. A cranky little voice inside keeps asking about "happily ever after." As you drift off, you remember that sex is about life, about creation, and that you could be pregnant. This thought startles you awake. You are too young for a baby, too young to be a mother! But your body doesn't care. Your body is going to sleep. "Happily ever after" will happen in good time.

～

Of course, even spiritually-grounded, realistic couples face devastations on the apple-blossom path of temple marriage. Childlessness, sickness, poverty, depression, and early death are incomprehensible to the young woman who believes that through obedience she will be rewarded with happiness. When she discovers that temple ceremonies and priesthood power cannot protect her from life's tornados or clay feet treading on her heart, the emotional and spiritual wreckage piles up. The concept of eternal life makes it easier to walk through the storm, but it doesn't allay the loss.

Tom and Cherie had been married nine months when a hulking Dodge Ram ran his Subaru off the road and into a tree. Tom died instantly, of a broken neck. Married just long enough to plan a family, Cherie had taken a pregnancy test that morning, and was planning a clever way to tell her husband at the end of the day. She couldn't wait to see the look on his face. When the officers came to the door, she fainted. She spent the next six months angry with God. Her mother and her sisters hovered nearby, asking what she needed, offering to do whatever they could. But Cherie refused blessings from the priesthood and would not accept visits from the Relief Society presidency or her visiting teacher. "This wasn't supposed to happen," she'd say when her mother pleaded with her to cheer up and get on with life. When she gave birth to a baby boy (named Tom, after his father), she reclaimed her faith. She opened her doors and invited the sisters of Relief Society in. They came armed with food and baby clothes and cleaning supplies. One of them helped her find a job she could do at home, using her computer, so that she could stay with her son. Cherie asked for and received the strength and healing of priesthood blessings. She found the courage to raise the little boy as his father might have wished. Two years later she marveled that she made it through the dark time, that time of utter aloneness. "You weren't alone," her mother murmured. "We prayed for you constantly. You had angels all around you."

Struggles with bitter disappointment descend on those couples who follow all the rules and then don't conceive children as scheduled. From every indication, they would be stellar parents, but somehow things don't work out. Faith is tested as they wonder why, when they married primarily to fulfill the commandment to multiply and replenish the earth, they have been denied the opportunity. The process of learning to embrace reality and celebrate life despite lapsed ideals and unexpected disappointments often provides a healthy orientation for the gritty realities of parenthood when such couples eventually do conceive or adopt.

Those who marry for the appearance of perfection, for the sake of a socially-acceptable image, often run into trouble. After young men complete their two-year missions for the church (usually begun before their nineteenth birthday) they often receive ecclesiastical counsel to get married within six months. This spiritual shotgun prompts many marriages. Another, more typical shotgun threatens a couple in love. Usually they are in college and can't keep their hands off each other. In Mormondom there's no permission for fornication, and the bishop counsels couples to marry before they break a commandment.

Lily had graduated from high school with an impressive array of options before her. With excellent grades and enormous athletic talent, she could choose any school she wanted. But she found it unnerving to be perched on the verge of the future, wondering what to do with the rest of her life. The strong cultural imperative to marry and bear children caught up with her as she neared graduation. When she met Dave at a nonalcoholic dance club, his patriarchal tone and strong, sure character had a calming effect. Dave took an immediate shine to her and soon talked with her nightly on the telephone. Their conversations centered on the Gospel. Dave's soft, firm voice reciting Scripture swaddled Lily in a cocoon of protective words. She might have to grow up and leave her father, but Dave was there to provide a similarly patriarchal aura. Soon they were talking of marriage. Lily's parents objected, reminding her that she had a college scholarship and a good deal of growing up to do before considering marriage. Lily took offense at their intrusion and seized an invitation to share an apartment with a woman who worked with Dave. When autumn came, Lily was working full time instead of using her college scholarship. She wanted to save up for the wedding, she said. Dave's parents worried that the two wouldn't remain chaste if they didn't hurry the wedding. Frustrated, the parents sought out Lily's new bishop and asked for his intervention. He testified that this marriage had been ordained by Heaven.

So the perfect temple wedding happened. Less than five years into the marriage, Lily blamed Dave for refusing to support her in getting an education. He reminded her that he never wanted her to have to work,

so why did she need to worry about an education? Dismayed by her impoverished circumstances as a full-time wife and mother, Lily accused
him of failing to support her dreams. Dave reminded her that her dream
had been to marry and have children, and they had agreed that she
would be a stay-at-home mom. Didn't she remember? Wasn't he working
eighty hours a week so that she wouldn't have to work?

Getting married in the cultural hall of an LDS ward house or chapel
doesn't really set your marriage up to win in the LDS culture. Even
though the ward building can be reserved for members who want to
hold special events, such as anniversary parties, family reunions, funerals, or weddings, church leaders express deep concern for couples who
want to marry in a civil ceremony. Bishops who get requests to officiate
in marriages in the ward house for couples not eligible to enter the temple find themselves conflicted. Privately, they sometimes refer to such
ceremonies as "performing a divorce" because the civil marriage vow,
"till death do you part," implies a divorce at death, while an eternal marriage "for time and all eternity" knows no end, as long as both partners
are faithful in the marriage.

But such beginnings are not necessarily doomed. Take, for instance,
the relationship of Regina and Mike. The two met while Mike was on a
30-day leave from the army, newly returned from six months in Iraq.
Rattled from the constant fear of attack, Mike was still living on the
edge. They met at a party thrown by a high school friend of Mike's the
day after he stepped off the plane. Shy yet seductive, Regina reminded
him of a rosebud unfolding. He turned the months of war into passion
for Regina. They married within three weeks so that they could honey-
moon briefly before his furlough expired. Both were practicing LDS, but
temple marriage wasn't an option, partly because of their rush to marry
before his leave was up. Temple recommends take time, interviews, worthiness. Although the couple refrained from sleeping together before
marriage, tithing had been the last thing on Mike's mind as he struggled
to survive boot camp and terrorists. Regina had other problems with
worthiness: Unbeknownst to Mike, she had met a marine, also home on
leave (she had a thing for uniforms), and became pregnant before she
found out he was married, hence the glow that so attracted Mike. Perhaps she figured that Mike would be somewhere far away when she gave

birth. In any case, their wedding was a subdued affair, Regina's shame and Mike's fear falling over them like a noxious cloud. They were married by an impatient justice of the peace during his lunch break. At the reception, in the cultural hall of the ward, people spoke brightly and hopefully about their future, but the remarks fell flat.

Maybe they were wondering if Mike knew Regina was pregnant. He did, and he knew the baby wasn't his. When a healthy, nine-pound boy made his advent two months earlier than he could possibly have been conceived, Mike didn't look for a reason to leave his wife. Moreover, Regina gave him no permission to treat her as damaged goods; she stood firm in the knowledge that, as a "daughter of God," she could start over. The couple went to the bishop separately and together to confess and to start anew. They went through separate processes of repentance and redemption, began attending church and temple preparation classes. Two years after they married in a civil ceremony, they married in the LDS temple and had their son sealed to them. That evening, as they celebrated with loved ones and ward members, the joy rose to the acoustic tiles of the cultural hall. Together, this young couple used their religious beliefs to emerge from shame and deception without breaking each other's hearts. They formed a strong, authentic union supported by family and friends and members of their community.

Temple marriage can't guarantee a blessed union, although it does increase the possibility. Many men and women use celestial marriage to create happiness, realizing that each moment is an eternal investment. We women stand in church during fast and testimony meeting (which happens the first Sunday of each month during sacrament meeting) and declare our gratitude for the priesthood in our homes and our thankfulness for eternal marriage. We weep as we relate midnight healings of our children's fevers, the calming voice of the Holy Spirit, the reassurance that all is well. We speak about peace and joy and love at home. Still, some women feel trapped in a golden cage, as if church membership and temple marriage keep them from fulfillment. Often, these women are frustrated by an ideal that's always out of reach.

Because of the doctrine of eternal progression, the dynamics of personal revelation, and the belief that "man is that he might have joy"[1] LDS marriages provide a context for high-functioning individuals to create excellence together. Maurine and Richard, for example, lead fast-track lives. Richard has a highly-successful medical practice. Maurine looks like she stepped from the pages of *Vogue,* sleek and chic and elegant. A vibrant, witty woman, she manages to be both warm and sophisticated, a devoted wife and a dazzling presence in any social scene. She has taken motherhood to new dimensions. The couple spends much of the year apart, while Maurine travels to New York and London and Paris to support their daughter, who models on high-fashion runways. She also manages to nurture three younger children in elementary school, and Richard makes sure nothing falls through the cracks while she's thousands of miles away. The support and synchronicity they bring to each other exemplifies the rich possibilities of eternal marriage.

Military personnel offer another, different take on the strength of LDS marriages. Alyce and her husband, Drake, married fifteen years ago, just after he graduated from the Air Force Academy. Since then he has been deployed on six different occasions, each hitch lasting from six to eighteen months. Alyce gave birth to five children and raised them to be good Latter-day Saints while fulfilling her callings from Primary chorister to Relief Society president in their ward. Drake attends church meetings wherever he serves: in a small billet in Korea, a bombed-out chapel in Bosnia, or a tent on the Iraqi desert. One bond that keeps them unified despite the thousands of miles between them is that every Sunday, they attend the same church at different ends of the earth, renewing the same covenants as they pray and take the sacrament and study correlated lessons while worshipping the same God. Soon Drake will be eligible for retirement, and they will be able to sit on the same bench at church. I believe they'll be blessed for their dedication rather than feeling deprived of autonomy, as with some retired couples. Once people learn that happiness is a do-it-yourself project, they have many positives to bring to eternal marriage.

I am grateful that one of my father's plural wives taught me to be responsible for my own happiness before I plunged into eternal marriage. From her I learned that internal commitment is a crucial ingredient whether the marriage is monogamous or polygamous. So many people get focused on the sensational nature of plural marriage, and they tend to equate the LDS Church with modern polygamy. This inflames members of the official church. In truth, the church will excommunicate any-one who practices polygamy and will deny a temple recommend to any-one who associates with apostates—including polygamists. The church has been known to quietly assist law enforcement agencies in the prose-cution of polygamists. Yet journalists, historians, and filmmakers con-tinue to reinforce the association between Mormonism and polygamy. In addition, "plygie kids" like me show up in the mainstream LDS Church like uninvited hillbilly guests at a wedding. We embarrass the church by exposing its roots.

Embarrassment has attended Mormon polygamy since the begin-ning and secrecy seems to have attended its practice all along. During the 1830s, soon after the LDS Church was established, polygamy was in-troduced surreptitiously by Joseph Smith, Jr. As early as 1831, he al-legedly told Apostle Lyman Johnson that plural marriage "was a correct principle"[2] but warned him to keep the practice secret, wishing to avoid the rancor of his wife, Emma, as well as the indignation of other people inside and outside the Mormon circle. In 1833 Joseph took Fannie Alger as a plural wife in an "exchange of women" reminiscent of old-world and tribal practices, telling Levi Hancock that if he would arrange for Fanny Alger to have him, he would allow Levi to marry Clarissa Reed. Fanny may have lived with the Smiths at the time, as a mother's helper or live-in maid, but Emma came to suspect the relationship between the two, and she threw Fanny out of the house. Some years later, she did the same with the Partridge sisters, Emily and Eliza Partridge, who became Joseph's nineteenth and twentieth wives.[3]

Most of the early Latter-day Saints, men and women alike, recoiled when faced with the subject of plural marriage. But realizing that they lived in "the last dispensation of the fullness of times," when all things would be restored to the earth, they found a way to accept polygamy as a biblical practice. Eliza R. Snow, esteemed as a high priestess and prophetess (terms that would later be diminished in the church) and a recognized poet who was second only to Emma Smith in LDS historical significance, reported that her first response to polygamy was repulsion, but she slowly converted: "As I increased in knowledge concerning the principle and design of Plural Marriage, I grew in love with it, and to-day esteem it as a precious, sacred principle, necessary in the elevation and salvation of the human family—in redeeming woman from the curse, and the world from corruption."[4] She paid a high price to live the principle. The circumstances surrounding the event are uncertain, but some sources indicate through "family stories" that Eliza may have lost her ability to bear children when Emma discovered that Joseph had taken Eliza as a plural wife. According to one account, Emma pushed Eliza, who was "great with child," and tumbled down the stairs to land at the feet of Joseph Smith, Jr. and Brother Charles Rich. Emma glowered above them, then burst into tears. Eliza reportedly lost the child and never bore another, and the hip she injured in the fall showed up in a limp for the rest of her life.[5]

Besides jealousy and outrage within LDS ranks, the practice of polygamy inflamed the neighbors of Mormons. Rumors about plural marriage (many of them circulated by former supporters of Joseph Smith, Jr.) and the formidable block of LDS votes (outsiders assumed that Mormons would vote in whatever way their prophet told them to vote) had raised ire throughout the country and galvanized mobs to move against the saints in Missouri and Illinois. The LDS people were forced to emigrate under severe conditions, often while being abused by mobs who confiscated their possessions and burned their homes.

Most people don't realize that a few early Mormons practiced both forms of polygamy: polyandry (a wife having multiple husbands) and polygyny (a husband having multiple wives). Joseph Smith, Jr. married women who were already married to other men. His bond with these women tested the husbands' commitment through their willingness to "give" their wives to him in eternal marriage. Often the women kept their civil marriages to other men intact after marrying Joseph in a spiritual ceremony. Zina Diantha Huntington Jacobs Smith Young is a case in point. Zina, a girl of nineteen in the midst of courtship with Henry Jacobs, was approached by Joseph Smith, Jr., who claimed that the Lord had instructed him to take her as his plural wife. This proposal came on the heels of some consoling encounters when young Zina went to Joseph in an attempt to reconcile her feelings regarding the death of her mother. She asked the Prophet Joseph if she would know her mother in the next life, and he responded, "Certainly you will. More than that, you will meet and become acquainted with your eternal Mother, the wife of your Father in Heaven."

"And have I then a Mother in Heaven?"

"You assuredly have. How could a Father claim His title unless there were also a Mother to share that parenthood?"

After much soul-searching (for she truly believed that Joseph Smith was a prophet of God) Zina decided to marry Henry, her fiancé. But after her marriage, Joseph Smith pressed his suit. Zina continued to live with Henry, who acted as a "proxy" husband, siring children and raising them on behalf of Smith's spiritual kingdom. No one knows for sure whether Joseph consummated the relationship with Zina, although most historians feel that it is a fair bet that he did. Some years after Joseph Smith died, Zina divorced Jacobs and married Brigham Young.[6]

Brigham Young always exhibited great enthusiasm for the Principle of Plural Marriage and partnered with Joseph to talk women into marrying one or the other of them. He recruited support from the other brethren, and once chose to phrase his encouragement with unfortunate precision in Provo, Utah, 1855: "We must gird up our loins and fulfill this, just as we would any other duty."[7]

In nineteenth-century Utah, the Principle of Plural Marriage created rapid growth, with between 20 and 40 percent of the population living it.[8] During this period, living the principle was regarded as essential to celestial glory, and many members felt that they would be denied exaltation if they refused to practice plural marriage. Meanwhile, the U.S. government organized a legislative campaign designed to abolish polygamy. In 1870 the Cullom Bill passed the U.S. House of Representatives. If it passed the Senate, the government would have unprecedented control over Mormons lives and would require wives to testify against their husbands. The women of Relief Society met to form a plan of action for, as Sarah Kimball declared in her introductory remarks, "if they make serfs of them [the LDS brethren] what do they make of us?"[9] The female leaders rose one by one, each voice strengthening the next as they declared their rights and asserted their freedoms: Presendia Kimball, Eliza R. Snow, and Bathsheba Smith, among others.

Eliza R. Snow declared that it was "high time . . . to rise up in the Dignity of our calling and speak for ourselves." She went on, "truth and justice . . . demands us to speak . . . . We are not inferior to the Ladies of the world, and we do not want to appear so." She added that Brigham Young had encouraged the women of Zion to take a wider sphere of action (indeed, he had urged women to receive educations in eastern universities and had called them to be in charge of various enterprises). As Relief Society president, Snow interpreted President Young's words as expressing full support for women to be granted their rights. The body of women decided then and there to petition for suffrage and to send representatives to Washington, D.C. [10] The voices of these women created upheaval in the Republican platform, for suddenly polygamy could not be described as "one of the twin relics of barbarism"—the other being slavery[11]—nor reviled as Abraham Lincoln and his running mate had done, not when articulate women who were also plural wives spoke fervently of their general civil rights. So powerful was the stand the sisterhood took that Abraham Lincoln confided to a journalist that the Mormon Church was like a huge and stubborn tree-stump in the fields, and the only recourse was to just "plough around it."[12]

But over the years, the intractable power of legislation had its way, confiscating church assets and locking up church leaders or forcing them to hide. In 1890, the fourth president of the church, Wilford Woodruff drafted a manifesto outlawing polygamy for Latter-day Saints. The practice continued covertly until 1904, when another manifesto passed. At that point, celestial marriage no longer meant plural marriage as inferred in the early days when LDS Church founder Joseph Smith set down the Book of Commandments for the fledgling religion as though celestial marriage and plural marriage were one and the same:

> "For behold, I reveal unto you a new and an everlasting covenant; and if ye abide not that covenant, then ye are damned; for no one can reject this covenant and be permitted to enter my glory" (Doctrine and Covenants: 132:4).

Because approximately 50,000 fundamentalists of Mormon extraction adhere to this passage, believing that the New and Everlasting Covenant, the scriptural name for celestial marriage, actually refers to the Principle of Plural Marriage, polygamy continues in underground cultures throughout the West, from Texas to British Columbia, from the Pacific Ocean to the green hills of Missouri. In polygamous cultures, the concept of celestial marriage requires that a man and woman include at least one other woman in their marriage, or they are not worthy to enter the highest courts in the kingdom of heaven. One modern-day plural wife who cleaned the home of a wealthy LDS couple said of her employer, "I'm cleaning her toilets in this life, but she'll be scouring mine in the next."

Although the New and Everlasting Covenant passage is still included in official LDS Scriptures, today it pertains only to monogamous marriages; any references to plural marriage are relegated to the past. Gordon B. Hinckley, the current president of The Church of Jesus Christ of Latter-day Saints and the Living Prophet for those of LDS faith, spoke clearly to the issue when he appeared on *Larry King Live:* "It [polygamy] was a very limited practice; carefully safeguarded. In 1890, that practice was discontinued. The president of the church, the man who occupied the position which I occupy today, went before the people, and said he had, oh, prayed about it, worked on it, and had received from the Lord a revelation that it was time to stop, to discontinue it then. That's 118 years ago. It's behind us."

In the fundamentalist underground, the sisterhood functions covertly, for the circumstances surrounding polygamous marriage dictate some degree of secrecy. When "polygamous round-ups" or "raids" are afoot, especially if someone has been arrested or is being pursued by the law, plural marriage ceremonies are performed so furtively that the only people present are the two getting married and the person performing, or "sealing" the marriage. Occasionally, other family members are unaware of these secret arrangements, the first wife assuming that her husband is working or attending religious meetings, only to find out months or even years later—usually when the second wife gets pregnant—that he keeps a second family. As with anything secretive, marriages performed under these covert circumstances reverberate with dark possibilities and painful outcomes.

One woman shared with me the circumstances of her plural marriage, performed when she was barely fifteen. People like to believe that plural wives, especially the young ones, are coerced into marriage by lascivious older men, and this may be true even when the young woman thinks that the choice is hers. Young Ellen felt a great sense of urgency about her desire to marry a thirty-eight-year old man who was about to serve a prison sentence for "illegal cohabitation" (living plural marriage). She spoke about her wish to marry immediately with her father, also a polygamist, who did not object. He understood when she described the strong spiritual prompting that this man should be the father of her children. The night before the prison sentence began, Ellen's father came to her as she sat at the kitchen table doing her homework, dressed in her flannel nightgown, long hair braided for bed. Her father hustled her outside, calling over his shoulder to Ellen's unsuspecting mother about "running an errand." They met her chosen partner at his darkened office in downtown Salt Lake City, slipping through the back door so that they wouldn't be seen. Ellen's father, who ostensibly held proper authority, performed the plural marriage, which took about three minutes. As her new husband bolted for the door, she called, "Aren't you even going to kiss me?" He stopped cold, sheepishly came back and planted a chaste kiss on her cheek.

Her father took her home, impressing on her that she should not tell her mother. "Let's face it, the woman likes to talk," he said. "If word of your marriage reached the authorities, it could be disastrous for your husband. His sentence could be doubled or tripled." Later that night her new husband crept into her bedroom, which she shared with a younger sister. He kissed her gently and whispered that they would consummate their union after he served his prison sentence and when she was older. Despite his sensitivity, and the fact that they eventually shared several children and were married for thirty-five years on this earth (until his death) and presumably for all eternity, Ellen continued to be uneasy about the circumstances of her marriage. Her mother was deeply hurt that she had not been trusted to know of her oldest daughter's marriage. The plural wives were likewise hurt that they had not been consulted. Although she had long served as their babysitter, and they all liked each other, the wives naturally wanted some say about who came into the family. Ellen began to wonder if her father had protected her properly, so eagerly had he supported her desire to marry. But the greatest hurt was Ellen's: In her hurry to realize her dream, she consigned herself to doubt that her husband truly loved her.

But often the wives choose each other, sisters or good friends suggesting to their husbands that they take the other as a plural wife. Because the friendship or sisterhood worked before the marriage, success in the union of marriage increases. When Alice met Helen, a beautiful sprite with an unusually ethereal presence, she knew that the young woman was a perfect fit for her family. Helen fell in love with Alice as a friend and spiritual mentor long before she met the man who would be her husband. Although he had a medical practitioner's education, a physical condition prevented him from practicing healing arts, so he taught his wives what to do. The three worked together, treating ailments with herbs and midwifing babies into the world. They delivered one another's babies, raised each other's children, baked bread and sewed clothing for each other. When Helen died, barely in her fifties, Alice was as bereft as if she'd lost a daughter as well as a sister-wife.

Sometimes plural families headed by an ambitious first wife can run into problems. The first wife wants to acquire many wives to increase her managerial responsibilities and to prove her willingness to live the principle. But the other wives don't necessarily agree with the first wife's decisions. When the plural marriage structure follows formal patterns, the first wife has "the right of Sarah," which is, according to the Doctrine and Covenants 132:65, "the law of Sarah, who administered unto Abraham according to the law when I commanded Abraham to take Hagar to wife." In other words, a first wife can choose when and which additional wives to give to her husband as long as she complies with God's wishes. In addition, any other plural wives should be allowed to give their consent before another woman can be added to the marriage. But a loophole was established when Emma resisted her husband, Joseph Smith, Jr.'s plural relationships, and in the Doctrine and Covenants 132:54, Emma gets a scriptural comeuppance: "And I command mine handmaid, Emma Smith, to abide and cleave unto my servant Joseph, and to none else. But if she will not abide this commandment [the Principle of Plural Marriage] she shall be destroyed, saith the Lord; for I am the Lord thy God, and will destroy her if she abide not in my law." Another Scripture, the Doctrine and Covenants, 132:65, reaffirms that the wife's rights and wishes are subject to God's plans for her husband: "Therefore, it shall be lawful in me, if she receive not this law, for him to receive all things whatsoever, I, the Lord his God, will give unto him, because she did not believe and administer unto him according to my word; and she then becomes the transgressor."

Many first wives enthusiastically embrace plural marriage, expressing a magnanimous, "the more, the merrier" attitude. But some first wives have entered marriage knowing that their husbands believe in the Principle of Plural Marriage, yet hoping that they will change their minds. And sometimes, if a husband converts after the marriage or if he keeps his belief a secret, the first wife will be broadsided when the reality hits home. A husband will sometimes neglect or abandon a first wife embittered by his plural marriages, which works to the advantage of his subsequent relationships. Because the Scripture clearly declares in favor of a man who wants to live the principle and the resistant wife faces damnation and denunciation at worst and being ignored at best, wives in plural marriages have very little real power unless they ally themselves with each other to get what they want. On this platform, strong sisterhoods sometimes form. More often they not, plural wives swallow the bitter pill of their husband's wishes, and they find happiness where they can, often in their friendship with sister-wives. This, of course, applies only to polygamous communities. The interpretation of this doctrine is a moot point to modern Latter-day Saints, who would be excommunicated for entering plural marriage.

Unless a marriage must be hidden even from family members, such as Ellen's, the plural ceremony is limited to family members and close fundamentalist friends. It looks something like the marriage between my sister's husband and his second wife. Or rather, it looks like the marriage *among* my sister Rebecca, her husband, and his second wife. For the very private ceremony between this woman and Rebecca's husband, Rebecca dressed in her own wedding dress (which I found at once charming and disturbing). Rebecca glowed as if it were her own wedding day. Truly, her radiant countenance tilted some of my suspicions about plural marriage on end, for she seemed genuinely happy, about to consummate the dream of a lifetime. I know from watching my mother and her sister-wives that plural marriage is more than a rite of passage, but a refiner's fire where charity becomes necessary for survival. I wondered what would happen in the aftermath: Would the dream turn out to be a nightmare? Would Rebecca find that her greatest aspiration was an endless source of hurt and disappointment? Would she awaken to find herself cruelly manipulated or ignored or cast off? The patrician bride, the soon-to-be second wife, stood taller than my diminutive sister, dressed in white lace, holding flowers in an elegant hand. She inspired escalating fears for my sister's happiness. Rebecca has always been obedient; how would she endure life with her quiet influence eclipsed by a woman "of the world" who knew how to wield her feminine wiles?

Rebecca seemed fearless. In fundamentalist circles, sealers rationalize their authority in a variety of ways, but she didn't seem to worry that the sealer might lack the proper authority to perform the ceremony. Rebecca, like our father and her mother, is a true believer, holding that celestial marriage and plural marriage are one and the same. As the ceremony began, she took the second wife's hand and gave it to her husband. Then she folded her hand over their two hands as the words of a formal sealing ceremony echoed in the hall. She said, among other things, "I, Rebecca, give you, Catherine, to my husband, Jeremy, to be his wife and to observe all the rights of marriage between you both for time and for all eternity."

As soon as the ceremony was over, the new bride and groom kissed. Then Catherine kissed Rebecca. Then Jeremy kissed Rebecca. These formal kisses in no way suggest anything like a future *ménage à trois*. The kiss represents Christlike love, and in fundamentalist communities, kisses are exchanged between men as "brothers in Christ" and between women as "sisters in Christ." The love represented pertains to plural marriage in that it symbolizes their mutual agreement to sustain each other in polygamy, which they regard as "God's law."

Historical plural marriages and those performed in modern underground cultures don't differ significantly when it comes to motive. Emma Smith resisted the principle, so of course she chose no plural wives. Joseph Smith, Jr. chose wives who promised some strengthening influence. By marrying the daughters and sisters of church authorities, he solidified his position as head of the church, which may have seemed necessary. Following rifts with founding members, such as Oliver Cowdery and the Whitmer brothers, who had been excommunicated for misusing church funds and selling church lands, Joseph Smith wanted to surround himself with people he could trust. He took wives who would shore up loyalty, including women who were currently married to his followers. In such unfathomable demonstrations of obedience, these men and women showed their unconditional trust in and obedience toward the prophet. In acting on his physical attraction to these women, Joseph could also fulfill the prophecy to "raise up a righteous branch unto the house of Israel"(2 Nephi 3:5, Book of Mormon) and to the Lord, thus restoring the Old Testament practice of plural marriage in restoring the fullness of the Gospel.

In modern plural marriages, a variety of factors influence husbands and their plural wives. My father, as the spiritual leader of our polygamous group and the only doctor, entertained many marriage proposals, some initiated by fathers and brothers, some initiated by the women themselves. The exchange of women for land or money or power echoes ancient tribal practices as well as those of the landed gentry in Europe and England. In some fundamentalist groups today, the patriarch maneuvers and leverages marriages, giving beautiful young virgins to powerful group members in exchange for loyalty or financial investment. But in more open and liberal groups, such as the one in which I grew up, the women themselves frequently engage in the process of forging an alliance. When the patriarchs are not tyrannical, the women tend to make their own decisions and choose marriages that will benefit everyone. Of course, they enter into these agreements as sexual beings, most of them yearning to become "Mothers in Israel" and desiring to "raise up a righteous seed unto the Lord". Most have fervent testimonies that they are living "the Fullness of the Gospel" when they enter plural marriage; they say they would rather "have ten percent of a hundred percent man than a hundred percent of a ten percent man." [13]

Plural marriage invites discussions of pecking orders and hierarchy. But is it possible to discuss monogamous marriage without exploring power structure? Well, certainly, in a different world. But in the LDS world, hierarchy prevails. The patriarchal hierarchy of marriage in the church sprouts from the Garden of Eden story, when Eve disobeyed God and partook of the fruit of the Tree of Knowledge of Good and Evil. As a result, according to Scripture, women are ruled by their husbands: "Unto the woman he said, I will greatly multiply thy sorrow and thy conception; in sorrow thou shalt bring forth children, and thy desire shall be to thy husband, and he shall rule over thee" (Genesis 3:16).

Some patriarchs believe that women are not only subservient by commandment, but also inferior to men. They take Eve's instruction to be obedient as carte blanche in marriage and with other female members of their families. But this is only a first glance interpretation of LDS Scripture. Deeper inquiry indicates that Eve demonstrated courage, partaking of the apple so that mankind could exist, and that Adam followed her example, deciding to join her in creation. This emphasis on mutual participation runs throughout LDS Scripture. Adam has consequences that match Eve's, toiling on cursed ground for bread to eat. Eve works beside Adam in the fields. They bear children together and raise them as partners. There is even an implication that Adam, having been created first, needs to be encouraged to step up and take responsibility. After all, he didn't take on the serpent himself, but left that to his wife. Many scriptural indications suggest that Eve completes Adam, that without her he is only half of mankind, and certainly not able to generate the race of man by himself.

In the polygamous marriage, the curse of Eve accompanies other fundamentalist beliefs such as "Blood Atonement". This actually refers to the Atonement of Jesus Christ, made through the shedding of His blood, for all our sins. But during the harassment and murder of Mormons in Missouri and Illinois, the term changed meaning to allow defense and even killing in instances where "innocent blood was shed." The Danites were a group of early Mormons led by Sampson Avard, who were convinced that they operated with authority from the First Presidency and thus felt justified in committing acts of robbery or murder to avenge wrongs against the church. When certain modern-day fundamentalists adopted Blood Atonement as another "lost principle," they opened a context for terrorism. "Blood Atonement" was invoked as an excuse to assassinate my father, even though he was a doctor who stitched up cuts and set broken bones and delivered thousands of babies. "Blood Atonement" has also been used to terrorize women.

One woman told me that she left her husband because of this interpretation of Blood Atonement. Her husband suspected her of adultery, and by way of questioning her, he sat her on his knee and held her chin in his hand. "If you ever leave me for another man, I'll be obliged to kill you."

"What?" she started, and tried to stand, but he held her fast.

"Adultery is the most serious sin there is, other than the shedding of innocent blood. The punishment of either is the same."

She stared at him, uncomprehending.

"If you left me," he said gently, drawing his index finger from one ear, along the underside of her jaw and to the other ear, "I'd have to slit your throat from here to here."

"You could do that to me?"

"For the sake of your soul I could. It's the law of Blood Atonement."

It took her a week to find a woman's shelter that wouldn't give out her name. She took the children and left.

Such beliefs don't exist in the mainstream Church of Jesus Christ of Latter-day Saints, where those being interviewed for a temple recommend are asked probing questions to assure that their treatment of family members and other human beings is beyond reproach. But sometimes, as in other human settings, the people asking the questions engage in the abuses they seek to suppress. One woman, Delia, went to a friend in her ward, asking what she should do about her husband, who was the first counselor in the bishopric in his ward. He had been very affectionate with the daughter of some friends, a young woman named Brianna, who had come to stay at their home while she attended college. Delia, alarmed at how much time her husband spent with this young woman, discovered that he had invested the entire family savings in getting Brianna a place of her own. Because of the priesthood structure, Delia had recourse within the church: She could report her husband to a higher authority. But she worried what he would do to her, what it would do to the children, what would happen in the ward and the larger community if people discovered that her husband was a fraud. Frozen between her loyalty to her "eternal partner" and her fear of repercussions, Delia slipped into a depression. Fortunately, her friend was there for her. She listened and commiserated and supported as long as it made sense to do so. Then, when the time for commiserating was past, Delia's friend confronted the husband and threatened to expose him. His behavior took an about-face, and he took steps to set things right. Delia has never discovered how her marriage turned on a dime from tyrannical to trustworthy. The desire of the third party who intervened was simply to serve the highest good of all concerned.

Whenever patriarchs invoke Eve as an excuse to dominate and demean the women in their lives, they violate the basics of fair play. But such an excuse also contradicts the second LDS Article of Faith, which states, "We believe that men will be punished for their own sins, and not for Adam's transgression."[14] In an enlightened democratic society, truth and consequences apply to women, as well as men. This sensibility, often expressed by the women of the early church, was sustained by the brethren. In 1870, the Relief Society sisters met in the Fifteenth Ward Society Hall to honor Acting Governor S.A. Mann for signing the law enfranchising women. Said Sister Presendia Kimball, "The day is approaching when woman shall be redeemed from the curse placed upon Eve."[15] When Eve represents all empowered women, and we celebrate her being courageous in perpetuating life, we gain new perspective on both the Garden of Eden story and celestial marriage.

Any structure that prefers man over woman seems to contradict basic Christianity, with its emphasis on the worth of the individual soul, regardless of race, ethnic background, gender, and age. "The Lord is not a respecter of persons," my parents often said to remind us that God doesn't care about status or money or worldly power. The saying also applies to gender. Enacting his message of universal love, Jesus freely included women among his friends, involved them as worthy spiritual entities, and spurned the double standard, enraging the orthodox leaders of his time who were accustomed to holding women separate and subservient. Jesus valued women and men; he broke bread with prostitutes as well as tax collectors; defended women who wanted to learn; he specifically acknowledged the woman who bathed his feet with her tears. He included women among his disciples. Close reading and insight gained from newly discovered ancient documents suggest that Mary Magdalene may have been one of Jesus' apostles. The risen Savior appeared to her before appearing to the others. She also seems to have had strong influence on organizing the early church. A clear exhortation to equality is found in Galatians 3:28: "There is neither Jew nor Greek, there is neither bond nor free, there is neither male nor female: for ye are all one in Christ Jesus" was ignored when Mary Magdalene was divested of power, presumably by Peter and other men in leadership. By the year 200, the pendulum had swung: The public position of women in the early phase eroded, the church became an institution, and patriarchal superiority was imposed on pure Christianity.[16] Despite the early Mormon stand for women's rights, The Church of Jesus Christ of Latter-day Saints organized in 1970s to suppress the Equal Rights Amendment. This is hard to fathom when considering that one hundred years earlier, the highest church authorities supported women in making their equality a matter of legal record. Even through the brethren were promoting the plural marriage agenda, the orderliness that characterizes God's household requires reconciliation. The developing church has changed its policies on certain issues over the years: on polygamy for instance, and on men of color holding the priesthood. The changes, emanating from the Living Prophet of The Church of Jesus Christ of Latter-day Saints, often reflect social and political demands but they always arise from prayer and revelation.

The contradiction between the current conservative mode of the church and the libertarian attitude of 140 years ago invites speculation about the demands on church leaders and the cycles of institutions. Were the brethren more or less pure in their response to women in the early days? Did the polygamous agenda encourage women to believe in a restoration that was never intended? Are the modern church authorities attempting to stave off forces that may undermine strong families: rocketing child abuse, homosexuality, and violence among children. Do families require full-time nurturers? Are women better off staying at home? Can they afford to stay at home in the current economy? Do women who work when their children need them waste their lives laboring for things that don't fulfill them or their children? In the world today, more women are raising their children alone, without the benefit of a life partner. Those who remain married are often saddled with all the family responsibilities—earning a living, taking care of the house, cultivating the children, preparing meals—because some men cling to the belief that "women's work" emasculates them; yet some men will happily allow their wives to provide for the family—traditionally a male role. By encouraging women to claim a context that allows them to stay home and raise their children, and encouraging their husbands to work to provide for their families, the leaders of the LDS Church are creating a latter-day haven for family.

We women in the church have always received considerable official encouragement to improve ourselves in all walks of life—so long as doing so does not require that we abandon our children. The LDS Church First Presidency and the Twelve Apostles have spoken at youth meetings, urging young women to obtain an education so that they can take care of their families should "something happen" to their husbands and also so that they can care for their families should the need for two incomes arise. They use the same advice in terms of family planning: be responsible.

Perhaps as a consequence of the church's strong stand for family, divorcees who are members often feel like outsiders. Women frequently feel pressured to give up their church callings when a divorce is in progress. Involvement in the church offers stability and comfort, so it seems a pity to reduce church participation in any way. Yet many divorcees feel shunned, reporting the loss of longtime friends and exclusion from "inner circle" events such as gatherings of high priests or elders and their wives. A divorcee might experience a loss of faith, but she doesn't always get the support she needs to regain it. Because divorcees must become autonomous and independent, they evoke discomfort in patriarchal settings. Their sexuality disturbs men and women alike, and they are seen as "free radicals" who can disrupt the integrity of established families. They often suffer not only from knowing how many regard them, but from the separate pain of watching healthy marriages. This could happen for divorcees anywhere, but the extraordinary success of LDS monogamous marriages exaggerates their sense of being on the outside looking in.

In the mainstream LDS Church, divorced women without children at home are encouraged to join singles congregations because church authorities want single men and women to aim for marriage. By attending singles wards it is hoped they will meet a single or divorced man. It isn't easy. Since most Mormon males receive serious pressure to marry, those who don't marry soon after their missions are completed often have some things to work through such as commitment issues, problems with pornography, or questions about their sexuality. Some are still avidly looking for "Princess Perfection." I find it interesting that this encouragement to attend singles wards doesn't apply to widows and it doesn't seem to be an issue with post-menopausal women unless they are actively seeking marriage.

Single women receive encouragement in developing their careers and in fulfilling eighteen-month missions for the church, but they are steadily reminded of the ultimate goal—marriage and children—which can be disheartening for a woman who feels she has dated every frog in the pond. After being single for sixteen years, Chris grew weary of disappointing blind dates and of hoping that her singles ward would serve up Prince Charming. She took it upon herself to gather information about all the LDS singles activities in the Salt Lake area and created a web site to compile and report singles activities, allowing people to advertise events that were not necessarily church-sponsored but that abide by LDS standards of conduct. It seems to have worked for her; she married her Prince Charming a few months ago. But so many single women populate singles wards, and so few dreams come true, I've privately wondered, drawing on my unusual background, if polygamy is a viable alternative for lonely hearts and lives on hold. But when a real-life fairy tale transpires, I'm told that it is definitely worth waiting for.

LDS people exercise extraordinary self-discipline because their attitudes toward sex follow scriptural lines. Regardless of the controverisal and foggy pronouncements about sex in Utah's pioneer days, church leaders have referred again and again to *The Holy Bible* and other LDS Scriptures. In keeping with 1 Corinthians 6:18, "Flee fornication . . . he that committeth fornication sinneth against his own body." Latter-day Saint leaders encourage their flocks to be chaste.

In polygamous communities, the Law of Chastity means something different from what it means in the mainstream LDS Church. In the polygamous context, the Law of Chastity dictates that men and women don't have sex unless they are committed to conceiving a child. So whenever a woman is pregnant, nursing, or menstruating, or when she has gone through menopause, engaging in sexual activity is considered inappropriate. This rigid rule discourages jealousy among plural wives, since the purpose of sexual activity stands foremost in everyone's mind: "to raise up a righteous seed unto the Lord."

In the mainstream Church of Jesus Christ of Latter-day Saints, the Law of Chastity means that fidelity in marriage is essential. This has sweeping implications for anyone preparing to marry for time and all eternity, suggesting that members refuse to participate in any semblance of sexual activity, including necking and petting, before marriage. Marital sex is regarded as a priesthood responsibility and the means for fulfilling the commandment to "multiply and replenish the earth." Latter-day Saints regard connubial relations as sacred, beautiful, and fulfilling. In heeding the call for purity and wholesomeness, Latter-day Saints recognize that sex is both a gift and an irrepressible force, one they need to be responsible in exercising.

In the late 1800s LDS Apostle Parley P. Pratt lectured about sustaining a healthy attitude toward sex:

> Some persons have supposed that our natural affections were the results of a fallen and corrupt nature, and that they are "carnal, sensual and devilish" and therefore ought to be resisted, subdued, or overcome as so many evils which prevent our perfection or progress in the spiritual life. . . . Our natural affections are planted in us by the Spirit of God for a wise purpose; and they are the very main-springs of life and happiness—they are the cement of all virtuous and heavenly society—they are the essence of charity or love. . . . There is not a more pure and holy principle in existence than the affection which glows in the bosom of a virtuous man for his companion.[17]

Unlike prevailing modern attitudes toward sex, behavior behind bedroom doors isn't a matter of "anything goes." Although bishops and other local church leaders are encouraged not to question married couples about their connubial practices, strong statements echo: "Sexual relations in marriage are not unrestrained. Even though sex can be an important and satisfactory part of married life, we must remember that life is not designed just for sex."[18] There's no permission at all for adultery or fornication, which according to LDS Scripture is "an abomination in the sight of the Lord; yea, most abominable above all sins save it be the shedding of innocent blood or denying the Holy Ghost"(Alma 39:5).

These restrictions may seem rigid. But in a world where people frequently die because of diseases caused by unwholesome sexual relations, such warnings carry a ring of truth. Even when death is not physical, relationships, families, and careers can be lost when people tamper with this powerful, life-giving force.

Married couples in the church seem to take to heart the challenge of staying within the guidelines of natural, normal sexual relations, and they receive huge rewards. After talking with various couples, I've learned that just as with other aspects of life, selfishness causes most problems in the bedroom. Success depends on a willingness to serve one another. Couples who are willing to focus on one another and on the relationship are more likely to cultivate intimacy, caring, and fulfillment.

With all the information made available through videos, books, and the Internet, people can be exposed to aberrant sexual behaviors without even leaving home. But LDS standards guard against this approach to sex, asking members to refrain from watching "R" rated movies, listening to suggestive music, or reading unwholesome literature. Some might worry that such emphasis on purity would diminish sexual interest, but the reverse seems to be true. Studies indicate that sexual innocence and ecstasy are strongly linked.[19] Ecstasy by its nature transcends reason and control, sometimes producing a mystic or metaphysical experience. The context provided by a loving, life-giving God makes possible the kind of rapture that everyone seems to be looking for. The price of bliss mirrors the consecration couples make of their lives in the holy temple: " . . . know ye not that your body is the temple of the Holy Ghost which is in you, which ye have of God, and ye are not your own? For ye are bought with a price: therefore glorify God in your body, and in your spirit, which are God's" (1 Corinthians 6:19, 20).

From speeches, journal and diary entries, and stories of Mormon women throughout time, one value emerges consistently: Being a woman in The Church of Jesus Christ of Latter-day Saints constitutes an act of faith. We will do our best no matter what we encounter. But both inside and outside of marriage, we women need to be valued as equals in order to feel fully empowered. Whether a woman finds fulfillment in this life depends not so much on the marriage, or even on whether she is married. It depends on whether she values herself and is valued by others as a daughter of God. If she is cherished and treated with respect, she is more likely to forsake the perception that Eve is cursed and, through faith, claim the full measure of her existence.

3

A Righteous Seed

We gathered in the living room for Family Home Evening, a Monday night ritual for all Latter-day Saints. Fundamentalists who live polygamy, like my father's family, claiming their relationship to the official church even though The Church of Jesus Christ of Latter-day Saints doesn't claim them, also participate in this family ritual. Thirty-five or so of us children sat on the floor or perched on our mother's laps. We sang an opening song, and my father asked my brother to say a prayer, our cue to fold our arms and close our eyes. Afterward my father looked at each of us, his blue eyes bright with unshed tears.

"You, my children, are the promise of the scriptures, the fulfillment of prophecy." One by one he met our eyes. "You, or your children or your children's children are the Children of the Millennium." Breathless, we poised to grab this clue that would yield a greater knowledge of who we were and why we were here in this life. But my father didn't explain. Instead he opened his heavy, dog-eared Scriptures and read Isaiah 40:31:

"'They that wait upon the Lord shall renew their strength; they shall mount up with wings as eagles; they shall run, and not be weary; and they shall walk, and not faint.'" He looked up and spoke in his own flowery prose. "By keeping the Lord's commandments and observing the Word of Wisdom, you will wax strong. We parents want nothing more desperately for you than that you achieve the full measure of your creation." His voice cracked and he stopped speaking until he regained his composure. Then he read one of his favorites, Matthew 18:5:

"'And whoso shall receive one such little child in my name receiveth me.'" We still didn't know exactly what being Children of the Millennium meant, but we were reassured that we children were precious and extraordinary, endowed with special gifts and talents. We were the reason for my father's many wives, the focus of his dedication. God mattered most, but we were next in importance to him.

My mother and her twin sister stood and Aunt Myrtle bustled to the piano to accompany them. From my place on the floor, back propped against my father's shins. I watched my mother's face, sweetness measured in her smile, eyes moist with feeling as her clear soprano reflected the music in her heart. Her sister harmonized the lower part just as wholeheartedly, and in that moment I felt privy to a stunning realization of just how much we meant to our parents.

> Favored little ones were they;
> Who towards him Jesus drew!
> Who within his arms he took
> Just as loving parents do;
>
> Christ, the Lord "Our living head."
> This of little children said.
> 'Such shall of my kingdom be,
> Suffer them to come to me.'
>
> Listen! to the Savior's plea,
> 'Let the children come to me;
> Let the little children come,
> Come to me; come to me.'[1]

This song, pulled from my trove of childhood memories, epitomizes the LDS attitude toward children and parenting. God and His Son, Jesus, are perceived as loving Father in Heaven and Savior/Big Brother, open-armed and welcoming, ready to receive us into their arms and Heaven's fold. They stand as the examples of what parents must be for their children. Ideologically at least, children are our most precious treasures, our dearest stewardship, our most important work. In 1995, as pressures mounted throughout the world to disrupt the traditional heterosexual family, the First Presidency of the Church of Jesus Christ of Latter-day Saints issued a document called *The Family, A Proclamation to the World,* which makes the importance of rearing children very clear:

> "Parents have a sacred duty to rear their children in love and righteousness, to provide for their physical and spiritual needs, to teach them to love and serve one another, to observe the commandments of God and to be law-abiding citizens wherever they live. Husbands and wives— mothers and fathers—will be held accountable for the discharge of these obligations." [2]

In a world always tempting, beckoning, tugging at our time and attention, families benefit enormously from such instruction. Making the family a priority means that parents and children spend the Sabbath day together (although they may be temporarily separated from anyone who has a demanding church calling). If friends show up at the door to play, they are told kindly that Cassie or Tyson can't play on Sunday: It's a family day. When homework and football practice and musical try-outs demand more and more of teenagers' time, there is spiritual and familial support for time with the family to ground and regenerate. In addition to the Sabbath, every dedicated LDS family observes Family Home Evening, also called Family Night, which is usually held Monday evening when no other church meetings are scheduled. In addition, when tempted to drink or do drugs or have sex, LDS youngsters can lean on the instructions of parents or the words of the prophet. In this way, the call to rear children in love and righteousness can shield them from many dangers in the world.

For the most part, children raised in LDS homes develop a strong sense of self. The Gospel of Jesus Christ can shore up a divine center in individuals, a self informed through prayer and personal revelation. Add a strong family to an attuned individual and you have a recipe for lifelong happiness. Even though Latter-day Saints are promised prosperity in return for keeping the commandments to pay tithing and observe the Sabbath day, devout members try not to become susceptible to materialism.

They try to keep their priorities straight, remembering that money cannot buy happiness or fulfillment.

Children attend church with their parents from the beginning. In addition to the congregational gathering called sacrament meeting, children attend meetings, almost always administered by women, where the little ones receive their own instruction in the Gospel. Children attend Sunday school and Primary, where they engage in age-appropriate activities, learn songs, and hear stories. They learn to help with the lessons and to give their own talks. At least once a year, and sometimes more often, they make a presentation in speech and song to the congregation. Nothing strikes the heart as poignantly as little children singing their gratitude for abundant life: "Child be glad with all that lives, but forget not God who gives."[3]

Despite strong support from the LDS Church in raising up a righteous seed, the instructions in the 1995 *Proclamation* are easier said than done: "We declare that God's commandment for His children to multiply and replenish the earth remains in force" poses a huge challenge in today's populated, economically-stressed world. The LDS belief that The Church of Jesus Christ has been established in the "last days for the restoration of his people" motivates members to do their part by providing spirits with mortal bodies and an opportunity for eternal exaltation. Many LDS couples go about family planning as if the population of Heaven depends entirely on them. Sometimes, in the pursuit of quantity, quality gets sacrificed when parents don't have the time or resources to meet the needs of burgeoning families. More than once I've heard of parents of large families unintentionally leaving one of their children at a service station or a restaurant or a national park. Sometimes they don't realize the mistake for hours, and the child trembles alone, feeling insignificant, overlooked and unloved.

The family system often groans under the strain when parents have big church callings. My husband, one of seven children, tells of a time when his mother, the Relief Society president, seemed to be in charge of everything. "If she had been a man, she would have been bishop," he says. His mother organized one ward event after another, for Halloween, then Thanksgiving, then Christmas, then New Year's Eve. He was thirteen years old and feeling severely neglected, so he stood in sacrament meeting to "bear his testimony." Fast and Testimony meeting is a monthly opportunity for members of the ward—and even non-members—to stand in sacrament meeting and speak their thoughts and feelings, following the edict to "let the Spirit direct the meeting." Little children often practice bearing their testimonies so that they'll be in the habit of professing their love for the Gospel and their families by the time they are teenagers. Even teens stand and say what they think and feel. Although no specific constraints are placed on members, there's an unwritten code that people will not say anything inappropriate such as grousing or making fun of people. Anyway, thirteen year-old Bruce stood not to testify of his great love for church and family, but to complain: "I hope you folks appreciate my mother because we sure don't see much of her anymore. While you were over here enjoying turkey and all the trimmings, we were home eating pork and beans." His mother pretended that his words had no effect on her, but she stopped giving so much time to the church after that.

"Train up a child in the way he should go: and when he is old, he will not depart from it" says Proverbs 22:6. What does this Scripture mean to an LDS woman? How does one train a child in the way he or she should go? Relief Society lessons delivered to women in the church imply that every good thing learned by sisters should be passed on to children through the example of parents and teachers. Manuals emphasize that children should learn to pray regularly, to study Scriptures, to obey the commandments (especially the Ten Commandments), and to attend church meetings. Children must imbibe the importance of Christian behavior: kindness, honesty, forgiveness. They are also taught foundations of chastity, that their bodies are sacred, temples for the spirit of God. They are encouraged to dress modestly, to date only after they've turned sixteen and under appropriate circumstances, and they are to be given love at home so that they don't go looking for it somewhere else.

From their earliest years, LDS children are acclimated to service, responsibility, and obedience, both in the home and through the programs of the church. From childhood, male children prepare for the responsibility of exercising God's power on earth by holding the priesthood, and to go on two-year missions for the church. Girls don't receive much encouragement to prepare for missions, although some young women who have not married will apply to go on a mission when they are 21 years old, serving for eighteen months. Girls focus on individual development, improving gifts and talents, growing spiritually and intellectually, learning homemaking skills, and helping with younger children. Both girls and boys aim for temple marriage. Children are encouraged to form good work habits, including a commitment to do the work in excellence and to complete tasks. Performing well in school, learning to meet personal needs, taking into account the highest good of all concerned, helping to manage family possessions and business interests, and learning to organize family projects all prepare a child to become an industrious leader and a team player. Special emphasis on caring for younger siblings creates brotherhood and sisterhood, so that individuals become caring members of the larger community—and the human race. The results are heartening: children who know how to take responsibility for themselves and assist those who need their help. In a world where toddlers typically get shuttled off to day care and elderly parents are stuck in nursing homes, this attitude of family interdependence reminds us that a gentler, more caring civilization is possible. As part of learning to serve, children and teenagers learn to care for their younger siblings, their nieces and nephews, and their elderly grandparents. They also engage in service projects such as lawn mowing, house repairs, and window-washing for the elderly of the ward.

But if it weren't for strong LDS youth programs, children could get lost in the gap between church-inspired idealism and the reality of everyday life. Fortunately, the concept that "it takes a village to raise a child" prospers in LDS communities where the whole ward takes part in children's instruction.

All LDS children are taught that they are sons and daughters of God from their first nursery classes as toddlers. When they are three years old they become "Sunbeams" in Primary. This children's educational program includes Sunday meetings, a monthly Achievement Day, and a variety of fun activities such as Halloween carnivals, Christmas parties, and perhaps the most outrageous and delightful, the Pioneer Day parade where children dress in the garb of their ancestors and walk or ride their bicycles in memory of the pioneers who trekked across the plains. As they parade, the children sing songs, including one entitled "Pioneer

Children Sang as they Walked," repeating 'walked' twelve times, only to start at the beginning and sing it again.[4]

This song can get little kids through a lot of walking, a lot of hot sun and bumps of the little red wagon. But the walking song doesn't do a thing for a runaway bicycle going downhill. My little brother always went to the Primary in our ward (despite our fundamentalist roots) and one Pioneer Day he rushed home with his skinny thigh split like a ripe watermelon. Neither his cowboy hat nor the Primary song protected him, and the doctor had to take sixty stitches in his leg. (Our father was out of town and having a stranger attend to him was as frightening as having his leg stitched up.) However, the treats and sweet ministrations of the Primary presidency and teachers, the visits from friends in his church class, and lots of family support restored him to full impishness. Influenced by this generosity and caring, he grew up and entered the official LDS Church, where he has served in the bishopric.

LDS boys also get involved in Boy Scouts, starting at age eight with the Cub Scout program; they are encouraged to continue until they become Eagle Scouts at sixteen. When I was called by the bishop to serve as a den mother or Cub Scout leader (something I ordinarily would not choose to do) I delighted in watching my son and nine other little boys race wildly in the fields behind our house. We walked together to the hill where an ancient structure for a teepee stood, and we went inside and told stories and speculated who had built it. We built a fire and roasted marshmallows. Being admired by ten eight-year old boys will always be one of the sweetest experiences in my life. By the time these boys became Eagle Scouts, they had developed character, learned survival skills, acquired appreciation for nature, and rendered substantial community service. Scouting is a major activity program for LDS young men. Although it has lost some significance among non-Mormons, LDS leaders consider scouting essential to prepare young men for adulthood, fatherhood, and citizenship. The boys learn about service, environmental responsibility, and other protective and reverential sensibilities, along with their "Duty to God" regimen. The annual Boy Scout Jamboree held in the vast Swanner Nature Preserve in Park City, Utah, filled fifty acres with tents and campfires of young men gathered with their leaders to sing songs, tell stories, and earn their badges.

The skill sets and secular instruction of the scouting program accompany the Aaronic Priesthood program which trains young men in their priesthood responsibilities. Twelve-year-old deacons are ordained to watch over the church and assist fourteen-year-old teachers who teach and exhort the members and assist sixteen-year-old priests who administer the sacrament and perform baptisms. Each young man is preparing to become "a minister and a witness" to Jesus Christ. As elders in the church—a position they can assume when they are eighteen years old—young men acquire the Melchizedek priesthood necessary for fulfilling a mission. All priesthood ordinations depend on worthiness (achieved through righteous living) as determined by their priesthood leaders.

LDS girls have Primary challenges specific to them, but no Girl Scout program. To many LDS people, the Girl Scout focus on selling cookies and worldly success seems out of alignment with the LDS picture of woman as homemaker and "sister in service." The LDS Young Women's program holds an annual week-long summer camp, feeble compensation for the absence of a scouting program.

At age twelve, girls enter the Young Women's program where they begin Personal Progress, a three-stage program that educates them spiritually, physically, emotionally, and mentally to prepare for their lives as women in The Church of Jesus Christ of Latter-day Saints. First they become Beehives, focused on being Daughters of God and the challenge to fulfill divinely-endowed roles as women. Beehives contribute to family life, learn about the priesthood, discover family history and temple work, get involved with ward and stake missionary efforts, and increase their spirituality through virtuous living. In this holistic approach to life, Beehives learn to maintain physical health, grow socially and emotionally, manage personal resources, and develop leadership skills. At age fourteen, young women are admitted to the MIA Maids program, (an anagram drawn from the early title of the church youth program, "Mutual Improvement Association") which focuses on drawing closer to Christ, developing spiritual gifts, and building the kingdom of God. These lessons reflect the commitments of the Beehive years, building on the foundation established there. At sixteen, Laurels are preparing to take their knowledge into the world, learning about their personal relationship with God, heeding the guidance that comes from within, and practicing the Gospel in their daily lives. Through their Personal Progress, they get a thorough education about Young Women's values, including faith, divine nature, individual worth, knowledge, choice and accountability, good works, and integrity. They learn some outdoor and camping skills as well as a variety of homemaking and survival skills, such as how to plant and raise a garden, how to crochet and knit, and how to be a good babysitter. As they get older, they have lessons in leadership and mentorship, they are groomed in appropriate dating and social behaviors, and they prepare for higher education. President Hinckley encouraged young women to "pray earnestly to the Lord for direction. Then pursue your course with resolution."5

Young LDS women attend special meetings and banquets where Rhodes scholars and beauty queens who have won scholarships encourage them to get advanced education. In addition parents, ward members, and church authorities strongly encourage young women to develop their gifts and thereby make a positive difference in the world. A yearly Young Women in Excellence night showcases their talents for family, friends, and ward members.

Brigham Young himself inspired the original organization of young Mormon women, encouraging his daughters to form a "cooperative retrenchment association" whose purpose was to retreat from the ways of the world and establish refinement in dress and deportment, to become proper Latter-day Saint women. Members of the Young Ladies Retrenchment Association joined the suffrage movement and, with the Relief Society, sent representatives to Washington, D.C., to attend the first meeting of the National Suffrage Association. The Young Women's program and the Young Men's association together claimed the motto, "The glory of God is intelligence" (Doctrine and Covenants 93:36). Over the years, the Young Women's program developed through the guidance of its leaders and in reciprocity with Relief Society until 1970, when it was brought into correlation with other church programs. The current Young Women's motto, "We stand for truth and righteousness," sums up the challenge given by Brigham Young to be examples to the congregation and the world in word, deed, and attitude.

It's challenging to be a Latter-day Saint in the making, while holding such high standards in regard to others. And the demands are even greater for the mothers of young women, who must attend to their own development while being accountable for the progress of their children. The resource pamphlet issued by the LDS Church Presidency and utilized by almost every LDS parent to define dating rules and other youth guidelines, "For the Strength of the Youth" outlines behaviors that set a higher standard than some fully achieve, but the standard still has enormous influence. Those who abide by the guidelines are rewarded with the order and equilibrium essential to developing character in an otherwise unstable world.[6]

The ward community, the village that helps to raise the child, offers guidance, comfort, and support to parents and children. Leaders in the youth programs, bishops, and home teachers offer a bulwark against adversarial influences. The sons and daughters of single parents get bolstered by Mormon neighbors, who include them in vacations, pick them up for youth activities, and make sure they get a ride to church if necessary. Since teens often look outside the home for someone to talk to, it is wonderful when that someone is a member of the church, someone who will encourage moral and healthy behaviors rather than taking advantage of the teen's vulnerability and leading him or her down a destructive path.

When church lessons remind couples of their purpose to "raise up a righteous seed unto the Lord," children have complex significance in a marriage. Many LDS couples consider their children to be the only measure of their success and become obsessed with how their offspring make them look. In fact, if LDS couples suffer any built-in stigma, it could be due to the notion that the relationship itself cannot possibly be as significant as what it produces. Couples who don't have children often feel inadequate and somehow wrong, as if their relationship has no intrinsic value. Once children are born, couples tend to set the marriage on the back burner and the family focuses on cultivating righteous little sprouts. This pendulum swing can hurt the marriage and disorient the children. If balance is not maintained, these children grow up with a superior attitude. Sometimes children become dedicated servants of mankind, devoted to making a difference for others and thus proving their extraordinary nature. Other times they act as if they stand above everyone else even if they don't contribute anything.

Obedience may be the most emphatic tenet in the official church. Obedience to the Ten Commandments. Obedience to the laws and ordinances of the church. Obedience to the words of the prophets and the apostles. Obedience to four different sets of Scripture: *The Holy Bible, Book of Mormon, Doctrine and Covenants,* and *The Pearl of Great Price.* Husbands obeying the Lord and their priesthood leaders. Wives obeying their husbands. Children obeying parents and teachers. Given that each of us is striving to discover and explore and grow, this maze of obedience can seem impossible to negotiate. If parents cannot induce their children to cooperate, the family image stands in jeopardy.

Too often, outpourings of love remain verbal rather than actual, which can further complicate the relationship between LDS parents and their progeny. When children don't measure up to expectations, everyone's heart gets burdened with the problematic emotions of shame, blame, and resentment. Raising children by the book can create a menu of "coulds" and "shoulds." and the child who is "too good to be true" can be exactly that: LDS parents sometimes reach out to the mental health community for help in curbing unwanted behaviors and readily receive medication for their children, which can contribute to the child's sense that he or she is broken. Perhaps this eagerness to produce conforming children has contributed to Utah's informal reputation as the Ritalin capital of the nation.

Even in the best of families, kids go south. Sometimes rebellion can be ascribed to simple oppositional behavior outgrown in adulthood, a means of establishing an identity separate from his or her parent. Sometimes the rebellion runs deeper and has to do with hypocrisy in the family: If you ask them, most teens in rebellion believe that family values are based on what others think, rather than genuine concern for modesty or discretion or diligence.

LDS leaders encourage parents to give their children room to be who they are and trust that they can make good decisions. Prophet

Joseph Smith said of governance, "Teach them correct principles and they govern themselves."[7] Most current authorities in the LDS Church agree that children should be cultivated, loved, and encouraged, practices that shore up self-esteem, rather than having their faults pointed out all the time.

When children are seen as extensions of their parents, the youngsters often pay for the parents' sense of inadequacy. Hierarchical by nature, a patriarchal culture inculcates subtle second-class citizenship. When children are regarded as appendages or possessions, parents (especially fathers and stepfathers) often believe that they can do what they want with them. The surprisingly high rate of child abuse found in Utah during the 1970s was ascribed to this fact, among others. Many people included in this category of abusers were those on the periphery of the LDS culture, people who felt alienated from the mainstream and somehow wrong. Many were stepfathers and boyfriends of women who had babies too young and who subjected their children to drug users, neglect and abandonment. Some were fundamentalists, patriarchs running amok with power and plural wives delerious with frustration. Some abusers deliberately identified themselves with behaviors in dramatic contrast to the Gospel. But a startling number were church members pretending to be something they were not. Some of these were mothers, frustrated by their inability to achieve perfection in themselves and/or their children. Some were fathers who felt that they should be able to control their families. [8]Currently, any member of the church who abuses spouse and/or children may be denied temple privileges. The child abuse rate has dropped significantly since the 1970s, which may indicate that screening through temple interviews is working in favor of the children.

In some polygamous cultures, children routinely endure abuse. Partly because of the secrecy surrounding their culture, partly because they have become "a law unto themselves," polygamists seem more inclined to visit their fears, frustrations, and appetites on their children. Old Testament law prevails in fundamentalist circles, so "spare the rod and spoil the child" is a common sentiment. Even infants are subject to strict and sometimes brutal treatment. New babies are typically swaddled so tightly they can't move, a form of control that sets kids up for disciplined lives. In the fundamentalist community currently under scrutiny in southern Utah, there are reports of toddlers being pinched till blood blisters form.[9] I have been told by fundamentalist refugees that when babies cry, they might be slapped or dunked in water until they learn to be quiet. Some fundamentalist fathers initiate their daughters into sexual activity as their "patriarchal right." Having decided to live outside the law, these men decide that even the ancient taboo regarding incest does not apply to them.

After I published my first book about growing up in a polygamous household headed by a kind and respectful father, several women called to tell me of being raped or molested by their fathers or other patriarchs in their fundamentalist group. As I questioned them, I learned that some fathers would ask male friends to their homes and invite them to partake of "my beautiful daughters" as if they were part of the hospitality—a sort of dessert to follow the evening meal. A covert belief that men are the only ones who matter and that women and children are property establishes a context where some mothers consciously endure the exploitation of their female children.

The violation of such ancient laws is only one of many reasons the Church of Jesus Christ of Latter-day Saints warns members to stay away from polygamous and other apostate groups. Indeed, the LDS emphasis on obedience supports healthy and safe living in other ways as well. The Twelfth Article of Faith declares that Latter-day Saints "believe in being subject to kings, presidents, rulers, and magistrates, in obeying, honoring and sustaining the law."[10] By also being obedient to the commandments and heeding the direction of church leaders, many children stay safe despite gang influences, drug dealers, and video violence. Families stay intact despite the forces that try to tear them apart. In a world where lives are career-driven, the LDS people see the church as a bastion of the family, pointing the way home. Although some accuse the brethren of sexism and tyranny, they nonetheless sustain a context where women can cultivate their young and where family life matters. Now if only we could insure the safety of everyone in the home.

Church instruction on homemaking and child rearing sets up LDS girls to be in constant demand as babysitters and nannies. It's not unusual for a nineteen-year old woman to forgo college for a year or two to accept employment as an au pair for a working couple in a big city.

Despite lifelong training in child care and a legacy of hard work, the nanny adventure does not always work out for the young woman—or her employers. People who expect these girls to behave as minions soon discover that they are clear about their personal rights, their relationship with God, and the value of their own lives. They assert themselves when they feel that something is out of order, and employers aren't always prepared for such strong demonstrations of character.

As they move toward adulthood, LDS teens go to the temple to be baptized as proxies for those who didn't receive the Gospel of Jesus Christ before they died. Teenagers have sworn they heard angels singing when they came out of the baptismal waters, and most who participate in these rituals feel that they have done a great service. According to the LDS belief in "Spirit Prison," unconverted souls are maintained in a gentle purgatory where they are taught the principles of the Gospel. As the baptisms by proxy are performed, souls are released to a higher glory.

Not surprisingly, in a religion that places so much emphasis on family and children, the LDS Church has always been concerned about maternity and infant care. Second Relief Society President Eliza R. Snow sought to establish a hospital for women, and her initiatives led to several women being sent east to receive medical training. An LDS preference that women rather than men attend births may have motivated Brigham Young to send so many women to earn their medical degrees. Romania B. Pratt Penrose became the first trained ophthalmologist to practice in Utah. Sister-wives Ellis Shipp and Margaret Shipp Roberts also became physicians as did Martha Hughes Cannon (who ran against her husband, Angus, to win a seat in the first Utah senate).[11]

In my family, babies were generally born at home. I remember returning from pep club practice with a friend. We had intended to stay only long enough to change clothes and meet the boys we were dating that night. But my sister-in-law was giving birth in my mother's bedroom, and my friend stood by the door, fascinated and awestruck. Something so normal to me seemed so exotic to her that we called the boys and told them we would be late. We hung around until we could hold my beautiful little niece. My friend (who'd rather have fun than study) was so deeply moved by the experience that she actually started studying and went to college to study nursing.

I took such earthy realities for granted. From the time my father delivered me at home, I had been exposed to the phenomenon which some call birth-light, an energy of newness and promise like no other. This natural birth experience dates back to the early days of the LDS Church, when midwives were preferred over male doctors. As the medical establishment grew strong and natural healing methods and lay nurses fell by the wayside, fundamentalists insured that the practice of midwifery would survive. Polygamists didn't trust official institutions in general, and for good reason: Hospitals kept extensive and potentially incriminating records. Even birth certificates could be used in a court of law to prove that a man was practicing polygamy. (This was why I never had one, for I was born close on the heels of my father's trial and imprisonment, when birth records had been used to prove "illegal cohabitation.") Midwives continue to be popular among those who prefer natural methods, including a small percentage of mainstream Latter-day Saints who refuse to trade the spiritual experience of birth for the safe but drug-laden delivery associated with hospitalization.

I didn't hear much about birth control when I was growing up. I only knew that every time a new baby was expected, everyone rejoiced. When I was older I came to realize that those babies were a mixed blessing and that the parents of a big tribe needed considerable courage and resourcefulness.

One mother of a big family struggled to feed her burgeoning brood. Her husband helped provide by taking their sons hunting. If the boys shot an elk or helped to skin a deer, they got extra meat at the dinner table. Despite encouragement from his father and brothers, Ben, the youngest boy, didn't want to kill the deer. He wept when his father slit the throat, and his brothers teased him. At dinner, Ben wept again, thinking of the deer, and soon he stopped eating meat altogether. Most of Ben's siblings grew up to marry in the temple. They became good providers and homemakers, and followed in their parents' footsteps by raising large families. Ben broke the pattern by telling the family that he was gay. As faithful LDS members, his mother and father couldn't understand it. Surely Ben was mistaken. Hadn't they raised him properly? Hadn't they set good examples? Hadn't they taught him to pray when they tucked him in at night, read the Scriptures with him, fed him properly? Hadn't his brothers and his father taught him to fish and hunt, to accept his priesthood callings, to date girls? Surely Ben would come to his senses and repent. Despite his parents' pleas, all Ben wanted was to have a life of his own. His mother continues to believe that in the hereafter, Ben will acknowledge his role as a patriarch and husband and become the father of all those unborn children he was supposed to have, whereupon he will be reunited with them in eternity. Parents who "train up a child in the way he should go" don't know what to do if the scriptural promise that he will "return to it when he is old" goes unfulfilled.

In a world where a booming population poses a threat to the fragile ecosystems of the earth, some people are repulsed by the religiously-motivated egomania that would produce huge broods of children. In this regard the LDS people do, indeed, suffer from an embarrassment of riches. Looking at the number of large LDS families, one might conclude that we're in competition for the size of families and numbers in the congregation. But while we're encouraged to multiply and replenish, the church does not interfere directly in family planning or prevent members from using birth control. Elder Gordon B. Hinckley (in 1984, before he became the prophet and president of the LDS Church and was serving on the Council of the Twelve Apostles) said "The Lord has told us to multiply and replenish the earth that we might have joy in our posterity. . . . But he did not designate the number, nor has the Church. That is a sacred matter left to the couple and the Lord." [12]

Fundamentalists do not have such a liberal view of birth control. (Extreme is to fundamentalism as yeast is to bread.) The first time I mentioned my preferred form of birth control to the fundamentalist family I grew up in, I had been married for eight years and had given birth to two children, yet my mother's sister-wife fixed me with an icy look and abruptly left the room. It took me awhile to understand how I had offended her. She had spent eighteen years trying to conceive before her prayer for a child was answered. That I practiced birth control only confirmed her suspicion that I didn't appreciate the gift of procreativity or the sacredness of life.

In polygamy, where children are the ultimate justification for women (one of my brothers once called me a "baby factory"), barrenness becomes a knife in the heart, a sword in the gut, a never-ending torment that can unbalance a mind and shrivel a soul. I have seen my father's wives and my own sisters agonize over childlessness, and sometimes I have seen their constant pleadings with God rewarded after twelve, fourteen, eighteen childless years. I have also seen them emerge childless but with dignity and beauty of character. These sisters have put the worth of a single soul in shining perspective; how much more thoughtful and deliberate a woman must be when she cannot make a half-conscious decision to pass her legacy through her genes.

Sisterhood can be a beautiful thing when it comes to bearing children. In some plural families, wives with children have been known to give their babies to barren sister-wives. Both in polygamous communities and in the mainstream church, women gather for the birth and coach the mother through her labor. They take care of the other children, fix meals, and do housework until the mother has recovered.

When a baby is born in the official LDS Church, women fill in for each other almost as readily as if they were sisters. I have enjoyed being at both the giving and the receiving ends of this reciprocal sisterhood. Through Relief Society, new mothers receive the support of hot meals, helping hands, and free child care. Then we members of the sisterhood get to actively celebrate with new parents: We bring casseroles and fresh bread and Jell-O salad. We bring potted plants and yardsticks to hang on the wall to mark the child's growth and baby books to record the first events of the baby's life. We bring baby booties and handkerchief bonnets and hand-crocheted blankets for the baby's blessing. In the ward, before people start bearing their testimonies at fast and testimony meeting, the elders hold the baby and bless him or her with a name and a promise of happiness if he or she obeys the commandments. Then the father holds the baby aloft for the congregation's oooh's and ahhh's. For the duration of the meeting, women pass the baby around, each of us sniffing the wondrous newborn fragrance, nuzzling the soft downy back of the neck, holding the fragile fingers and counting the months or years since we held our own tiny being this way.

In some especially close-knit wards, nursing mothers will take care of each other's babies while their sister in the Gospel is teaching a lesson or leading the choir. If the baby cries in hunger, the mother will nurse this sister's child as readily as she would her own. The child, in some sense, belongs to everyone in the ward, and the joy in this new baby becomes everyone's joy.

Although they don't agree on polygamy or birth control, one subject on which the official LDS Church and the fundamentalist groups agree is abortion. Both regard it as a grievous infraction, and warn those who tamper with unborn life that they are succumbing to evil. The LDS position on abortion reflects the overarching respect and reverence for life that I have come to associate with the religion. (I know, of course, that religion has been used as bludgeon and cannon, as an instrument of torture and of death, as well. But I am one of those who directly owes her life to religion.) The LDS Church acknowledges that, in rare cases, abortion may be justified: when rape or incest is involved, or when the life of the mother hangs in the balance, or when competent medical authority states that the fetus has severe defects that will not allow the baby to survive. But even these are not necessarily reasons for abortion, which the church dictates should happen only after a couple has consulted with one another and their ecclesiastical leaders, and after praying about it.

LDS Church leaders have declared that "the practice of elective abortion is fundamentally contrary to the Lord's injunction, quoting the Doctrine and Covenants: 'Thou shalt not steal; neither commit adultery, nor kill, nor do anything like unto it.' We urge all to preserve the sanctity of human life and thereby realize the happiness promised to those who keep the commandments of the Lord." [13]

In 2006, during the Commission on the Status of Women at the United Nations, LDS women joined with other conservative Christians to encourage delegates to shift the vote on women's health issues from building abortion clinics (a major plank in the European platform) to more emergent issues regarding women's health (including cancer, heart disease, and other primary causes of death). I was there to witness when the United States stood with a few nations to confront a strong push to construct more abortion clinics. The LDS contingent also supported the distribution of information about research pointing to a link between abortion and breast cancer. [14]

To counteract the strong inclination of pregnant teenagers to seek abortion, the church offers solutions for unwed mothers and pregnant teens; they can stay in homes for the duration of their pregnancy and offer their baby up for adoption to a temple-worthy couple, with the assurance that the child will have a good life with sound spiritual foundations. Of the babies so adopted, over 90 percent end up in loving homes where they become devout church members and grow up to marry in the temple themselves. [15]

Of the young LDS women who give birth out of wedlock and give their babies up to a temple-worthy couple, most continue their education, marry in the temple, and bear more children. Of those who try to keep their babies and raise them as teenage mothers, a very small percentage marry in the temple, many do not marry at all, and most live in circumstances marred by poverty and a lack of education.[16]

High LDS standards can backfire. In one case, a married woman had an affair while separated from her husband. She conceived a child, and everyone knew it was illegitimate. She went through with her divorce and stood alone, pregnant and unwelcome in her ward. All the mothers refused to let their children play with her children, and she finally moved to another ward, rather than have her children grow up with such heavy condemnation hanging over their heads. Mormons can be as judgmental as any other group of people, even when the happiness of little children is at stake.

Yet Latter-day Saints are capable of incredible courage on behalf of their children. The desire to give birth, to be obedient and follow the laws of life in spite of the risks, waxes strong in LDS women who confront adversity with faith. A sister in the Gospel and dear friend of mine, Trudy, discovered melanoma in two spots, one on her back and one on her arm, thanks to years of sun-bathing as a teen. Following successful surgery, doctors, friends, and loved ones warned her about the enormous danger of the disease's return, the high mortality rate associated with this form of cancer, and advised her to be content with her three children, for the stress of pregnancy was likely to cause the cancer to recur. Trudy accepted this at first. As the years passed, however, she had dreams and impressions that led her to the strong belief that another spirit waited on the other side longing for a body and an eternal family, a being she had promised to bring to earth. Her eleven-year-old son Landon told her that he knew, somehow, that Jesus would not let her get sick if she had another child. She gave birth to a beautiful little girl who is almost six years old, and the melanoma has not returned.

Perhaps more than anything else, children test the faith of LDS parents. What happens when a child is born with a birth defect? Most Latter-day Saints participate in our high-tech world of ultrasound and amniotic testing, so they usually know ahead of time if a fetus has problems but they rarely elect to interrupt the birth. Sometimes the parents have faith that blessings and prayers can heal the baby. Sometimes they share a faith that the baby, with its defect, is being born into their home for a reason only Heaven understands, and that to shirk the responsibility is to interfere with God's plan.

Once in a while, someone in the church may lapse into judgment, deciding that God is punishing the parents of a birth-defective child for unknown sins. But there is really nothing in LDS Scripture to support this point of view. In fact, LDS parents are more likely to receive comfort and meaning through their faith and their fellow members. For example, Jessica gave birth to a baby with a defective heart who lived scarcely a week. Throughout the process, Jessica maintained faith that the Lord's will was being done. When the baby died, she concluded that this little spirit had needed to stay on earth only long enough to secure a body. The couple had the child sealed to them, and Jessica believes that the child will receive a glorified, perfect body through the promise of the Resurrection.

Unlike those who believe that babies are born into original sin, Latter-day Saints adhere to the Second Article of Faith which states: "We believe that men will be punished for their own sins, and not for Adam's transgression."[17] We believe that babies are born good and that they are not accountable for sins until they reach the Age of Accountability—eight years old, when they become eligible to be baptized.

One couple, Robert and Susan, married in middle age. A few of years later, they were delighted to discover that Susan was pregnant. Tests motivated by the fact that they were both nearing fifty soon revealed that the baby had Down syndrome. The grandparents were devastated; was Susan somehow being punished for waiting so long to marry? But Robert and Susan believed that the surface of things obscured a beautiful truth. Mainly to assuage her mother and father, Susan made an appointment with a prominent church leader. He told them that in the Pre-existence, during the War in Heaven, their child had been a most valiant spirit for Christ. Such an enlightened being needed to be protected from Satan during his earthly existence; hence, the Lord had given the child this condition to assure his return to paradise. This reassurance allowed the grandparents to wholeheartedly embrace this child of love and faith.

In fundamentalist communities, the rate of birth defects is higher than in the mainstream because of intermarriage and substandard birthing practices. Not all fundamentalists allow intermarriage (my father, being a doctor, refused to let cousins marry, knowing the genetic roulette involved), but the belief that eugenic breeding will produce a noble bloodline encourages a few proud patriarchs to rationalize cousins marrying cousins, uncles wedding nieces, and so on. The result: birth defects. This, combined with the fundamentalist paranoia that keeps them away from mainstream medical doctors and hospitals, puts mothers and babies at serious risk. Since midwives deliver most of the babies, even when a doctor is involved, most polygamists do not have medical insurance or money, or trust in the system. Consequently, even when the birth isn't going well, they stay at home, laboring with difficulty until damage occurs to mother and baby. After my father, the doctor attending thousands of polygamist births, had died, women who had little or no training attempted to midwife in his place. Their lack of knowledge showed up in a disturbing number of botched births.

Unlike fundamentalists who are wary of the "ways of the world" most members of the modern LDS Church have been quick to ride the waves of scientific knowledge and have welcomed enlightened methods of maternity and infant care. In the 1800s, the strong Relief Society tradition of maternity care was established and made way for forward-looking infant and child welfare. With the passage of the Nineteenth Amendment to the Constitution, women who had been organized for suffrage turned their attention to improving the lot of women and children. As national public health practices improved in the 1920s, Relief Society President Clarissa Williams took a strong stand for maternal and child health care. Her main concern was that the interest on the wheat raised and sold by the Relief Society would be used to lower the maternal and infant mortality rate. By 1924 the death rate among LDS children had decreased significantly, allowing the church to claim that by cooperating with local health authorities, 500 young lives had been saved. The establishment of fine maternity care and excellent nursing programs paved the way for LDS Hospital, which flourishes in Utah today.[18] Similarly, the devotion of Primary President Louise B. Felt generated treatment programs for sick and injured children, which led to the establishment of Primary Children's Hospital, one of the best pediatric care centers to be found.[19]

During the Depression, funds went to bishops instead of Relief Society presidents, and money earmarked for maternity and child care was often rerouted to fund buildings or more food storage. (Food storage has always been important in LDS culture, the prophets continually encouraging members and organizations within the church to put food and other necessities aside for a time of emergency.) Despite rerouted funds, the success of those years prove how powerful an alliance of women can be. Together, they changed the plight of the sisters and their children; the cooperative efforts of Relief Society and various public agencies had produced the most significant reduction in maternal and infant mortality rates in the nation.[20]

Always, the challenge of creating an uplifting environment at home trumps everything else of importance. The charge to make home seem a "heaven on earth" for husbands and children poses a tall order, but that's the instruction given to women in the LDS Church. This includes teaching each person to be sensitive and respectful of one another's feelings so that the spirit of the Lord will dwell in the home, kindling in each family member the sense of being wanted and needed. In this heaven on earth, the family gathers for prayer, individuals are encouraged to pray, Family Home Evenings convene regularly, and everyone engages in daily Scripture-study. Books, music, laughter—these are the elements of a happy home, habits encouraged among the sisterhood that women instill in their families.

"By their fruits ye shall know them" (Matthew 7:20). Results don't lie; they are the litmus test of religion and of every reality. Christ often referred to children, holding them as a standard of innocence, of clarity, and of alignment with Father in Heaven, whose loving concern was infinite and eternal: " . . . it is not the will of your Father which is in heaven that one of these little ones should perish" (Matthew 18:14). The ability of Latter-day Saints to give prodigiously to the children of the world extends not just to youngsters but to all God's children—to the entire human family:

> "I am a child of God
> And He has sent me here,
> Has given me an earthly home
> With parents kind and dear."[21]

In general, the fruits of Latter-day Saint living are sweet, especially in regard to children. Fewer instances of drug abuse, teen suicide, and child abuse (in families sealed in the temple) and a lower divorce rate—all these point to safe LDS homes. Higher-than-average grades, civic involvement, and school attendance indicate that children are encouraged to succeed. Community commitment manifests in members' contributions of time, energy, money, and heart to the children. The two-year mission expected of all LDS males and that of women who choose to fulfill an eighteen-month mission before marrying puts the capstone of service in place. By committing to something greater than themselves, LDS youth become world-class participants in a happier global community. Rabbi Harold Kushner, addressing the students of Brigham Young University in 1995 remarked that the commitment manifested by a two-year mission, even if it yields no baptisms, improves life on earth because of the purity of service rendered.[22] Life on earth becomes better for everyone when we commit to serve our Heavenly Father's children, our brothers and sisters in the human family.

The "Every Member a Missionary" program, in which all members of the church, including little children are encouraged to participate, exemplifies the love for fellow beings cultivated in the LDS people. By sharing the message of the LDS Church—that we are all children of a Heavenly Father who loves us and wants us to lead joyous, fulfilling lives, that we have been given a Savior who atoned for our sins, and that families can be together forever—members find an appropriate expression for their caring. New Missionary Training Centers have been built in the last ten years to assist members and full-time missionaries in sharing this message with their brothers and sisters throughout the world. In a sense, we truly are all children, all in need of a brother or a sister who will lend a helping hand, each of us longing for loving parents, all in search of home. By reaching out to one another, we can find our way together. If we can reach out to those who are suffering or lost, then the children within and without, the children at home and in foreign lands, will thrive.

4

Call the Man

"**B**ecause my husband holds the priesthood, I feel like royalty," one LDS woman told me. "I know that no matter what comes along—sickness or injury or disaster—I have the power of the priesthood to see me through it. Because my husband is willing to honor his priesthood, I can have whatever I need and most of what I want, as long as it doesn't conflict with God's plan."

"What is the power of priesthood?" I asked my son, Jeff, thinking that he would know since he has grown up in the mainstream of the LDS Church.

He gave a characteristically succinct answer. "It's the power of God on earth . . . the power to act in His name."

"How do you honor your priesthood?"

"By striving to live righteously. By using my priesthood to benefit people and serve them. Rather than . . . something else."

The "something else" refers to not only the secular values that beckon, but also to the potential abuses and illusions that accompany any sort of power, religious or secular. The claim of genuine priesthood authority separates The Church of Jesus Christ of Latter-day Saints from other churches. As my nephew, Ben, who had just returned from a mission said by way of explanation, "The ice cream man can't dispense traffic tickets because he has no authority. Proper authority makes all the difference."

My son-in-law, Todd (whose father was a bishop throughout most of Todd's youth) gave me a more extensive answer regarding what is expected of men in the church. Being a male Latter-day Saint means being the best father, husband, priesthood holder, and servant to mankind one can possibly be. It requires participating wholeheartedly in your family, your career, your church, your neighborhood, and the outlying community. The church gives us a consistent message that men must be eligible to attend the temple and engaged in upholding commitments made in the temple. To be temple-worthy, a man must observe the Word of Wisdom (abstaining from coffee, tea, alcohol, drugs, tobacco, and more), keep high moral standards (being faithful in his marriage, refraining from masturbation, pornography, and other unchaste, unnatural, or unwholesome acts), maintain financial integrity (providing for his family and paying his tithing), and truly be a servant of the Lord by serving in the church and the community, thus honoring his life's purpose.

For LDS women, men who fit this bill are potential Prince Charmings. A man who serves God first, his wife and family second, his career third and thereby his community engenders respect and inspires dedication. Such clean-living, service-oriented, and honorable sons are a dream to raise. As friends, such men show up when needed and do their best to see fellow beings, including women, through God's eyes, rather than passing judgment or trying to take advantage. That is, they can be all these things when they actually live according to the precepts of the Gospel. When they don't, they can be sanctimonious, self-righteous, hypocritical con artists.

From the time they are old enough to aspire to spiritual maturity, boys train for baptism and missionary service. Boys regularly sing "I Hope They Call Me on a Mission" in the Primary program. According to Todd, until boys become teenagers—and sometimes not until they embark on their mission—they don't realize that they actually have a choice in the matter. Although they are expected to be in control of themselves and their lives, many follow along by rote rather than making their own decisions about such basics as getting baptized, going on a mission, choosing a life partner, and getting married in the temple.

Of course, this tall order of qualities and behaviors isn't easy to fill. In the gap between what is expected and what actually occurs, a lot can get lost or stuck, leaving part of a young man's personality buried or imprisoned.

According to my husband, Bruce, an LDS man must stay in alignment with the Gospel and align his values with the church—which means exercising a lot of discipline and honoring a lot of covenants. Given each member's right to personal revelation, Bruce feels that people must fulfill these covenants according to their own lights, rather than succumbing to a sea of expectations and manipulations. He knows that fulfilling one's calling in life might require doing something that others judge or criticize. Because of his work as a communication trainer, Bruce encourages people to look deeply into themselves and speak honestly from their real experience, rather than delivering a sugar-coated account of their lives that omits doubts, fears, and contradictions. When the social veneer is penetrated, people reveal alarming inconsistencies and proclivities that can be disguised by a church-generated image, or any other image, for that matter. The insincere take advantage of the sincere; meanwhile, those who want to pretend that "all is well" in Zion don't want to deal with the cognitive dissonance resulting from contradictions of ideal and real. "As an LDS man I sometimes feel judged and criticized, that I'm somehow lacking when compared to others' notion of what I should be. Sometimes the criticism comes from the world outside, and I can handle that. But when disapproval comes from a clique within the ward, it hurts. It feels like I'm being sent the statement, 'We are more valuable than you are because we are more righteous than you are, therefore God loves us more.'"

In his work, Bruce travels extensively to conduct communication workshops for the general population and often returns on Sundays after church is over. He believes that he has been subject to criticism because he isn't always available to serve in traditional church callings. "I feel that my work requires a hundred percent, and it's a huge consecration of my time—especially whenever I donate my time." (He has freely shared his abilities with various community programs over the years.) Because his seminars sometimes save lives and always enhance the well-being of others, he says, "I think of it as being better than nine-to-five land-grabbing and exploitation, or getting people to buy expensive things they don't need that won't make them happy, and then showing up to pass out the program or teach a class on Sunday. But instead of being given a calling that reflects the specialized quality of my skills and talents, I'm ostracized because I don't readily fit into the system."

Thanks to my peculiar background, I always did relate to men who feel like they don't fit perfectly into the system. When I was a teenager, with little experience to make comparisons, most LDS boys seemed like rice pudding: somewhat sweet, good for you, a little bland. My father often ate rice pudding to calm his ulcers, and I imagined LDS men to be a similar balm. Why then, I wondered, was I always attracted to my brothers' rougher, tougher friends, the ones who were marginally religious or perhaps weren't even LDS? Parents within the mainstream church frequently remind their sons and daughters of the supreme importance of dating and marrying those who believe in the Gospel. Despite their fundamentalist backdrop, my parents were no different. Although most parents tolerate their children dating nonmembers, there's an unwritten, often unspoken expectation that they'll convert anyone who isn't a member before considering them as a potential mate.

Too preoccupied with leaving the polygamous group and jumping into the mainstream of life to worry about whether my dates were LDS or not, I dated a gamut of young men. One Saturday night my senior year of high school, I had two dates, the first an obligatory arrangement with a young man named Jed who had been very kind to me. The list of his kindnesses had grown long, beginning with his crush on me. He'd invited me to prom, had nominated me to a student-body office, and had made sure I was a candidate for homecoming queen. When he asked me to go out with him, I felt obligated to say yes.

Jed was a good LDS kid: He didn't swear, at least not around girls, he didn't drink or smoke or drive too fast. He came to the front door to pick me up, took me to dinner and an indoor movie, parked in the driveway to talk when he brought me home. We spoke of things I considered peripheral: grades, college entrance exams, football. I did care about those things. But my whole being itched to resolve the issue that had taken over my life.

The previous spring, after I had turned sixteen (deemed officially old enough to date), I had been raped. Now, at the overripe age of seventeen, I engaged in a labyrinthine plan to avenge myself. My second date, once Jed dropped me off, would be with the man who had raped me.

But Jed was talking about God and the church and how grateful he was for the power of the priesthood. I looked at him out of the corner of my eye. "Why are you so grateful?" I asked.

"One night we were playing pool in a friend's basement. He had an Ouija board and we started playing with it. We asked some questions that . . . well, we shouldn't have asked, like 'Will we all live long lives? Will the world be destroyed by nuclear war?' That sort of thing. The board wouldn't give us an answer. Instead it rose up—I swear, it did, it sort of floated and tipped over and I could feel Satan in the room. We were all pretty scared, so I raised my arm to the square and I cast out the devil. I said, 'In the name of Jesus Christ, I command you to depart.' And it did. Then it was peaceful in the room. We threw the Ouija board in the garbage can outside and went back to playing pool."

He'd grabbed my full attention. For a moment, I was more focused on his bête noir than my own. Then I wondered if, through the discerning power of the priesthood, he had any idea what I'd been planning. I half expected him to raise his arm to the square and cast the demons out of me. He didn't. And, young gentleman that he was, he didn't try to kiss me good night.

It was a crossroads moment in my life; I might have dated him for the next several months, and such a shift in companionship could have made all the difference in my future. Instead I decided he was too good for me to date. I told myself that as soon as he discovered I wasn't a virgin, he wouldn't want anything to do with me. I decided that I would be bad for him, that I would hurt him in some way. The next time he asked me out, I told him no as kindly as I knew how. He didn't understand, and I don't know if he ever forgave me.

Despite a rough patch or two, my life path reflects the legacy of most LDS women: We are rich in good men. My father. My brothers. My husband. My son and my sons-in-law. Most of them started out as members of The Church of Jesus Christ of Latter-day Saints. All of them bear the influence of the Gospel, although some tried to dispel it. Even those who have left the religion have been exceptionally loving and generous with me and with others. They have been affectionate, tender, protective, and adventurous. They have inspired me to go after my dreams, encouraged me to "run for the roses," and have been my champions when I needed someone to believe in me. Their magnanimity of spirit can't be separated from the religion in which they were raised, although certainly they cultivated the good in themselves, bringing heart and authenticity to a system that could be reduced to play-acting and game-playing as readily as any other. I have looked at these good men more than once and felt the eyes of Jesus smiling at me. They would give their lives to protect me and those I love, and such heroic values dominate their daily lives, governing their thinking, and determining their behavior. Emanating from an effulgent spirit that brightens and betters everything, these men encourage life in all its forms. When hit by the undertow of destructive forces, they stand strong in their reservoirs of faith.

Such men tend to call forth the best in their wives, daughters, sisters, as well as in themselves. A woman married to such a man also aspires to a standard of honesty and clean personal habits. She's more likely to be kind to him, to the children, and to herself. When a woman feels safe enough to grow, she thrives. When a woman feels that she is being served and has an example of service in her husband, she's more likely to be in service to her family and community, if nothing else so that she can be evenly yoked in her marriage.

Among men who humble themselves before God, a desire to serve keeps greed or overweening ambition at bay. Regardless of gifts and talents, such men seem to respond to a divine center, rather than running on ego-drive, and they refuse to give up native sensibilities such as tenderness and kindness. Even professional athletes of LDS background reveal sensitivity that runs contrary to some of the brutal physical encounters of football or basketball. Pro-football quarterback Steve Young and pro-basketball star Shawn Bradley exhibit nice-guy attitudes that contradict the bad-boy aggression manifested in some teammates. While highly skilled, these men seem to back away from anything that hurts their fellow beings or themselves Violence would keep them from fulfilling their ordained callings to be good fathers, husbands, sons, and to be "a minister and a witness" for Jesus Christ as called for in Acts 26:16. Such is the possible destiny of those who are taught reverence for life and who dedicate themselves to transforming the darkness into light.

Religion is a tarp that cannot contain everything and no matter how neat and tidy everything appears, human nature leaks out around the edges. Consequently, very good men still demonstrate the capacity to domineer, condescend, and control. They will ridicule women in order to get the upper hand, aggressively argue with them to gain control, and discount a female point of view in the name of being right. They have teased, thwarted, and belittled women. (Of course, the same could be said of some women regarding their treatment of men.) Some men have actually tried to commandeer the dreams of wives and children. One acquaintance opened a boutique that thrived until her husband, who read too many *Fortune 500* magazines, pressed her to expand. After opening five stores in one year, the whole thing—including the original shop—went bankrupt. Some LDS men seem to hold women's aspirations as less important than their own. When it's convenient, they forget the religious encouragement to treasure their wives and daughters, remembering only when doing so works in their favor.

Some women in the church are troubled that men who hold the priesthood have all the power to make decisions. Men as heads of households. Men as the direct connection to God. When we pray, we address Father in Heaven. (Even though Joseph Smith assured us that there is a Mother in Heaven, ecclesiastical leaders discourage praying to her.) We are taught to recognize a male trinity: Father, Son and even the Holy Ghost. Women's feelings that men run the show are exacerbated by a belief that they don't play fair. The brethren make all the powerful decisions about the body of the church. The Relief Society, which doesn't control its own finances, takes direction from the priesthood. All this control over half of the adult population, plus male and female children, can go to a man's head with dire consequences for individuals and families. When men don't respect needs that strike women as significant, those needs go unmet and resentment sets in.

In her writing, Carol Lynn Pearson expressed her worry that men are preferred in The Church of Jesus Christ of Latter-day Saints, and exposes the fear that God loves men more than women. Even though Pearson resolved this for herself, and most LDS women don't really believe that God plays gender favorites, we sometimes succumb to our doubts, especially when we find ourselves in a paradox perpetrated by men we count on to protect us: The LDS brother who sides with his sister's husband even though he's being disloyal. The LDS counselor who urges the wife to sleep beside her unfaithful husband. The LDS adviser who encourages a wife to return to her abusive spouse even though his violence has put her in the hospital. In these situations, women often contribute to the problem by coddling their men like tempestuous little boys who must be handled with kid gloves. So many women quietly walk behind men who act like willful adolescents, cleaning up their messes.

When a woman needs help from the man she's cared for, a return on her patience, hard work, and long-suffering attitude, he doesn't always step up. Perhaps women set themselves up for this by not asking for assistance when the weather's clear. Then when the storms come, we find out what's real. One woman, call her Ruth, had raised a family of seven children, all of whom moved far away to escape their father's self-righteous tyranny. Dominated by a man who wanted to control rather than love her, when she discovered that she had advanced breast cancer, Ruth had to call on the sisterhood to help her through the ordeal of chemotherapy. As she said, "My husband can't handle it. He doesn't know what to do." She said this of the man who had made every decision pertaining to their lives for the thirty years they'd been together. He had directed or expected her to clean up one mess after another. Now that the "mess" was hers, he wouldn't do what needed to be done. Every time she threw up, every time she needed help to use the bathroom, every time she cried out, he fell apart. She died painfully, and much of the pain came from processing the monstrous anger that had accumulated over the years capped by the ultimate betrayal, his refusal to support her when she needed him most.

But even ego-driven men thirst for redemption, and enough upstanding LDS men sustain an environment for fair play, compassion, and kindness, that reprobates get called to account within the priesthood framework. Recently, the head of the LDS Church, President Hinckley quoted from Scripture in a biannual conference meeting to remind men to exercise their priesthood authority "by persuasion, by long-suffering, by gentleness and meekness, and by love unfeigned; [b]y kindness, and pure knowledge, which shall greatly enlarge the soul without hypocrisy and without guile"(Doctrine and Covenants 121:41–42).

In the same talk, he pointed out the injustices done to women. "Notwithstanding this preeminence given the creation of women, she has so frequently through the ages been relegated to a secondary position. She has been put down. She has been denigrated. She has been enslaved. She has been abused." [1]

Containment systems in the priesthood correct some abuses. Home teachers who hold the priesthood visit families to assure that healthy conditions prevail. Priesthood heads follow up with men in their area of responsibility. They remonstrate and remind them that priesthood authority is not an excuse to tyrannize. Most church leaders listen to women and gratefully share their authority and responsibility with those women appointed to leadership positions. One Sunday I taught a Relief Society lesson about child abuse. After I finished, a sister came up to me and said that I had delivered a great lesson, but taught it to the wrong group of people. Upon inquiry, I learned about some instances of child abuse in the community—all perpetrated by men. Even though most of the abuse had happened long ago, with the abused children grown and gone, I knew I had to act on the information. I sat with it all that Sunday, prayed about it, and finally called my bishop. First we discussed the necessity of reporting abuse to the state. Then we talked about the need for education such as the sisters had received. I was expecting that he would assign one of the high priests or elders to teach the lesson I had taught in Relief Society. Instead, the bishop challenged me to teach it. So the next week I went to a combined elders and high priests meeting where I taught the child abuse lesson again. By the time I finished, three of the men had tears in their eyes. Several asked me after class what they could do to correct abuse. I was moved by their humility, their desire to repent and repair mistakes. I wondered why the priesthood hadn't been taught the lesson about abuse before. I wondered if it would ever be taught to the priesthood classes again, or if I needed to be watchful, rocking the boat now and then to make sure that men received the lessons that perhaps only women will deliver to them.

This quintessential dilemma plagues women who want change in a world where children, abused spouses, handicapped and mentally ill people, and senior citizens get the short end of the stick. My uncle, who took over the leadership of the polygamous group after my father died, called me a troublemaker because I have written and spoken about injustices that had been kept secret and most of all because my brothers and I insisted that the "priesthood council" in the polygamous group (who named themselves the United Apostolic Brethren after my father's death) return the deed to my mother's home. She had quit-claimed the house to the council to prove her willingness to live the United Order and the Law of Consecration, but the patriarchs had not taken care of her after my father died. When her home needed repairs and when she required major surgery, they did not respond. Their willingness to use her assets without honoring her needs enraged me. This myopia and exploitation in the fundamentalist group reflects what happens in some large systems of patriarchy where the leaders are not accountable to anyone but themselves.

Most LDS women aren't sure how much boat-rocking to do. We aren't sure what changes we can make when our concerns are screened through a patriarchal system. Some of us have difficulty discerning between those who exercise righteous dominion, providing necessary leadership and protection for the family and the flock, and those who abuse power or who put on a show to satisfy their own agendas. Those who desert their own sensibilities are much more likely to turn themselves over to wolves in sheep's clothing. If we're in touch with life, we turn toward real light, real energy. Rather than looking for someone to tell us how to live our lives, we're looking for support in taking responsibility for our own lives. We know that all changes begin within ourselves, so we get on our knees and ask for guidance. Some of us hit brick walls of contradiction. Will the needs of women and children be met if men make all the decisions? Will the children be fed and loved and protected if women have no voice? Will the sick and afflicted and the elderly get help? And will women get what they need when they need it from the men they've loved? If all men met the LDS standard, there'd be no problem. But men fall short of the ideal just as women do.

Regardless of clouds and storms and aberrant weather, and regardless of hypocrites and scoundrels in their midst, men of God proliferate in the LDS Church and their lives form a beautiful arc. Their thoughts seem illuminated by eternal light, their wisdom formed through a consciousness of the grand design. They consistently "school" their feelings, for they get frustrated or angry as anyone, but their dark feelings are transformed to a kind and caring form of truth that people can actually respond to. They seem to serve tirelessly: their wives and children, their parents and siblings, their brothers and sisters in the ward and stake, their coworkers, etc. They have strong work habits and stringent ethics. No wonder so many strong LDS women regard their fathers as heroes. Lacking explicit knowledge of the feminine divine, they begin as children in their aspiration to be like these magnanimous men rather than identifying with their mothers, who have been similarly denied a corollary for divine power. (It has been said that Mother in Heaven is so sacred that Father in Heaven doesn't want Her name to be spoken aloud.) Some women identify so thoroughly with admirable, powerful men that they succumb to gender confusion. Although I'm happy to be a woman, I nonetheless wanted to be like my father when it came to speaking my mind and asserting my wishes.

Like many LDS boys, my father wanted to serve God from the time he was a tiny child. His father's first wife had died after the family returned to the United States from Mexico, leaving his mother as the only wife. Thereafter the family dedicated themselves to activity in the LDS ward in Blackfoot, Idaho. When he was ten years old, my father had an accident with his horse that amplified his spirituality. The horse stumbled and threw him from the saddle, but his boot caught in the stirrup and he was dragged a long distance. He was unconscious by all indications, but in his account, he left his body and hovered above it, watching. He saw the horse stop, panting, in the yard. He saw his mother rush to him, breathe into him, pray over him, and call him back. And then he was back, reluctantly occupying his aching, broken body. Forever after he knew that he was more than his body. He had a body—a temple for his spirit, a place where he could lead a clean life dedicated to the Lord. But he always knew that he was more than his physical presence, more than his feelings, more than his mind. He knew that he was the spirit-son of divine parents, a child of God.

My father also knew about the power of the laying on of hands. Hadn't his mother's prayer and her tactile command, the power flowing through her hands, brought him back to his body? His mother's mother had been a renowned nurse and midwife, and he'd seen her use faith as an instrument of healing whether a priesthood holder was present or not. This realization expanded my father's relationship with women, but he didn't ever relinquish his own divine authority. His egalitarian posture about healing arts and women generated an unusual respect for womanhood that empowered me. As a father and as a husband, he showed how well he had learned to school his emotions and use them to serve the highest good. As the oldest living child of my grandfather's second wife, he did his best to set a Christ-like example for his brothers and sisters. He showed remarkable courage as a teenager when chased by wolves in Canada one winter night when he had gone some distance from home to gather wood for the family fire. He stood his spiritual ground during the same period when some older boys pushed him around and mocked his religious zeal by calling him Elijah.

By the time my father was old enough to have a social life, his devotion to the mainstream LDS Church preempted any contrary desires. Each new responsibility, whether in scouts or the priesthood, he met with eager joy. When he was old enough to consider marriage, he took his bride to the temple to be sealed to him for time and all eternity. He and his wife moved to Los Angeles, where he earned degrees in osteopathic, naturopathic and chiropractic medicine and fathered four children. He dedicated himself to being a physician with the same kind of zeal he had brought to his religion, learning everything he could about the built-in resources the Creator has instilled in each human being for healing themselves through faith, clean living, and natural supplements. He saw his profession as a naturopath as being in full alignment with the Word of Wisdom and the Gospel of Jesus Christ.

When he was twenty-nine years old, he began a dialogue with his father that turned his life upside down. Through prayer and fasting, Scripture study and doctrinal research, my father became convinced that his calling in life required him to live the Principle of Plural Marriage. He wrote in his journals and autobiography about powerful answers to prayers and being visited by angels. Still I wonder what motivated his choice psychologically. Perhaps he discerned a mantle of spiritual leadership that would fall on him if he seized this opportunity. Perhaps physical attraction to his female patients or his wife's constant jealousy demanded resolution with honor. He certainly knew the Scripture that placated Joseph Smith's misgivings about the Principle of Plural Marriage: "Behold, mine house is a house of order, saith the Lord God, and not a house of confusion." (Doctrine and Covenants 132:8) It would be so unlike my father to get involved with any woman without committing wholly to her well-being and that of their children. Certainly he would have to marry a woman before he slept with her. In any case, he made a choice that would justify the terms of his own existence, as a child of polygamy. But he paid dearly for his choice to live the principle, for his first wife took the children and left him, and he lost membership in his beloved Church of Jesus Christ of Latter-day Saints, experiences he described as being "like limbs being torn from my body."

Despite these losses, my father spent his life in service, either as a healer or as a spiritual leader. He married and remained committed to six of his eight wives (the first and the seventh divorced him) and he took on more wives in his later years, although those relationships may not have been consummated (because those who live the Principle of Plural Marriage practice the fundamentalist Law of Chastity, which precludes sex for postmenopausal women.) He fathered forty-eight children, most of whom have lived productive lives, lives of service to their fellow beings. He stitched up countless cuts, set hundreds of broken bones, cured a man who had had the hiccups for four months, and facilitated miracles large and small. Eventually he was assassinated by a woman acting on the orders of a man who tried to force my father to give up his religious conviction. In the sense that he gave up his life to honor his relationship with God, he followed in the footsteps of Jesus Christ and Joseph Smith, the beings he held as heroes.

Regarding men like my father, it's easy to see why women would share a husband. The practical, psychological subtext goes like this: "My husband is more than enough. He provides for me and so many others that I'd be self-indulgent to keep him all to myself. I'll be glad to share this man with you, a worthy sister, as long as you don't betray me and you don't betray him."

As with the benevolent and powerful men in the official LDS Church who inspire awe and admiration in the women around them, my father was so good that I sometimes didn't feel worthy of his love, especially since I didn't possess a tenth of his religious zeal. When I began to act out as a teenager, I felt the need, as many young women do, to stay away from my father; like Eve, shamed in the Garden of Eden, I hid myself from my father, afraid that he would see my troubled spirit or the stains on my soul. So, of course, when I began looking for another way of being in the world, I chose men and boys who were very different from my father. The boys like Jed, with their deep religious devotion, made me as uncomfortable as my father did. Fortunately I married someone who struck a happy medium.

My son, Jeff, showed an interest in spiritual matters at a very early age, but his real concern was truth rather than religion. He wanted to know how God would hear his prayers, how God could listen to everyone's prayers all at once, and how He could possibly answer them all. The first time he dealt with death (he was nearly five years old, and a neighbor's dog had been run over), he came to me, white-faced and stricken. "Will that happen to me?" he asked. I nodded sadly. "Everything that lives must die, son." He looked to my mother who sat with me at the kitchen table, hoping she'd dispel this horror, and she nodded. "Unless, of course, you are translated," she told him. "What's that?" he asked. "It's when you're so good you don't die, but you're lifted up in a twinkling." (My mother was referring to the doctrine of translated beings described in 3 Nephi 28:7 and 38 in the Book of Mormon, and in the Bible when Elijah who was taken to Heaven without tasting death, according to 2 Kings 2:11.) Jeff put a hand on one hip. "So what are the rules?" he asked, ready to take them on.

When he was older, Jeff wanted to understand how he would know when God answered his prayers. He wanted to know what would happen if he didn't go to church. I did my best to be neutral, to allow him to discern his own truth and have his own relationship with the divine, just as I had insisted for myself.

When Jeff was in his teens, he dreamed that President Hinckley caught him napping in church and reprimanded him. "Wake up, Jeff," he said. And Jeff did. Suddenly he came alive in his Sunday school and priesthood classes and in his seminary class. He prayed about going on a mission and eventually chose, on his own, to do so. After putting in his papers, he was called to serve in Guatemala.

I wept daily after Jeff entered the Missionary Training Center (MTC), where he spent two months studying Spanish and learning how to preach the Gospel of Jesus Christ. His girlfriend, Jennifer, would come to our home to visit in the evenings and on the weekends; she would lie on my bed, listening to music or watching television, and it seemed to me that we felt a similar shell shock. Like me, she didn't know whether to be proud or angry with God, whether to be grateful for Jeff's strong character and capacity for commitment or wish he would bail on the whole thing and come home before it was too late. Together we sent letters and treats, including a "Birthday Party in a Box," so that he could celebrate in the MTC.

The day came for him to leave for Guatemala to fulfill his mission, and we gathered at the airport to see him off. He stood tall and scared and excited in his dark suit and white shirt, surrounded by friends and family members who had come to say good-bye. More tears from Jennifer and his sisters and me. But our hearts swelled with the knowledge of his courage and extraordinary commitment.

His plane flew into the eye of Hurricane Mitch, and I watched CNN and the Weather Channel as the storm raked Honduras and pummeled Guatemala. When Jeff—Elder Solomon, as his letters to us were return-addressed—arrived in Guatemala City, the streets were flooded, and he slogged through three feet of mud. But he took the people into his heart. He lived with them, ate with them, prayed with them, and converted them. He wielded a machete to help them build houses out of cane and bamboo. He worked alongside them and read to them and helped them find ways to kick a smoking habit, or get married, or find enough food for the day's meals so that the children wouldn't go hungry. When we visited Guatemala, I was deeply moved by Jeff's pure love for the people there, the knowledge that he had given them something they didn't have, wouldn't have had without him: the Restored Gospel of Jesus Christ and the opportunity to be together forever. His district was one of the most dangerous places in the world some of the time, but he doesn't speak of his confrontations with evil, in much the same way that my husband will not discuss the details of horrendous firefights in Vietnam. Valiant—that is how I would describe them. Heroes. They each went into the unknown and faced the unthinkable to bring back something valid and true, a testimony of life tempered in the refiner's fire.

It isn't always easy, but women do their best to accept the decision of their sons, brothers and fiancés to leave for a two-year mission, often on foreign soil, sometimes in dangerous situations. Many women express faith that their sons are protected by the Lord. But some struggle with enormous anger because their sons go to drug-running or war-torn or environmentally-toxic capitals, and their sons' missions become the greatest trial of their faith.

Good men in the church transcend the understanding of pedestrian souls. Somehow they walk the talk of their belief system without eclipsing or distorting their true selves. They seem driven by a pure connection with the divine that yields joy and love and enlightenment, a state of being that sets them apart, just as our most devout leaders always transcend ordinary agendas. Men like President Gordon B. Hinckley stand in such dedication that there's no room for pettiness, ulterior motives, or selfish desires.

President Hinckley's perspectives stand so clear that even in the paranoia and nationalism of post – 9/11 America, he did not forget that everyone is our brother or sister in the family of man. Less than a month after the attack on America, he was conducting LDS Church conference on international television when the United States entered Afghanistan; he learned of it when someone brought him a note as he stood at the podium. He sadly announced the news and then immediately offered a prayer to "Thou great Judge of the nations, Thou who art the Governor of the Universe, Thou who art our Father and our God, whose children we are. We look to thee in faith in this dark and solemn time." After praying for faith and love and charity, for democracy and for those sent into battle, President Hinckley closed with these words: "We humbly plead with Thee, asking that Thou will forgive our arrogance, pass by our sins, be kind and gracious to us and cause our hearts to turn with love to Thee."[2]

Some of the most powerful missionaries and compassionate servants in the church have encountered the dark side. Having returned to the light, they stand firm, grateful and knowledgeable. Consider Brother Early, a father of nine children who lived down the street from me as I was growing up. He had tattoos—marks of his former life—up and down both arms and across his chest and back that showed through his white shirt and temple garments. He always knew what to say when a young man or woman in the neighborhood engaged in rebellious behavior. They always trusted that he knew what he was talking about when he warned them about the Adversary. After a session with Brother Early, they turned on a dime, gave up the image associated with drinking, smoking, fast driving, and they usually started attending church and school again.

But image matters a lot in LDS culture, so Brother Early (and his wife) paid for his 'tats' when certain members took his outward appearance as a measure of his worth and judged or dismissed him. They missed knowing an extraordinary man, all for the sake of image. The LDS people seem to be trying to make up for a century of public misunderstandings by being correct to a fault, pretending that every skeleton in our church closets has been exhumed and properly buried. This sometimes makes us slow to respond as individuals to real problems, such as child abuse, spousal abuse, sexual perversity, and other outcomes of tyranny. Because image matters so much in the LDS Church, unhealthy sublimations become part of the scene. Some men develop fetishes. Others spend so much time and energy getting approval that they lose track of themselves. Some get stuck in an adolescent mode of always trying to please others, and they mistake their own narcissism for homosexuality.

Does God make homosexuals? LDS Church authorities don't condone this idea and in conference talks they've made the church's stand regarding homosexuality very clear. According to President Hinckley, "Prophets of God have repeatedly taught through the ages that practices of homosexual relations, fornication, and adultery are grievous sins. Sexual relations outside the bounds of marriage are forbidden by the Lord. We affirm those teachings."[3] The LDS Church encourages professed homosexuals to pray for a change of heart and mind as well as a change of passions and attractions. The church teaches that people can overcome homosexual desires and inclinations, and that they should do so in order to achieve eternal exaltation. According to most bishops, those who can marry should; those who can bear children should, since we have been commanded to multiply and replenish the earth. But recently, church leaders have indicated that marriage is not considered to be a cure for homosexuality and should not be hidden from the prospective bride, who would suffer if an ill-founded marriage takes place.

Persecution is a strong LDS and Christian tradition. Those who suffer for their testimony of Christ believe that they will be rewarded in the hereafter. The idea of suffering for the truth is mightily attractive to Latter-day Saints, who are fed the stories of the suffering of the early pioneers and whose appetite for martyrdom is whetted by accounts of Joseph and Hyrum Smith, Parley P. Pratt, and, of course, Jesus Christ. Most LDS people perceive that the surrounding world culture supports homosexuality by concluding that homosexuals are born rather than made, forged by the Creator rather than self-created. As a religion of accountability, the LDS Church maintains that all human beings have their free agency, and suggests that people choose their behaviors, if not their preferences. Some homosexuals feel persecuted by the church, while others feel persecuted by their appetites. Either way, their suffering fits into a religious scenario focused on pain, rather than joy, which ultimately is out of alignment with eternal happiness.

The LDS Church firmly encourages members to love homosexuals "as sons and daughters of God."[4] Moreover, church leaders encourage members to help them as needed, but we are also instructed to remind them of the danger should they participate in immoral activity or engage in same-sex marriage: "To permit such would be to make light of the very serious and sacred foundation of God-sanctioned marriage and its very purpose, the rearing of families."[5]

Certain elements in the LDS lifestyle are discussed as possible contributors to homosexual behavior, and the mission is one of these. At the height of hormonal activity, young men are strongly encouraged to go on missions. They are coached against spending long periods of time alone and directed to refrain from masturbation and any practice that might tempt them to sexual activity. They are bred to "listen to the Spirit" rather than to be too tough or macho. This combination of patterns can drift into homosexual exploration. Because the LDS Church makes no provision for homosexuality, men or women who have homosexual inclinations have limited support, the most prevalent being an organization called Evergreen International which orients its therapy to LDS standards and touts a high success rate in turning homosexuality around.

What of a woman's torment when she learns that she has committed herself for time and all eternity to a man who doesn't desire women? What happens when she realizes that she shares children with a man who wants to claim another man as his life partner? In Carol Lynn Pearson's devastating and beautiful book, *Good-bye, I Love You,* we learn of the enormous anger and pain associated with realizing that you are bound to a man who will never be attracted to you.[6] Love you, yes. Admire you, yes. But never attracted to you, no, not even in the beginning.

A psychologist told me that of all the emotions, respect is most likely to create sexual attraction. Many LDS women I've spoken with over the years grapple with complex questions: Do patriarchal cultures where men are perpetually first-class and women perpetually second-class citizens orient men to prefer their own sex, rather than the opposite sex? To what extent does the patriarchal structure unwillingly contribute to homosexuality? What prices do individuals and families pay because the standard is immutable?

Some of those who suffer most are also the ones who make the biggest difference. Pearson, a woman of surpassing empathy, has recognized the terrible torment of gay LDS men and their families. Noting the high suicide rate, the immense loneliness, and the paucity of support systems, she has taken on a challenge to enlighten her fellow saints—with or without help from the brethren. She has written an off-Broadway play and established a Web site that confronts and explores these issues in depth.

Utah's past, replete with the controversy surrounding polygamy, contributes to the confusion and pain surrounding sex. The LDS community gets rocked by books and other media perpetuating the idea that all Mormons are fundamentalists. We are defensive, intently concerned about how others perceive us, ever eager to correct any misapprehension. We are tired of being regarded as a cult. When fundamentalist cousins show up in the news, the audience hungers for lurid details and we meet a world that looks at us askance. Our only recourse is to continue to communicate clearly through speech and behavior that we are disciples of Jesus Christ.

In some fundamentalist communities, priesthood leaders wield so much power that its abuse seems inevitable. Warren Jeffs, the leader of the Fundamentalist Latter-day Saints (FLDS) recently made the FBI's Top Ten Most Wanted list and has been arrested for allegedly participating in the sexual abuse of minors. He was charged with rape as an accomplice because he arranged the marriage of a fourteen-year-old girl to an older man. He reportedly had nearly a hundred wives at the time of his arrest in August 2006. Many dirt-poor fundamentalists believed that Jeffs was God's prophet on earth, and they consecrated everything they had to him; even little children collected their "Pennies for the Prophet," contributing about $145,000 to their fugitive leader, whom they now regard as a martyr. Like other fundamentalists, Jeffs openly used religious belief in the Principle of Plural Marriage to justify violations of state and federal laws against bigamy and illegal cohabitation. When a man discovers that he can change the rules in the name of God, he can appoint himself the maker of laws and can give himself reason to ignore even the most ancient codes, including taboos against incest and abuse of children. Jeffs' treatment of all his followers—men, women, and especially children—reflects a disregard for life. He used men's devotion to their wives and children as leverage, taking their families away if they didn't follow his orders. He was the nephew of one of my father's wives, my "Aunt" Leona, and when I was twelve years old, Leona took three of her four children (my half-brothers and sister) and left my father to follow her brother, who by then had gained considerable power in the Colorado City/Short Creek fundamentalist group. Jeffs used his patriarchal authority to authorize "spiritual incest". Absolute power promotes abuse and exploitation, perpetrating the phenomenon described in the Scriptures, "That which breaketh a law, and abideth not by law, but seeketh to become a law unto itself"(Doctrine and Covenants 88:35). Such beings, according to Scripture, abide in sin and cannot be sanctified by law. In other words, even the powerful don't get away with corruption. As the Doctrine and Covenants 88:36 states, "All kingdoms have a law given."

One Sunday in 1990, I went to church at my ward, and during the Gospel Doctrine class, my feathers were seriously ruffled by a man who seemed convinced that his version of the Gospel was *right*. I found myself comparing him to the self-righteous men in the fundamentalist group I grew up in and quickly determined that he did not welcome a female point of view. To make things worse, this man expressed anger at his grandfather for living polygamy even though he would not be alive if it weren't for his grandfather's convictions. (How liberally, I thought, he willed away our existence.) Since he did not ask for my point of view even though it was widely known in my ward that I was a child of polygamy, I left feeling discouraged, believing that it would take more perseverance than I could muster to explain our complex history.

That day, following the Gospel Doctrine lesson, as a statement of rebellion I went directly to the grocery store even though it was Sunday and shopping violates the Sabbath. As I stood impatiently in the cashier's line, I saw a new copy of *Life* magazine. I picked it up and it fell open to a page that highlighted two versions of patriarchy. On the right-hand side was a photo of a girl in Cairo undergoing a ritual clitoridectomy. Her mother holds her down while the religious surgeon removes her clitoris, and with it, most of the pleasure in the act of procreation. The expression on the girl's face exposed a scalding betrayal. In the facing photograph, a circle of LDS elders hold a baby girl dressed in pink and white, all ruffles and froth, the men in white shirts and dark suits balancing her on their extended right hands, as they close the prayer circle by placing their left hands on the shoulders of the men next to them, forming a force-field of love and protection around the little girl. They tell her that she is born good, that God and her parents love her, and that they want her to have a happy life.

I raised my wet eyes and looked around the grocery store. All the fight went out of me. I took back the items I intended to purchase, bought the magazine instead, and left the store, chastened. Patriarchy is everywhere, myriad in form and focus; I had chosen the most benign I could find and deliberately stayed in the LDS Church. I was so grateful to have the choice, something one ego-driven teacher could not destroy.

Regardless of the contradictions women experience living in a paternalistic society, most LDS women are confident that the patriarchy of The Church of Jesus Christ of Latter-day Saints stands as the kindest, most loving and generous-spirited of the patriarchal orders on the face of the earth. As one woman explained, "The attitude in my ward and stake is very favorable toward women. My bishop and stake president have been very interested in hearing what the women in leadership positions have to say. I have felt heard and validated." [7]

Some Mormons argue that men hold the priesthood and women do not because women are inherently flawed or unenlightened. Others argue that men need the priesthood because they (men) are inherently flawed or unenlightened. Neither argument does justice to the topic. Belittling men *or* women as an explanation diminishes everyone. Most LDS women prefer to regard the matter of priesthood as a 'gravity issue.' "You don't get out of bed and complain because the earth's magnetic core creates gravity, do you?" said one LDS woman. "Without it we'd be in chaos, no order at all. For me, the fact that men hold the priesthood is a gravity issue."

The men in The Church of Jesus Christ of Latter-day Saints aspire to be like their leader, Jesus Christ. Jesus invited women to sit at his table and be his friends. He taught women just as he taught men. He gave his life for His brothers and sisters, and He offers an alternative to the abuses of hierarchy. His example—of unconditional love for men and women alike—presents the greatest possible antidote to tyranny. He has offered an even and equal playing field in the meadows of life—if we have the courage to play there. LDS people will continue to struggle with their egos, but men with faith in Jesus Christ will reflect what He taught. They will transform their behavior, and women of faith will benefit.

5

Love at Home

Families pass down legacies or curses. Some families pass down both. Whether we bestow legacies worth perpetuating or curses that ruin lives determines the prosperity of the family. We are influenced by our families, regardless of our relationship to them, and whether we like it or not.

I remember sitting in the car with my father's legal wife, waiting outside a doctor's office. My mother had been getting chiropractic and naturopathic treatments daily ever since my baby brother was born. Although my mother was in the office, "Aunt" Myrtle (my father's legal wife) got out of the car and told me to stay there. I didn't mind; even at the age of five, I entertained myself by watching the people on the street. The man walking up and down the sidewalk, wearing an old and bedraggled soldier's cap—I felt his despair and knew where it came from: from the war, the one my uncle fought before I was born, and from something else too. I could see into this man's life, could see where he lived: two small rooms on a second floor somewhere not far from where we were. The rooms were dark and cluttered and lonely. He didn't like to go home to them because there was no one there. He had no family. They were gone and he missed them like he would miss his legs if they were gone. And then I felt tears rolling down my cheeks, splashing on my knees. "Aunt" Myrtle returned and wanted to know what happened; did that man hurt me? After I nodded, she shook me and asked if he had touched me. She started shouting at him, and I cried no! The lonely man with no family went away, more miserable than ever.

I've always intuited that everything centers on family. Most human beings know this despite all the tinkering that goes on today with gender roles and family unity. When families fall apart, individuals lose their center, cultures break down, and civilization threatens to topple. Social workers testify that home pulls so profoundly on the heart that foster children still long for the biological hands that beat them. Even in its worst manifestation, and even as the ghost of experience, family—our hunger for it and our inevitable attachment to it—rumbles through our bloodstreams and in our deepest consciousness. The Church of Jesus Christ of Latter-day Saints has always underscored the importance of family and given it priority. The preeminence of family is trumpeted in LDS Scriptures and has been emphasized in the speeches of LDS prophets throughout the last century. Consider these words from *The Family: A Proclamation to the World:* "We, the First Presidency and the Council of the Twelve Apostles of the Church of Jesus Christ of Latter-day Saints, solemnly proclaim that marriage between a man and a woman is ordained of God and that the family is central to the Creator's plan for the eternal destiny of His children."[1]

According to LDS Church doctrine, the family is at the heart of the Lord's plan for His children, which includes the plan of salvation, the promise of redemption and the reward of happiness. In order to avail ourselves of this Gospel Plan, we must choose between good and evil. Given the many dangers and temptations in the world, we need support in this discernment and the most potent and enduring support comes from family. "The divine plan of happiness enables family relationships to be perpetuated beyond the grave. Sacred ordinances and covenants available in holy temples make it possible for individuals to return to the presence of God and for families to be united eternally."[2]

A typical LDS family might remind you of a 1950s- or 1960s-style television family like the Cleavers or the Partridge family, with lots of enthusiasm, lots of goodwill, and a few problems that get resolved through a common effort. In fact, once you get the hang of it, you can spot an LDS family in any crowd, in England or Central America or anywhere in the United States. If you want to see the results of LDS living, look at the Osmond family. Squeaky clean. Look at Mitt Romney and his wife. Most people can't find anything wrong with them, except that they are LDS, which to some people is a good reason to vote for him. Look at the Mormon Tabernacle Choir, essentially one big family singing the same song at the same time with emphasis on harmoniously worshipping God and celebrating life . . . together.

> There is beauty all around
> When there's love at home;
> There is joy in every sound
> When there's love at home.
> Peace and plenty here abide,
> Smiling sweet on every side.
> Time doth softly, sweetly glide
> When there's love at home.[3]

Whether the home is a Victorian structure situated on the ten acres Brigham Young prescribed in Huntington, Utah or a modern McMansion on a quarter acre in Las Vegas, Nevada, or anywhere else in the world you know when you've entered a Mormon home. Portraits adorn the walls—of Jesus Christ; of Joseph Smith and other presidents of the church, especially the Living Prophet, Gordon B. Hinckley; and family, past and present. Orderly and clean regardless of income, this home displays some touch of Heaven, perhaps in the curtains or the crochet-edged scarves or statues of LDS temples or ceramic praying hands. Always, set in a place of honor are the heavy, leather-bound Scriptures. Usually you can look around a Mormon home and know what the most recent homemaking project has been, the "glass grapes" of yesteryear adorning end tables and curio cabinets in LDS households giving way to today's messages on tile: "Christ is the Center of Our Home: A Guest at Every Meal, A Listener to Every Conversation" or "Families Can Be Together Forever." Almost always there's the fragrance of cooking or baking or the sweetness of potpourri, underscored by the sharper odor of cleaning products.

In fact, "Cleanliness is next to godliness" has become a credo for most members of the LDS Church, based on Scripture: "Let all things be done in cleanliness before me" (Doctrine and Covenants 42: 41) and "Cleanse your hearts and your garments, lest the blood of this generation be required at your hands" (Doctrine and Covenants 112:33). This commitment to cleanliness usually shows up in comely appearance, laundered and mended clothing, generally a clean-cut look for both men and women. The commitment also shows up in a strong desire for inner purity, which manifests in friendships as loyalty, in marriage as fidelity, in the business world as honesty, and in the church as devotion. The sisterhood holds this together, establishing these standards of cleanliness in the home and teaching these principles of purification to the children.

In the LDS family, men and women have separate roles, based on a belief that, as essential beings, our gender was established in the Pre-existence, before we came to earth. Combined with the belief that natural and spiritual laws act in harmony and are essentially eternal, the doctrine leaves no room for sexual deviation. The commandment to multiply and replenish the earth fits into the Eternal Plan, providing time on earth for God's spirit-children to gain a body. This body allows us to experience life and to exercise choice. In other words, we come to earth to distinguish the cause and effect of good and evil and to make life-affirming choices. In this plan, motherhood stands as a holy calling. Women don't hold the priesthood because their preordained relationship with the Creator requires utter devotion. According to church leaders, "Motherhood is near to divinity. It is the highest, holiest service to be assumed by mankind. It places her who honors its holy calling and service next to the angels."[4] "There is nothing in the revelations which suggests that to be a man rather than to be a woman is preferred in the sight of God, or that He places a higher value on sons than on daughters."[5] In the LDS view of family, men and women must respect and honor each other and work together to serve one another, their children, the community, and the kingdom of God.

Mutual respect and love between husband and wife sets an example for children. In LDS families where parents walk the talk, siblings treat each other and their parents with respect, and friendship develops. Certainly this happens in any family where love prevails, LDS or not, but the Gospel boosts this phenomenon. Love at home gets reinforced at every stage of human development. Siblings are taught to respect and serve one another, and to do the same for their parents. I'm still amazed as I watch the friendships of my own children. I can trace the strengthening of their relationships to periods when my husband and I treated each other lovingly and respectfully and when we stood together in the church and in the home. Regardless of our temporal struggles—with time or health or finances—we taught them to look at the big picture. Occasionally I can see glitches in their relationships which can be traced to periods when we were successful and busy in secular pursuits or lost in our personal insecurities, when we neglected to conduct Family Home Evenings regularly, or when we skipped going to church together. When we didn't pray together or meet with the bishop for tithing settlement, we paid in big ways. In heeding our own faulty compasses, we drifted away from each other. The family struggled during those times, and the children's self-concept suffered as did their relationships with each other. Thankfully, the Divine Center holds once it is established, keeping us together. Even when our children don't agree with each other, they love each other. Love moves through the weft and the weave, as strong and immutable as the blood in their veins.

Human beings need love at home, and we need to be taught to serve one another. Left to our own inclinations, we tend to think primarily about ourselves. Life unravels our expectations and we sometimes harbor contradictions and lies, so we don't always like ourselves. Consciously or not, we tend to hide our insecurities. As parents, we prefer to disclaim any connection between how we treat each other and how we treat our children, but we are accountable for the lives we create. We believe that we can betray each other, break our vows, talk disparagingly to a spouse, and then we expect our children to be kind to one another. It doesn't follow. Parents establish context for their progeny. In a context of love and respect, love and respect fill the home and spill into the larger world. In a context of contention, then anger, blame, shame, and regret spawn separation and misery. "By their fruits ye shall know," the Bible tells us, and our children are our 'fruits'. They are the measure that tells us how we are living our lives, whether we want to face it or not. "For whatsoever a man soweth, that shall he also reap" (Galatians 6:8, and Doctrine and Covenants 6:33). The teachings of LDS Church consistently remind us of this Law of the Harvest, a major tenet of Christianity.

Consider one couple, Ann and Devon Cristobel. They knew that their relationship was a shambles. The family occasionally attended church, but the children quarreled and rebelled, refused to follow house rules or do what they promised to do. Then their oldest dyed his hair green and sported a variety of body-piercings and tattoos (contrary to instructions of church leaders) and a recent plunge in grades and abusive treatment of younger siblings alarmed the parents. As every parent knows but doesn't always admit, physical indicators represent behaviors and attitudes, and the parents had glimpsed only the tail of the monster roiling beneath the surface. Devon blamed Ann, and she blamed him for their oldest son's wrong turn. They took their teenager to counseling, hoping the therapist could fix him.

Things didn't go bad overnight. For years the couple's relationship had been tangled in unhealthy ways, with Ann trying to control every moment of her husband's time except when he was at work, and Devon generally ignoring his wife until she made it impossible to do otherwise. A dreadful contest had developed, where Devon, instead of freely fulfilling the measure of his creation (as we are charged to do in the Gospel), decided to play possum whenever he was at home. His limp presence burdened his wife with all household responsibilities and many related outside duties such as paying bills, getting the cars repaired, and meeting community obligations. At work Devon exercised all the freedom denied him at home. He was well liked because he was funny, playful, innovative, and hardworking. Consequently, he spent more and more time at work, and his children hardly knew him. Ann deeply resented him and his lack of partnership. The more she resented him, the more he stayed away. She began to resent the children who didn't appreciate the career she'd given up to be a full-time mother, and now she had no self-esteem and no gratitude. With all these contradictions, going to church became increasingly difficult because the couple saw other LDS families who seemed to like each other, which made them feel worse about themselves and each other. As the children grew, they followed their father's example and avoided home. They hung out at friends' homes and got more involved in extracurricular activities. Before long, they too spent as little time at home as possible. Ann was still the tyrant of the home front, but soon she'd have no people to control.

"If you want to fix your teenager," the therapist told them, "you need to fix your relationship." They took the challenge and got some marriage counseling (which is available through LDS Social Services). Eventually they turned their lives around. As they learned to treasure one another, they started regularly going to church as a family, and they remembered to hold Family Home Evening, to have morning and evening prayers, to read their Scriptures. The piercings no longer held jewelry, the green hair grew out and the siblings stopped slugging each other. They started to play games together, and once in a while they actually threw a friendly arm around each other.

In another family, the Jensens, the parents refuse to quarrel. They discuss rather than argue. You can see them searching for sensitive ways to request assistance, to work out problems, to communicate difficult messages. They use metaphors, and they make room for the other to reach his or her conclusions. They take responsibility for their own thoughts and feelings, and for communicating them, rather than expecting the other to be a mind-reader or a magician. Their family meetings and dinner-table conversations are conducted like a class, everyone thinking hard, feeling deeply, and doing their best to come up with a response, a solution, a contribution. They don't interrupt and they acknowledge each other's opinions even if they don't agree. They're open to learning from each other and from other sources as well. Mom and Dad ask the children to get involved when the subject matter is appropriate. You can see the kids racing to get the dictionary or the encyclopedia, or looking things up on the Internet. They take turns in leadership roles, Mom giving Dad a break and Dad assigning the older children to guide discussions, lead Family Home Evening, read Scriptures and say prayers. The shared responsibility assures everyone that they each have an important role in the family. They refuse to blame each other, remembering their Sunday school lessons in accountability. The parents treat the children with the same kind of basic respect with which they would like to be treated themselves. When discipline is needed, it's given kindly, respectfully, and firmly. On Sunday mornings, when everyone's hurrying to get to church, the parents help each other with breakfast and other preparations, so of course the older children help the younger ones get ready. When something goes wrong or feelings run high, the parents have set an example of spending some time alone praying and doing their best to understand what they're feeling and thinking before they talk to others. Only the baby throws tantrums; the older children and the adults like the idea of being mature enough to be in charge of their emotions. When it's time to say what's on their minds and hearts, they continue to communicate until the message is delivered and received. Of course, the children treat each other the way their parents have treated them because this is how they learned what relationship is. Because the children don't fight with each other, they have a lot of time to play together. When you walk into the Jensens' home, you notice the light, not just from the tall windows, but a spiritual light that lifts your heart. It might seem boring to someone who likes high drama, but it offers an island of peace and light to those who want to preserve a "clean, well-lighted place" in the hearts and minds of family members.

One family, the Tracys, play a game invented by their mother, Trudy, called the "the Accountability Game" where they do their best to accept accountability for any mishap or misunderstanding in their family. In the LDS system of belief, accountability is a birthright, something you acknowledge and take responsibility for at age eight, when you are baptized, and for the rest of whatever. The process of being accountable for one's own behavior quickly resolves differences in a family (and in other relationships) and creates a strong environment where individuals excel. Children and parents alike wax strong and confident, knowing that if they make a mistake, they can learn from it and go on. This process also encourages the family as a whole and as individuals to face problems readily and to resolve them through effective communication.

As protector and provider, the father of an LDS family holds responsibility for family finances, but of course that requires cooperation. When family members don't abide by the budget, the provider finds himself on a never-ending treadmill, unable to produce enough income to meet the family's voracious needs. If Mom is a shopaholic or teens have no self-restraint, everyone's quality of life suffers, especially the provider who has to work harder to make ends meet. One big danger of the patriarchal system is that women and children might not learn to manage money. When the patriarch dies or the teens grow up, the wife and kids don't know what to do with their newfound freedom. Like the children of Israel leaving Egypt, they are inclined to make poor decisions and worship golden calves.

LDS leaders continually urge families to stay out of debt, suggesting that only the only good reasons to borrow are to acquire a home or get an education. They also urge every family member who has an income to give ten percent of their income to building up God's kingdom. Paying tithing fulfills a commandment, yields blessings and abundance, and one thing more: it establishes fire insurance for the Last Days when, Scriptures predict, the earth will be destroyed: "Behold, now it is called today until the coming of the Son of Man, and verily it is a day of sacrifice, and a day for the tithing of my people; for he that is tithed shall not be burned at his coming" (Doctrine and Covenants 64:23).

This ancient law of increase has a huge influence on family solidarity. The last month of the year, when most of a holidays-crazed world spends its excess income and some of what it doesn't have, LDS members are scheduling a yearly tithing settlement meeting with their bishop. Even children participate in this practice, paying ten percent of their allowance ("How do you give 10 percent of a quarter, Daddy?") Somehow we Latter-day Saints manage to finish the year feeling good, knowing that although 10 percent seems like a lot of money to give unconditionally, 90 percent is enough to live on. Just knowing we tithed creates effulgence of the heart, and the sense that we are blessed in giving and that we will be blessed in ways we can't anticipate bolsters everyone as we face the new year.

But even devout LDS families can make financial mistakes. They can get carried away by greed; they can fail to budget; they can sink deeply into debt. Family Ship Swain hit the rocks when father and husband Brit decided to invest all their assets in a tax-free real estate venture. His wife, Greta, did her best to talk him out of such speculation, but Brit had been fully convinced by a chum from high school and went ahead without her blessing. Within a year they had lost their savings and their home, and Brit lost his job because he had involved so many coworkers, including his boss, in a scheme that ruined everyone except the scam artist who invented it.

Greta had to put their little children in day care and went back to teaching seventh grade. The whole family took a downward plunge. The teenagers seemed to mind the change the most, but everyone suffered, even the uncomplaining toddlers. As one might expect, Brit had lost all confidence in himself. Without references from his last employer he couldn't seem to land a job. When Greta pressed him for news of his job-search, he blamed his former boss for giving him poor reports. Greta would roll her eyes, as if to say, "What did you expect?" Brit sank into deeper depression, the family sank deeper into debt, and it seemed that the world was closing in.

Finally, after three years, Greta brought up the "d" word, hoping that the shock would jump-start Brit into action. Instead, he nodded morosely and said, "Whatever you want to do." As her anger cleared and Greta thought about it, she wondered if her life would be easier without Brit. She didn't want to start all over again, build a solid base and then have Brit make some stupid investment and lose it all. But she didn't want to make the biggest mistake of her life either. Because they had married in the temple, the two agreed to talk things over with the bishop before they actually filed for divorce.

The bishop told them things neither of them wanted to hear: that their lives would be even harder if they split up. That they had forged an eternal commitment, and that eternal commitments are not made to be broken. That they were setting an example of grudge-holding for their children that would hamper them all their lives. That the Lord has commanded us to forgive.

Greta didn't think she could forgive Brit. Brit didn't think he could forgive himself. The bishop quoted Scripture, the Lord declaring through revelation "Wherefore, I say unto you that ye ought to forgive one another; for he that forgiveth not his brother his trespasses standeth condemned before the Lord; for there remaineth in him the greater sin. . . . And ye ought to say in your hearts, let God judge between me and thee, and reward thee according to thy deeds" (Doctrine and Covenants 64:9, 11).

Greta looked at her husband. "I don't know how to forgive him," she confessed.

The bishop looked from wife to husband and back to wife. "You start with prayer," he said.

Prayer establishes a citadel for LDS families, offering unification, sanctuary, inspiration and enlightenment. LDS people carry many kinds of prayer in their quivers: individual prayer, at least twice a day, and then as often as needed. Couples prayer, especially at bedtime. Family prayer, morning and evening. Blessings over food, offering thanks and requests for health. Priesthood prayers. Father's prayers and blessings. Mother's prayers and blessings. Prayers at baptism and confirmation. Prayers that dedicate businesses and homes and graves. Prayers for blessing the sick or for those about to embark on passages. Prayer becomes an opportunity to ask for blessings, repent of sins, catalyze a change of heart or behavior, turn over fears and angers, and express gratitude. Although certain rote qualities attend Mormon prayers, other than the Lord's Prayer and the ordinance prayers such as those for baptism, conferring priesthood, and consecrating oil for healing the sick, prayer generally affords immediate experience, a spontaneous process of communing with the Creator. The immediacy makes way for the two-way communication called personal revelation, wherein God responds to individuals regarding their needs and desires. According to protocol, the husband may receive revelation for his entire family and the wife may receive revelation for her children. Thus the family watches out for each other, using the divine binoculars of prayer.

People of the LDS faith regard children as "an heritage of the Lord" (Psalms 127:3). Parents are encouraged to recognize that God has entrusted them with His spirit-children, that He expects parents to treat their children with respect and love. As custodians of these divinely conceived beings, parents should seek to meet each individual child's needs. The child born with a gift of musical talent might require different treatment from the child with a gift of athletic ability. The child with dyslexia might require different homework help from the child with attention-deficit disorder. But one thing all children have in common: They need a safe place where they are loved by parents and siblings, where their basic physical needs are met, and where they can learn without fear.

But not all children in LDS homes experience a safe and loving environment, even though the LDS Church holds that child abuse is an offense to God and to life. Although the Old Testament ways are included in LDS Scriptures, members are much more likely to uphold New Testament dictums, in word and in deed. Anyone guilty of abuse takes extra precautions to ensure that no one knows and no one tells, for if he or she is discovered, everything comes crashing down. So even abusive families go to church and do their best to look like every other LDS family, for if an abusive family is discovered, the image shatters, the law gets involved, and everyone *knows.* The increased pressure resulting from the fear of being discovered exacerbates feelings of hypocrisy, the stress is unbearable, and a Jekyll and Hyde dichotomy springs up: Mr. Clean and Wonderful at church and Raging Lunatic at home. It happens with women too. Mrs. Sweetness and Light leaves Relief Society and on the way home she becomes Maleficent, the Wicked Stepmother, and Cruella DeVil rolled into one. Typically, the abuser takes out his or her frustrations on the weaker family members: the children. But the prices for abuse are beyond comprehension. As Jesus said, "Whoso shall offend one of these little ones which believe in me, it were better for him that a millstone were hanged about his neck, and that he were drowned in the depth of the sea" (Matthew 18:6).

We live in a time when children can create a lot of grief for parents, who are liable for any destruction their children cause. We've seen it happen: A teenager manipulates for control, perhaps to regain lost privileges. The parents, sensing that the child hasn't sufficiently matured or learned from past mistakes, withhold the privilege. The teen retaliates and the parents walk on eggshells, unsure of the best way to guide the family through these difficulties. Fortunately, when parents raise their children in an environment of love, the chances of out-of-control behavior diminish. When parents raise their children in the Gospel, exercising the Golden Rule, they are much more likely to receive love in return. Rather than having their children turn against them, their children are much more likely to bring them joy.

When abuse rears its ugly head or contention rips at solidarity, LDS families receive support from various organizations and individuals in the church, just as they do when illness or tragedy strikes a home. All households in a ward are supervised by the bishop and his counselors, plus priesthood holders from the elders' quorum or the high priests group who bring perspective, love and support. Every family in the ward has home teachers who come to talk with the family, to offer prayer, lessons and blessings and any practical assistance needed. Visiting teachers from Relief Society also visit to offer prayer, lessons, and tangible support to the sisters in the household. LDS Social Services stands by to deliver professional counseling in alignment with Gospel principles. Careful supervision and love from members of the ward insure that families receive help to alleviate abusive situations.

Years ago my husband and I moved to a new city. We had very little money, as my husband had just started a new job. We lived in a small town house with a fireplace, and one day while we were cleaning together, eight-year-old Layla decided to vacuum up the ashes, including some hidden embers. The vacuum caught fire. Even though we unplugged it immediately and dragged it onto the front stoop, the smoke alarm went off. The baby started to cry, the toddler screamed. While I comforted the two of them, Layla filled pitcher after pitcher of water to douse the smoking vacuum cleaner. Just then, the home teacher showed up for the first time. He took in the scene—our financial difficulties evident in our scanty furnishings—then introduced himself and met the children. Because my husband wasn't there, he offered to return at another time and he took the smoky, dripping vacuum cleaner with him. I thought he was doing us the favor of disposing of the ruined appliance, but I worried about how we would afford another vacuum cleaner. When he returned for his second visit, he brought the vacuum, fully repaired. Layla has always been very sensitive. She knew we couldn't afford to buy a new vacuum cleaner and she was worried about it. When the home teacher returned the repaired vacuum cleaner, tears of gratitude welled up in her eyes. The willingness of church members to reach out and support families can make a big difference for little children as well as adults, can reinforce their faith and make them feel safe and protected by the larger family of the LDS ward.

I was particularly grateful for such support from this church member with my huge birth family so far away. Although I had no desire to stay in the fundamentalist group I had been born into, I missed the strong family ties and the sense of many shoulders to carry life's burdens. Even though I grew up outside the law, to parents without a marriage certificate, I grew up in the Gospel. I knew that an eternally-connected family, no matter how different, is the most important thing in the world.

My mother kept a clean, well-organized home despite our material paucity. What we lacked in goods or money, she filled with love and music and prayer. She made everything work, whether it was whipping up a meal out of couple of potatoes and carrots or making a new dress for me out of an old dress of hers. She filled our hearts with joy and our minds with light by reading good books and Scriptures and telling us stories. Oh, she worked hard! But she didn't complain, and she never seemed to resent the demands we made. She was the most Christlike woman I've ever met. How strange it was for me to speak at her baptism when she returned to the official Church of Jesus Christ of Latter-day Saints, after she'd spent sixty-five years in the polygamous group, this woman who taught me the ways of Christ.

My bond with my parents and brothers and sisters was galvanized by secrecy, by the knowledge that the family must be protected. Due to the insularity and illegality of polygamy, abuse happens too often. Even in my kind and caring family, something akin to abuse went on. When a child has to lie about who she is in order to protect the family, that's abuse—whether the parents or the society or both are perpetrators. As society forces the family to turn back on itself in shame and fear, the likelihood of abuse increases dramatically. One man operating outside the law and claiming to have all the authority can amplify abuse exponentially, putting plural families in terrible situations. Recent news reports reveal the terrifying potential for harm when one man controls the minds and souls of huge polygamous clans that have no trust or recourse in state or federal governments. No wonder the leaders of The Church of Jesus Christ of Latter-day Saints want to distance themselves from these sects claiming relationship to the mainstream church.

Children are our greatest legacy, an unknown potential embodying our ability to progress eternally. A boundless and replenishing treasure to their parents, both earthly and spiritual, children become a force for good in the world if raised to serve and contribute. A beautiful passage involving children appears in LDS Scripture. When Jesus came to the New World and ministered to the Nephites, he asked them to bring their children to him:

So they brought their little children and set them down upon the ground round about him, and Jesus stood in the midst; and the multitude gave way till they had all been brought unto him. . . . He said unto them: Blessed are ye because of your faith. And now behold, my joy is full. And when he had said these words, he wept, and the multitude bare record of it, and he took their little children, one by one, and blessed them, and prayed unto the Father for them. And when he had done this he wept again; And he spake unto the multitude, and said unto them: Behold your little ones. And as they looked to behold they cast their eyes towards heaven, and they saw the heavens open, and they saw angels descending out of heaven as it were in the midst of fire . . . and the angels did minister unto them" (3 Nephi 17: 12, 20–24).

To preserve the innocence and unconditional love of such pure spirits, families must learn to serve one another. One of the most heartening aspects of my life comes from watching my children serve each other. They call each other to vent pent-up feelings, to gain perspective, and for advice. They get together to watch movies, to go to football games, to shop. They show up to help each other paint and redecorate their homes. They help each other move from one house to another. My oldest daughter, a labor and delivery nurse, has moved mountains to assist with the births of her sisters' babies. My children take care of each others' children, both in time of need and just so everybody can know and enjoy each other. They travel long distances to sustain their connection. They seek friendships with each other's spouses. They set up family vacations together. They can be critical of one another, but nothing surpasses their love for each other and nothing dampens their desire to serve. Yet their lives are not limited to or by each other. My husband and I agree that our children's love for one another validates our parenting like nothing else.

In the family, the role of the father is to work with the mother to provide a shield of faith against the barbs of the Adversary and the stings of the world. Peter's words to the elders in Christ's church sum up the importance of being armed with the Gospel. "Be sober, be vigilant; because your adversary the devil, as a roaring lion, walketh about, seeking whom he may devour" (1 Peter 5:8). Truly our world teems with dangers, so many ways to be stripped of one's soul, one's health, one's family: whether the seduction involves spending too much of one's precious lifetime on a computer or playing a video game or on a full-scale addiction to pornography or gambling, dangers truly threaten the family. I've seen how easily hearts break in a world where relationships matter less than money, and where people squander their lives on meaningless or destructive past-times. A father presiding in love and righteousness exemplifies mercy and justice. A father who provides his family with the necessities of life and protection creates safety for his loved ones, so he doesn't question his manhood or his role as an elder or high priest in the hierarchies of faith. A father who establishes his own values in reality will raise children to really fulfill their lives.

Children raised by caring fathers who establish a strong presence in their young lives tend to take more healthy risks as youngsters and as adults, expressing their points of view, trying out new things, and aiming for success. These children tend to trust themselves and others and life itself. People who take meaningful risks are much more likely to succeed (since we miss 100 percent of the chances we don't take). People who don't take risks shrivel or just get by. Those who aren't taught to calibrate risk might engage in life-endangering risks. Who wouldn't want to raise children who want to take healthy risks, who love to grow? When mothers and fathers live what they teach their children, their example can be a potent influence on their future.

In the Latter-day Saint community, mothers occupy an unparalleled place as co-creators with God of human lives. As such, they directly participate in God's work. Even before the moment of conception, a mother's responsibility revolves around nurturing children. By respecting her body (living a clean life by obeying the commandments and observing the Word of Wisdom) and listening to the dictates of the Holy Spirit, a woman preserves herself for her most important calling. Perhaps the high value we place on keeping ourselves healthy for motherhood correlates with statistical indications that women in Utah have a very high fertility rate (the number of live births per 1,000 women).[6] This can be attributed to Mormon couples' eagerness to be blessed with many children as well as the healthy LDS lifestyle.

LDS mothers work with fathers as equal partners in the family, teaching the children about equality (which does not mean "the same" in LDS doctrine) and about mutual respect and support. By working together, the couple creates synergy in the family. Parents who do not work together fail to teach their children how to be part of a greater whole. Children—especially teens—often display the hidden problems of a family and sometimes blame themselves for family dysfunctions. Kids are real results, and like it or not, results don't lie.

But even wonderfully synergistic, Gospel-centered families have members who go astray. Some who leave the paths of their fathers are heroes-in-the-making, seekers or artists who, in the classic definition of "hero" leave the tribe and venture into the unknown in order to meet challenges and discover something of value to replenish the home, genetically or otherwise. The wide circle they descry while finding their way back home includes a wider sphere of knowledge and humanity. Church doctrines promise parents that if they fulfill the responsibility to teach their children through example and instruction, they will be rewarded with family togetherness and eternal happiness.

Parents receive guidance and assurance in patriarchal blessings, in temple sealings, and in scriptural promises that they will be inspired in teaching their children. By learning to listen to the still, small voice, they can overcome anger, fear, and doubt, and bring a spirit of love to their instruction. Children taught with love are much more likely to receive Gospel principles—or anything worth learning—and to put them into action. Over a lifetime, the principles bear wholesome fruit, and children thus stay strong in the faith of their parents, and in life. Such children are less likely to see the challenges of a religious life as stumbling blocks; they are more likely to eagerly follow the Gospel Plan, getting baptized, attending church and seminary classes, dating only when old enough and in groups, going on missions, and marrying in the temple. The low rates of suicide and of death by heart disease and cancer among LDS members indicate the obvious: A healthy lifestyle leads to a healthier, longer life. (We like to point out that the Word of Wisdom revealed to the Prophet Joseph Smith preceded the health cautions concerning tobacco, alcohol, caffeine, and eating habits by at least a hundred years.)

Children who grow up in harmonious environments seem to develop better social skills by learning to be kind to siblings. By learning to serve one another and by exercising compassion they become better citizens. As long as the family doesn't succumb to the social conspiracy of pretending to be perfect while harboring hearts full of lies, children learn to exercise honesty. As children learn to respect family property, their own things, and the possessions of siblings and parents, they learn to respect public property and personal property of people outside the home. They learn to work hard by working alongside their siblings and their parents. By learning from their parents' example "to pray, and to walk uprightly before the Lord" (Doctrine and Covenants 68:28) children can become strong adults, committed to personal growth and to family solidarity while being conscientious community members. They are capable of making their own decisions from a foundation of strength; having been ransomed by the sacrifice of Jesus Christ, they are "free forever, knowing good from evil; to act for themselves and not . . . be acted upon" (2 Nephi 2:26). They are more likely to remain married to their "eternal companions" and to raise their children in loving, healthy homes. They learn to pray as a family, per scriptural instruction: "Pray in your families unto the Father always in my name, that your wives and your children may be blessed" (3 Nephi 18:21). When love prevails at home, then all good things seem possible.

Parents are in the prime position to teach children about wise use of free agency. Parents everywhere seem to believe that if you hold high expectations and browbeat children into meeting them, everyone will live happily ever after. But focusing on failure affects relationships adversely and damages an individual's sense of worth. If teaching accountability isn't a matter of holding up various hoops and telling your children to jump through them, then it must be a matter of teaching them to make good decisions by giving them guidance and letting them find out for themselves the consequences of poor decisions. It also means loving them even when they screw up. LDS parents strive to think of the prodigal son, even if the children who walked the straight and narrow feel neglected when the prodigal son or daughter returns.

Family prayers reinforce family solidarity, but they differ in style from family to family. In my sprawling, polygamous family, we always knelt facing north, toward "Kolob," where, my father said that God lives. My father or some other member of the family would be "mouth," offering a line of the prayer which we would repeat together.

In most mainstream LDS families, members fold their arms across their chests, close their eyes, and someone is called on to offer the prayer. Little ones usually offer blessings on the food, a prayer they are capable of giving. Certain phrases are passed down and become ritual: "We ask thee to bless this food to nourish and strengthen our bodies to do us the good we need." (From this my little Laurie created her own phrase, "nourshthen our bodies".) In my little family, we often knelt in a circle, holding hands as we prayed. Now that our children are grown, my husband and I embrace each other when we pray, and there's a beautiful sense that God is hearing a prayer offered from our shared heart.

In my father's house and in my own we always started our Family Home Evening with song and prayer. In the tradition established by the official church and taught to me by my father and the mothers, my husband and I would gather our children together. After the opening song and prayer, we'd have a lesson (with family members teaching on a rotation basis) then a game or an activity and a treat, and the closing song and prayer. The meeting could last half an hour or all evening long. Afterward the family went back to homework or friends or TV programs, feeling happy and more deeply connected.

In reality, our Family Home Evening went so smoothly only occasionally, which is how this special family night acquired the reputation of "the family fight that begins with a prayer and ends with a prayer." Children harbored little gripes and wrongs they could bring up in the meeting, and they usually expected to be called to account for any lapses in chores or homework. People can feel these confrontations coming, so prying them away from the phone or getting them to turn off the TV or computer can be a struggle. The opening song went smoothly unless someone who hadn't yet learned to read music wanted to accompany on the piano or guitar. Then the prayer. That was always good, even if the phone was ringing or the microwave was beeping. Then the lesson. This worked out fine if the person assigned had actually prepared the lesson. A lapse in this area usually set the stage for a quarrel. Actually it began with a benign reminder that we have a schedule and if we don't do our part, everyone suffers. The same problem, my husband or I could not refrain from remarking, characterized lapses in the schedule for dishwashing and laundry, bed-making and bathroom-cleaning. If everyone did their part, what a happy family we would be!

How long did it take me to figure out that Family Home Evenings were a time for encouraging, inspiring, and connecting rather than a time for upbraiding, guilt-tripping, and manipulating? It was not a time for "taking care of business"; it was a time for taking care of each other's *hearts.* I think I learned this lesson in fits and starts, and gradually realized that Family Home Evenings provided a forum for our children to share their thoughts and feelings, a time for them to take part in determining the quality of our shared lives. Only then did I realize what a magnificent asset the Gospel can be in raising children. I am a rebellious soul and a slow learner; I hope I learned it in time to do my children some good.

We began to have discussions: why it is important to bless the food, to express our gratitude for each day, to communicate our love for one another. Why it works to acknowledge each other, even the youngest of the family. On the good nights, we would read Scripture and an article from *The Ensign* or *The New Era,* the church magazines. Each child would take turns saying something about the topic of the day (a topic chosen by whoever was in charge). Then each family member would express concerns and desires and allow the rest of us to respond. It was a great time for Denise to update us on her busy life. Always, Layla, our animal lover, would speak for the dog. "What about Zackie?" she would say, with tears in her eyes that no one else had mentioned this important member of the family.

Now, with my children raised, we still tend to seek each other's company, especially on Sundays and Mondays. Sometimes we have Sunday dinner together at one house or the other. Other times our children opt to bring their children and share Family Home Evening with us, or they invite us to attend theirs. I know that this interconnected future was established when they were children, despite their parents' slow learning curve.

In new, unknown environments, the bonds of family are subject to severe tests, and commitment to family values takes on a whole new meaning. When LDS families move to new locations for work or school, they sometimes have to fight to hold onto their values in the fast-paced, money-driven societies of large cities. The children, especially the boys, sometimes get singled out for ridicule and bullying at school. Fathers sometimes find themselves on the outs with work teams since they don't go to bars with the happy-hour crowd. Mothers can feel especially stranded without a network of stay-at-home LDS moms and a strained family support system. When families see their faith ebbing day by day, LDS parents know how to reestablish family solidarity. One mother in this situation called her family together every night. When she called to them, they were expected to set aside their homework or their phone calls or their TV program, and they soon excelled at assembling within a minute, had a prayer, a song, a lesson, a little discussion, and a closing prayer. Twenty minutes later, everybody went back to what they were doing. Gradually their spirits rose. Soon the parents were certain that the family would make it through their difficulties. In fact, when they look back on this period of their lives, they testify that during this time, they made their biggest leap of growth, both as individuals and as a family.

Family Home Evening stands prominently among the many tools offered by The Church of Jesus Christ of Latter-day Saints for raising children and keeping families intact. Grown LDS children seriously consider their reasons for wanting to leave home: instead of breaking away in a huff, they tend to get college educations, serve missions, and have a job or two before taking off to make their own way in the world.

Family Home Evenings and bedtime prayers present opportunities for parents to share their testimony of the Gospel with their children. Often, children spark the spirit's expansion, and a miniature testimony meeting takes place, where the little ones express their love and gratitude for life, family, and Jesus. Testimony meetings provide a great way for family members to get to know each other and to restore their conviction and reiterate their covenants with God. The few minutes I spent sitting beside my son, reading him a bedtime story and hearing his prayers, opened the space for us to tell each other the truth. "How do you know if God is answering your prayer?" he asked one night. I shared my experience, how I'd wait for an answer, and then look to the Scriptures. Then I referred him to his own experience of God, remembering 3 John: 4: "I have no greater joy than to hear that my children walk in truth."

Of course, there are other, less desirable facets of close-knit families. The guilt-ridden, "I have to take care of you because you took care of me" side. The "I'm not enough and I'll never be enough to please you" side. The "you only love me because you are my family but no one else will love me" side. The system of "families can be together forever" works when we use our time together to make it a desirable reality. Pretending doesn't work any better with the LDS system than it does with any other. In fact, the price of denial may actually be higher in this system, driving people over the edge more readily and with greater force. Fathers and especially mothers are charged with the responsibility for making home a heaven on earth. How does one do this without adding an element of the ethereal, the ideal? Can heaven on earth accommodate baby poop and holey socks and breast cancer? Can heaven on earth deal with hormone explosions and petty grievances and honest doubt? Well, probably, if you learn to talk and laugh and pray your way through it. And if you exercise faith.

The basic truth that family matters more than any other unit applies even to church leaders. This has been emphasized following a spate of problems surrounding absent fathers with big church callings who missed time with their wives or children while attending to the flock. By mandate from church authorities, administrative meetings have been consolidated and shortened so that all members may spend more time with their families.

The Gospel indicates that all human beings are brothers and sisters in the same big family, siblings all, regardless of skin color or ethnic origin, children of a Heavenly Father who loves us, redeemed by our older brother, Jesus Christ, so that, by our faithfulness, we might have new life. This message of tolerance wasn't always manifested in the church. In the 1970s, I taught in a junior high school with a high percentage of minorities, and I writhed internally with the knowledge that my religion discriminated against African American males by withholding the priesthood. I felt like a hypocrite, and couldn't bring myself to go to church. When the church presidency received the revelation in 1978 that all eligible males could receive the priesthood—thereby alleviating this discrimination—my attitude shifted dramatically. I felt that the church was "truer" and more in alignment with Jesus Christ and with a loving Father in Heaven. Certainly millions in the family of man have been and yet will be affected by this expansion of the priesthood.

My children had been going to church ever since our oldest daughter, Denise, began attending with a friend. Then she decided that she wanted to be baptized. At that time I was so busy sorting out my fundamentalist roots, and my husband was so alienated after his Vietnam experience, that we neglected our children's religious education. In a way, Denise called us to account for our membership in the church. She reawakened the Gospel in our lives and in our hearts. Many parents rediscover or keep themselves on the straight and narrow path that leads to eternal life because their children "get it" about the Gospel. The children begin asking their parents difficult questions, and the parents are moved to make a choice: Either jump in all the way or get out; no more fence-sitting.

I recently heard about an exchange between six-year-old Christopher and his father, Brandon, who wanted to stay home from church to watch football. Surprisingly, Chris said, "Aw, Dad, I want to go to church. Our teacher is gonna dress us up as Pilgrims. We're doing a play about how they helped God with His plan for our free agency." Brandon blinked. "Wouldn't you rather watch football?" "No," Chris said, "we can watch football another time." Resigned, Brandon herded his son toward the door. "Let's go get our church clothes on so we can be there on time." Marie, the mom, had been standing by, listening to the exchange. Although she had been upset with her husband, she allowed Chris to influence him. Everything worked out, saving her from one of those uncomfortable marital conversations about walking the talk.

Perhaps the greatest beauty in the LDS religion is the concept that families can be together forever. The New Testament says it clearly: "Whatsoever thou shalt bind on earth shall be bound in heaven and whatsoever thou shalt loose on earth shall be loosed in heaven" (Matthew 16:19). The Church of Jesus Christ takes this Scripture into deep space. When families begin with a couple sealed for time and all eternity in the temple of the Most High God, then that couple marries forever, providing that they are faithful to covenants they have made in the temple. The children born to this couple are automatically sealed to them as "children of the covenant." Children born to parents before they are married in the temple must be sealed to them after the bond for time and all eternity is secured. A child over eighteen must go through the temple and receive his or her own endowments in order to be sealed to his or her parents for time and all eternity.

After my father was assassinated, I wondered if the sealing implicit in my parents' spiritual marriage would hold up, given that my father had been excommunicated from the church for living the Principle of Plural Marriage. That night I had a dream that my father came to me and spoke with me. He clarified some misunderstandings that had marred our relationship, and then he embraced me. I felt his body pressed against mine, felt his energy, his love. After I woke up, I still felt the imprint of his presence. The experience reassured me that life goes on after death and that in some way our being continues with a glorified physical presence, as do the bonds we have established here on earth.

After she was re-baptized into The Church of Jesus Christ of Latter-day Saints at the age of eighty, my mother had all her temple blessings restored by one of the Twelve Apostles. When she died following surgery, I anguished over losing her, but I knew she was happy and safe and exalted. I also knew that the burden had fallen on me to live my life in such a meaningful and enlightened and productive way that I would be worthy to see her again. Denise, my daughter who is an RN, stayed with my mother throughout her ordeal in the hospital, holding her hand, telling her how much she was loved. My mother slipped away when all of us were gone; it was as if our presence, our love, was holding her there. I met my daughter and my younger brothers at the mortuary to plan the funeral. My mother's body had been bathed and covered with a sheet. When I saw her lifeless form, the reality pierced my heart and I couldn't keep myself from crying out. The next day my daughters met me and we performed the sad office women have always performed for their dead loved ones: preparing them for burial. We dressed my mother's body in her temple clothes; we put on the mother's necklace and mother's ring we had given her, with each of our birthstones. My niece, who had taken cosmetology classes, came to do her hair and makeup. It was my mother's body, the body that had once grown and carried me. But my mother wasn't there. She was off somewhere, dancing and laughing in the light, her aches and pains and depression gone. She was having a good time with long-departed loved ones: her mother and father and brother and sisters; my father and her sister-wives.

We all want to return home to our parents, both earthly and eternal. The worst kind of loss seems to be the loss of home, the loss of family, the loss of meaningful relationships. What comforted me as I buried my mother, what comforts me when I hear sirens in the night, is this belief in eternal families. There's a balm and a joy I'd love to extend to every person on this earth, to every person who has ever lived. The recognition that we are part of one family inspires us to encompass all brothers and sisters through all time. If energy is never lost but only changes form, we need to keep aligning and organizing energy as it is released into the universe so that we don't lose track of it; that way we can stay connected to it. That's what I believe the work in LDS temples addresses: In completing temple ordinances on their behalf, we are bringing home the lost and lonely members of our family.

There's no overestimating the power of family synergy. Think of the family of Elizabeth Smart. Through the kindness of Lois and Ed Smart, a drifter named Brian David Mitchell finds a way to make some money doing odd jobs for the family. Mitchell, a lapsed Mormon, then decides that fourteen-year-old Elizabeth will be his second and plural wife and he kidnaps her. He supports his choice with doctrinal evidence from the LDS Church's early history and with his own delusional interpretations of Scripture. The Smart family might have fallen into hopelessness or blamed themselves or blamed the police for their daughter's ordeal. Instead, they focused all their energy on finding her. Their efforts paid off, of course. She was found through the kind of miracle that only seems to happen through the synergy of perfect faith. And the foundations of her family were strong enough to withstand everything that ensued, strong enough to help her recover from the abuse she'd endured.

When the family is orderly, enacting traditions and rituals that render meaning, energy is contained, protected, focused, and used for the purpose of enhancing life. Even when chaos visits, the family, like life itself, develops an ascending order, becoming more refined and sensitive and capable of variety as it becomes more complex. Strong spiritual families that stay grounded in reality produce gifted individuals, people who make meaningful contributions to society as a whole. LDS families learning to work together throughout eternity strive to bring their best as individuals to the great banquet of life, where we all get to share in the feast.

6

Charity
Never Faileth

aroline Van Zee never expected to be the spiritual head of her family. She grew up in a devout LDS family "out in the mission field" as we say in Utah. She'd been raised on a farm in Iowa, and vowed that she would marry in the temple, but that was before she went away to college and met and fell in love with Utah native, Erik Van Zee. Erik had been baptized into the LDS Church, served a mission in France, and came home, duty fulfilled, ready to LIVE his life. To Erik, that meant following strong urges to master every musical instrument, to write music, to record and rehearse and perform, to celebrate his life's purpose. When he met Caroline, he told her that he would be the best husband and father he could be . . . as long as these roles didn't interfere with his deep, driving purpose. He promised Caroline that someday he would take her to the temple to be married, but first he needed to establish himself as a musician. They wed in a simple civil ceremony, a justice of the peace performing the rites, and Caroline's parents promised to host a lavish celebration in a year or two when the couple married in the temple.

For the next twenty years Caroline held her family together and maintained a foothold in the church while her husband followed his dream. She persevered even through the dark times because she believed in the eternal life they would share. She represented his work while he rehearsed or went to music camps or traveled to symphony capitals around the globe. She took evening classes and correspondence courses to complete her own education. She also took care of their children, and during the lean times, she took in secretarial work she could do at home to keep bread on the table.

She accepted and fulfilled church callings as they came up: Primary chorister, Young Women's advisor, and Relief Society compassionate service leader, a role that put her in touch with everyone in the ward. If someone's great-aunt died in a rest home in southern Utah, Caroline knew about it. If someone in the neighborhood was injured in a boating or a skiing accident, Caroline lined up sisters to feed the traumatized family. If someone had a baby or graduated from college, or got called on a mission, Caroline was on the phone offering congratulations and support. As part of her church calling, as well as her nature, she reached out to the larger community. When the Great Salt Lake rose in 1984 and flooded homes, Caroline coordinated with the Elders Quorum president and High Priests Group leader to sandbag levees and sump basements. When she felt overwhelmed or discouraged that there wasn't enough of her to go around, or that her husband would never give up his quasi-secular attitude toward life, she reached out to her visiting teacher or her friends in the Relief Society, and they talked until she could turn it over to God and laugh about her situation.

As the years passed, she waited for Erik to initiate their temple marriage, but he didn't. She decided to get her endowments anyway, risking the possibility that he might be turned off by her temple garments, which covered more of her body than not. This commitment brought her considerable comfort and strength, but it made her sad and angry, too, knowing that her husband hadn't been there with her. As anyone knows who has raised children with an inactive partner, she carried a big burden, and she carried it alone. How could she communicate the importance of observing the Gospel to her children when life with Erik was laissez-faire? Occasionally when the kids acted up or one of them committed an egregious offense, she asked Erik for support. More often than not he remained wrapped up in his music; and when he wasn't literally gone, he might as well have been.

The consequences of this arrangement didn't really show up until their oldest son crashed his motorcycle into a tree while driving under the influence. Erik woke up and realized that half of his family had grown up and he still hadn't kept his promise about the temple. If he died, he would lose them forever. He might lose them anyway. His children were being raised outside the covenant, vulnerable to a brutish world of drinking, drugs, and extramarital sex. Erik considered his now well-established career as a musician and thought how meaningless life would be if he lost his family. He cleaned up his act: He gave up coffee, late-night jam sessions, and nymphet protégées. He stopped traveling to San Francisco and New York and London. He went to church with Caroline and the children. Soon they set a date to be married in the temple. The largest sealing room in the temple was packed with well-wishers and witnesses. Every temple-worthy couple in the ward attended as well as members of both families who had waited and prayed for this day.

It wasn't exactly too little too late, but the weeds had sunk deep roots. Determined to make up for his lapses, Erik committed himself to church activity with zeal. Soon after their temple marriage, he was called to be a high priest, which took him away to other meetings some Sundays. Then he was called to the stake high council, which meant he didn't get to go to church with his wife and children most Sundays. But their spiritual relationship grew strong, and Caroline was proud of Erik's newfound authority and commitment.

Erik's biggest challenge was converting their oldest son's partner. In the way of the world, their son had been living with his girlfriend without the benefit of marriage. Calling the children who still lived at home back into alignment wasn't so tough. Persuading those who were living on their own to be obedient . . . well, that was next to impossible. It took a lot of prayer, a lot of fasting, a lot of talking and loving and forgiving. But it worked. Gradually the young woman embraced the Gospel and was baptized, and the two made plans to be married in the temple. Erik had just been called to be a counselor to the stake president when he went out to shovel the snow on his walk. He had just finished the job when Caroline called him inside to take a phone call. He said hello and then collapsed: an aneurysm.

That quickly, he was gone. Caroline, who'd grown accustomed to being more or less alone, had reawakened her heart and spirit to include him, and his death shook her to the core. Being married to Erik hadn't been easy, but it had grounded her. Now that he was gone, she could not find herself. She didn't go to church, she didn't work. She sat and stared out the window. She would awaken in the middle of the night, go to his grave, and lie on it and weep. Knowing that they were married for all eternity made losing him bearable in some ways, but it didn't help much in the here and now. The bishop or the high priests leader would respond to her children's midnight calls, go and find her at Erik's graveside, wrap her cold body in his overcoat and take her home. This went on for two years, the strange behavior, the sleepless nights. The night her first grandchild was born, Erik came to her in a dream, smiling. "Live well," he said. "I will wait for you." She awakened, her heart filled with joy. All at once she could concentrate, she could hold up her end of a conversation, and she wanted to be with people. She picked up the pieces and put them back together again. She reintroduced old patterns: family celebrations, gatherings of friends, church involvement. She continued to be the agent of Erik's music, finding ways to distribute it. She filled in as best she could for the absent father and grandfather. She didn't give up. She went on living.

She didn't want to marry again, even though she was alone—her nest empty, with the two youngest off to college and the other two married. She took comfort in her quiet evenings, attending firesides on Sundays and empty nesters' Family Home Evenings on Mondays. She said her prayers, did her church work, and made her contributions to the community. Her children came to dinner on Sundays and spent holidays with her. They were loving, concerned, and clearly self-sufficient. The day she received a humanitarian mission call to Indonesia, to help people rebuild their lives in the wake of the tsunami, she knew she was ready for the challenge. Her children were thrilled for her, and offered to take care of the house and the business in her absence. She boarded a plane with a suitcase of blue jeans and cotton blouses; she was more anxious and excited than she had ever been in her life, but she knew she could fulfill the mission. After all, she had rebuilt her life, and with God's help she would help the tsunami survivors rebuild theirs.

~⌐

Strong faith while confronting adversity has characterized LDS women since the beginning. Whether they were burned out of their homes or raped by mobs enraged at the church in its early days, burying babies or husbands who perished from exposure or disease as they crossed the Great Plains, or challenged by a jealous plural wife or a greedy, self-right-eous neighbor, LDS women have generally held up under duress. This faith that we can "endure to the end" and that we can perform difficult tasks with joy activates a desire to serve based on the knowledge that we are all one family and that we're on this earth to love and serve one another. When one's family is grown or dead and gone, there's always another, larger family to serve.

A woman's role can be best understood by getting to know the Relief Society, the women's organization within The Church of Jesus Christ of Latter-day Saints. In 1842, the Prophet Joseph Smith, Jr. set the stage for the Relief Society by transmitting a revelation regarding his wife, Emma. In this revelation, Emma, having been forgiven of her sins, is called to be a scribe for Joseph and she is assigned to put together a se-lection of sacred hymns. According to the revelation, Emma is "an elect lady" who would "expound scriptures and exhort the church." Such spir-itual callings for women in any patriarchal church in those times, when women were rarely allowed to speak in religious settings, stood out as re-markable. The revelation clarifies that God speaks not just to Emma but to all women who become part of the fold. In this sense, Emma Hale Smith becomes a paradigm for all women who aspire to exaltation.[1]

The growth of the LDS Church reflects the advancement of Ameri-can civilization. In the early 1800s, a profusion of benevolent women's so-cieties accompanied the expansion of American culture. The LDS people who settled Nauvoo, Illinois in 1840, building chapels and temples, lyceums and universities, felt the fervor and inclination of this move-ment. Sarah Granger Kimball organized a Ladies Society to help the workers building the temple, and asked Eliza R. Snow to write bylaws and a constitution for the group. When Eliza put the document before Joseph Smith for approval, the prophet invited the organizing women to meet with him. Joseph Smith praised its excellence, but advised the group to organize under the direction of the priesthood. The women agreed that an organization of Daughters in Zion should differ from those out in the world. Smith then invited the women to elect a president who would choose her own counselors. Elizabeth Ann Whitney nominated the founder's wife, Emma Smith; she was elected and promptly chose her counselors.[2]

In being supervised by men holding the priesthood, this early version of the Relief Society stood apart from worldly ladies' societies. Even though Sarah Cleveland, the first counselor who assisted the president, was not a Mormon, the Relief Society would be defined by sacred promises linking women to divinity and to one another in acts of service. From the beginning, the women offered charity and relief, giving from their own means and from the generosity of others, watching out for each other as well as those outside the organization. Their meetings proceeded harmoniously and were marked by intelligence and observance of parliamentary procedure. "Charity never faileth"—a quote taken from 1 Corinthians 13:8—guided the organization from the start, and so became the appropriate choice when the Relief Society sought a motto. According to Joseph Smith, charity characterizes a woman's nature, and as a gift instilled by God, charity would be the main purpose of the Relief Society and of all women in Zion.

Over the years, the Relief Society united women to influence politics, education, economics, social work, and culture in the church and in the nation.

The unlikely liaison between plural wives and women's suffrage leaders was shored up, at least in part, through the empowering influence of the *Woman's Exponent,* a newspaper founded in 1872, which became the unofficial voice of the Relief Society. Most of the LDS women involved in the political movement received the support and blessings of church patriarchs. In some cases they were officially "called" to their responsibilities, as were Lula Greene Richards and Emmeline B. Wells, who were set apart by the church presidency to be editors of the *Exponent.* In January 1870, when a series of Relief Society meetings to organize women's political influence attracted the national press, one reporter asserted that, "in logic and in rhetoric the so-called degraded ladies of Mormondom are quite equal to the women's rights women of the east." [3] Phebe Woodruff, whose husband, Wilford would be the church president who signed the Manifesto of 1890, said "God has opened the way for us." In one of these stirring sessions, Bathsheba Smith, wife of the Prophet Joseph Smith's nephew, urged "that we demand of the Gov[ernor] the right of Franchise."[4] In response to these fervent Relief Society meetings, acting governor, S. A. Mann signed the bill granting women the right to vote on February 9, 1870.[5] Thus, the women of the Utah territory were the second body of women in a U.S. *territory* to be given the vote and twenty-five women exercised their franchise on Election Day, February 14, 1870, becoming the first group of women to vote in a general election.[6]

Women's activists Susan B. Anthony and Elizabeth Cady Stanton visited Utah in 1871 to address the largest body of enfranchised women anywhere in the United States. The Relief Society committed to support the National Woman Suffrage Association (NWSA) and enlisted the support of the Young Ladies' Mutual Improvement Association. The two LDS women's organizations became charter members of NWSA, sent representatives to Washington D. C., and collected thirteen thousand names petitioning the U.S. legislature to grant women the right to vote. The Relief Society and the young women's organization in the LDS Church continued to be members of the National Council of Women and the International Council of Women until 1987.[7]

A major factor in Mormon men supporting women's franchise involved their desire to preserve the Principle of Plural Marriage. Much of the persecution of the early Latter-day Saints had been focused on polygamy. Several legislative forays against polygamous patriarchs and the church itself motivated men to support women's franchise so that their wives could endorse plural marriage with their votes and their voices. Plus, plural wives needed greater autonomy to exercise other rights that would enable the plural way of life, such as the right to own property, the right to an education, and the right to engage in commerce and to run for public office.

By and large, early LDS women were strong-minded and strong-willed, and felt themselves endowed with the power of God to choose the character of their own lives. Most had been born into the freest society known to mankind, and some were daughters and granddaughters of men who had fought in the Revolution, so they knew the price of individual freedom and democratic government. Their religion granted reminders of their free agency, with doctrinal and spiritual connection to all human beings, and with a mission to spread the truth and to share their substance. They spoke and wrote of gender equality as a blessing of the Restored Gospel of Jesus Christ and the outcome of living on American soil—that the time and place had been established for women to openly own and exercise their God-given rights and their native power.

Ironically, given that polygamy tends to diminish females, plural marriage in those early days enhanced women's independence. The principle required each wife to make more decisions for herself and her family. The Law of Chastity gives women the implicit right to decide if and when she will bear children, which awakens women to physical self-possession. Perhaps not having a husband nearby to command all decisions induced women to be more decisive and creative. Owning land and business enhanced women's leadership, political acumen, and financial abilities. The absolute necessity to make one's own living empowered women to lead lives of their own volition and creation. Perhaps their manifested capability in business, arts, and public office encouraged church leaders to support them. Certainly the men had their own interests mind, but their enthusiasm may have reflected the relationship between Eliza R. Snow and Brigham Young—she a brilliant visionary, he a gifted organizer and entrepreneur—exemplifying the possibilities of partnership. But there's little doubt that the attack on the Principle of Plural Marriage galvanized the issue of women's rights in Utah Territory.

Some have suggested that the principle was not designed to be subjugating but rather to be freeing and empowering for women. Others suggest that the commandment was given so that men and women could "raise up a righteous seed unto the Lord" (as my father used to say of his purpose in living the principle). The struggles of the beleaguered Mormon pioneers to survive forced immigration, harsh wilderness, and other hardships brings to mind the behavior of animals during times of distress: the Canada geese, for example, become polygamous until their population has restored itself, then return to monogamy. But some have suggested that the principle's primary design was to teach charity, that by being willing to share everything, we reach transcendent being.

But even charity has limits. Many balked at practicing the principle, especially when it was first introduced. Understandably, women objected more often than men. But many men refused to take another wife, even under the threat that their refusal would keep them from progressing in the church and in the eternities. Despite their devotion to the Gospel, some women extracted an engagement promise from prospective husbands that they would never take another wife. This constituted rebellion, for in the early days devout Latter-day Saints believed that God had given a commandment to live the Principle of Plural Marriage, and those who were "called" should respond.

The radical protest and passionate rhetoric of Utah women—40 percent of whom lived the Principle of Plural Marriage in the 1860s, and all of whom stood for it as a sacred principle protected by the U.S. Constitution under the freedom of religion—didn't jibe with the perspective that polygamy enslaves women. Clearly the principle inspired a peculiar, yet resolute emancipation from traditional marriage systems.

The women in pioneer days seemed to prosper, gaining significant power and freedom under the principle. As they claimed their rights, they celebrated their recently-won freedom and recognized that a new and valuable status was being granted that transcended polygamy. I imagine that these women held their breath in some ways, hoping that any men who sought to control instead of empower would not notice the gates of freedom flung wide.

Women understood that their liberty and quality of life was at stake, as were those of their children. They cared about liberation for their sisters and their daughters as much as for themselves. As Emily Partridge, who had been plural wife to both Joseph Smith and to Brigham Young, wrote in her journal, "Long live womans suffrage and equal rights. No need for four-fifths of the inhabitants of the earth to grovel in the dust in order that the other fifth may stand a little higher." [8]

"God has opened the way for us," rejoiced Sister Woodruff, president of the Fourteenth Ward Relief Society. When some men predicted that women would have as much difficulty as the men would in dealing with their newly conferred status, Bathsheba Smith, a strong and devout woman who would one day be Relief Society general president, declared, "there is nothing required of us we that cannot perform." Some women approached this new freedom with trepidation, as if it might trample them like a runaway horse: "I have never had any desire for more rights than I have" was a typical feeling in this regard, but even these reluctant suffragettes seemed pleased when exercising the franchise.[9]

Unfortunately, Utah women soon found themselves disenfranchised and again fighting for their right to vote in 1887 when the Edmunds-Tucker Act retracted their civil rights and escheated church properties, including temples. Suffrage leaders in the East expressed their dismay, calling the legislation despotic and praising the optimism of Mormon women in the face of this discouragement. Realizing that the work of the church would be halted and that Utah would not be granted statehood as long as polygamy was an issue, President Wilford Woodruff presented the Manifesto of 1890 abolishing polygamy. As Utah approached statehood in the early 1890s, LDS women anticipated the restoration of their right to vote. They did not expect that they would have to fight for suffrage with their fellow Mormons, but Susan B. Anthony advised weaving their franchise into the state constitution. Timely advice it was, for the issue of women's suffrage became the most controversial issue of the Utah State Constitution. This controversy was easily blamed on the non-Mormons (who believed that the vote of LDS women would be dictated by their husbands) but the strongest opponents were LDS men of such caliber as the noted journalist and orator B. H. Roberts.[10] Despite his passionate rhetoric, women were guaranteed the right to vote by the state constitution, which also banned polygamy in Utah forever.

Relief Society ended its involvement with some national women's organizations after the Nineteenth Amendment to the United States Constitution was ratified to guarantee women's suffrage in 1920. LDS Church President Joseph F. Smith worried that "woman-made" organizations might compromise the divinely ordained institution and encouraged Relief Society leaders to forgo their historic participation in secular organizations. These twentieth century Mormon women, newly ensconced in nationally-established legitimacy, allowed themselves to be divested of financial autonomy. They also gave up editorial rights in their publications and no longer nominated and elected their own leaders. How did this happen? By the 1920s was a different sort of women leading Relief Society than those who led the sisterhood from Nauvoo and Winter Quarters across the plains? Those women had told their daughters through the *Young Women's Journal* of 1902: "To women there belongs a right which lies deeper than suffrage, higher than education, sweeter than enforced virtue. It is the right of choice; the right to choose what she shall be." Why did they relinquish their power? Emmeline B. Wells, president of Relief Society during many of these changes, had been among the early voices to declare the redemption of Eve. In 1907 she told the National Council of Women, "The man and the woman will be equal . . . awakening woman and her cooperation with man in the world's great work."[11]

Wells's vision had not changed. Could it be, then, that a different sort of prophet was receiving revelation for the saints? Could the son of martyred Hyrum Smith and the nephew of the Prophet Joseph Smith be all that different from his forebears? Certainly it was a different time. The church was trying to live down its polygamous past and busily proving compliance with the law. Society was changing too, the world growing more liberal, so church leaders worked to shore up the moral fiber of its members. As with people who have been radical in their youth, the church has become increasingly conservative as it matures. The larger the institution has become, the more formal the patriarchal hierarchy and the less inclined it has been to empower creative freedom in individuals, men or women.

Without the communion provided by the *Woman's Exponent,* which was dissolved in 1914 and replaced by the priesthood-edited *Relief Society Magazine,* women's voices faded. When the Nineteenth Amendment passed, Relief Society President Emmeline Wells, in a fulfillment of her years of radical feminist leadership, sent her congratulations to suffrage leaders in Washington, D. C. Although her predecessors held office until death, LDS President Heber J. Grant released Emmeline Wells from office when she was 92, stating that Relief Society required a person "of greater strength of body."[12] She was heartbroken and died soon after her release in April of 1921. For LDS women, a groundbreaking era ended with her life.

From 1914 through the 1920s, war, influenza and industrialization were taking their toll on the American home. In the process of claiming their rights, some women lost their moral bearings. Liberated women cut their hair, cut their skirts, and cut the strings that tied them to the hearth. Latter-day Saint leaders struggled to keep women and children on track with the Gospel. LDS women of energy and vision who held a path of dignity in exercising their new freedoms dedicated themselves to social and charitable work during the World War I and afterward.

As the moral upheavals of the Roaring Twenties and the scarcity of the Great Depression influenced church members, people turned their hearts and minds toward home. Women were admonished to focus their energies on raising children. They lived in households ruled by priesthood-holders: their fathers, their husbands, and their sons. As leaders of the LDS Church and as individuals, Mormon men discouraged their women from working outside the home. As women committed to their duties at home, they were often ignored, dismissed, and patronized by their men. Of course, they were also protected, adored, and put on pedestals. An unwieldy standard emerged as men dedicated huge amounts of time to work, politics, and church work and less to direct participation with their families. Although women had traditionally involved themselves with social issues, LDS participation with the Prohibition movement was led by men, and women were consigned to support them.

When the men went off to "fight the good fight" during World War II, women again took charge of the home front. And as they had done in former times when their men went off with plural wives or went on missions that took them to distant lands, women again proved that there was almost nothing they couldn't do. But when the men came home, they did their best to get women back to the hearth. As activists like Betty Friedan and Gloria Steinem began to make national noise about women's rights and dreams in the 1960s and 1970s, men of the church stiffened even more.

One of my friends in junior high school, Serena, had an older sister who married an ambitious patriarch. Serena and I occasionally babysat while the couple attended ward gatherings. His jaw was always set, his attitude hard. He didn't spare us a glance. We did not matter to him. Neither did he seem to care about his wife. He had certain expectations of her—that she keep the house clean, mind the children, prepare meals. Otherwise, she had the television to keep her entertained. What more could she possibly want or need? Once, when she brought up the possibility that she might return to college, he lost his temper. The next day they went to the temple to pray that there would be no more contention in their home. We babysat for them while they arrived at a "divinely inspired" decision that more schooling provoked contention, and contention being of the devil, an extended education would no longer be considered.

When I was fifteen one of my teachers, an elegant woman with a truly beautiful spirit, had the gift of teaching all-thumbed people like me to make elegant things. She had been in love with her husband since she was sixteen, had been a cheerleader while he was on the high school football team. She had gone to BYU for the two years he spent on his mission. When he came home, she married him in the temple, then stayed home with the babies. Everything went along well until their children entered their teens. Then he started having affairs. He couldn't live with the guilt and confessed, but blamed his behavior on ancestors who lived polygamy. He couldn't stop, he said, and he didn't know what to do about it. Maybe the church would bring plural marriage back someday, and then everything would make sense. She divorced him, but it tore her heart out. She felt she was giving up her eternal happiness in order to have peace of mind in the here and now. She aged a decade in one month, went into a deep depression and moved from her ward, feeling that the bishop and his counselors, in their efforts to promote her husband's redemption, had taken his side and discounted her pain.

Circumstances such as these may have prompted church leaders to see that women's issues need to be handled differently. So many Mormon women suffered from depression in the 1970s and 1980s that the media focused on the epidemic, probing the whys and wherefores. No longer could we sweep the dirt under the carpet. LDS social workers and counselors began to address some of the root causes, In addition to finding therapies and drugs to treat depression, people sought transformations that would empower women. Bright, intuitive LDS women who survived this period of pretending began to write and speak out, to communicate with each other, and to lobby for change. Some became discouraged and left the church, yet found they couldn't leave the issues they carried inside. Others stayed, committed to creating change by leading fulfilled lives within the church.

In the 1970s I would come home from classes at the University of Utah to the little apartment I shared with my husband, my heart aching for a world rife with war and confusion. I listened to the music of social change as I washed dishes and diapers, my mind alight with huge and beautiful ideas, about the power of education to effect transformation, about men and women and equality. As I began to grasp the imperative of our nuclear age, I knew at last why my father had emphasized that we were living in the last dispensation in the fullness of times, the reason The Church of Jesus Christ must be restored in every aspect. This magnanimous view gave me some comfort about my parents' choice to live the Principle of Plural Marriage. It also gave me hope in a world of glaring inequities regarding gender, race, and quality of life, a world at war with itself. I recognized that we must learn to live in peace or succumb to global destruction, and that we weren't doing so well when it came to learning to live together. We verged on nuclear annihilation, but we also verged on global transformation: The choice was ours, as a species, as a nation, as individuals. We could usher in the Millennial Reign of Christ, or we could fulfill another prophecy and destroy the earth by fire. I realized that choices manifested at an international level, such as war, begin in our own hearts and homes. I began to see that equalizing matters between men and women could introduce a new dimension of peace, and must be must be part of the deal. I would tentatively share these ideas with my Vietnam veteran husband and his friends. Bruce remained remarkably silent. His friends said painful things: "You live in the Emerald City, Dorothy." Of women's liberation, they said, "Those libbers are either ugly or they're gay." I wondered, noting the yearning for equality in my own heart, which of the adjectives they applied to me.

Often I was more of a feminist on behalf of my mother than on my own behalf. I grieved her lost opportunities, her long periods of depression, the anguish of unfulfilled dreams and the squandering of her vast talent. Like most women of her generation, she tried to love the box she lived in, but her soul protested anyway and her nerves crawled with the knowledge that "all was not well" in Zion. Yet sometimes I envied her. Sometimes I thought I had too many freedoms, too many choices, and too much responsibility.

Being a mother realigned my values. I wanted my child to be healthy and safe. I wanted her to be free of nightmares and settled in a safe neighborhood within a kind community. I wanted to keep her with me through hell or high water. The childhood teaching that families can be together forever had caught up with me, and I wanted to believe it with all my heart.

I didn't try to work out all the quirks of the national women's movement. I was preoccupied, a "plygie kid" struggling to be part of the mainstream, and since I had never been in full alignment with society, I didn't expect to be now. I survived one day at a time, stayed a course of personal development, prayed for change, and celebrated the revelation that permitted all eligible males to hold the priesthood. I was too busy and too burdened to yearn for my own priesthood authority as some of my contemporaries did; I just wanted my husband to be a guide and protector and provider in our little family. It didn't bother me much that I didn't have official recognition of priesthood power, because I knew that any of us can call on God in the name of Christ. But a few of my peers complained about the inequities and even compared our plight to prisoners in concentration camps.

Most women in the church waved off the feminist movement. Others spoke and wrote about our radical feminist history and the early suffrage movement and in that way found personal meaning and connection to the national movement.[13] Still other women who were firmly entrenched in the religion had experiences that accentuated the gap between the radical, reformative nature of the original women's movement and increasingly conservative attitudes in the LDS Church. In the 1970s, Sonia Johnson, at the request of her church leaders, began attending firesides — small gatherings held at the homes of LDS people — to protest the Equal Rights Amendment, then asked herself "Why?" She discovered that the LDS Church had mounted a carefully-orchestrated campaign to stop the ERA. By the time she wrote her book, *From Housewife to*

Heretic, Johnson had trumpeted what she had learned about the clandestine move to put down the ERA, and had publicly criticized her religion, sharing her perception that Mormon women are victims of a patriarchal plot to usurp the rights and power of women.[14] She had been excommunicated and she and her husband divorced. She had lost her spiritual legacy, the songs and prayers and practices of her childhood. If the doctrine holds, she had also lost her eternal family—her husband, and her eternal bond with her children.

Obviously, most LDS women do not agree with Johnson or her methods. Many have made their personal odysseys to freedom and enlightenment the subject of essays, poems, stories, and speeches without reviling their religious leaders and usually without sacrificing their membership in the LDS Church.[15] Many others worked out their issues in the privacy of their own souls as women have done since Eve chose to bite into the apple and as Mary pondered the circumstances of Jesus' conception and birth in her heart. Some spoke of these things to their husbands or their closest friends, while others simply thought and whispered the truth to themselves as they waited for a new day to dawn.

Education

"The glory of God is intelligence" (Doctrine and Covenants 93:36) is one of our most frequently quoted scriptures, for LDS people believe that we can take knowledge with us into eternal life. This belief contributes to LDS women being counted among the best-educated groups of women in America.[16]

Early in the inception of the Relief Society, leaders discovered that attendance and participation increased as long as members were learning, so the presidency began working education into meetings. While women sewed their rags into rugs, sisters would take turns instructing and entertaining each other. Sometimes the lesson would be scriptural or doctrinal reading. Other times the lesson would be drawn from periodicals. Entertainment might include a song-fest or a Shakespeare recitation or the sharing of other talents or abilities. *Woman's Exponent* evolved similarly, supporting women in edifying their minds, their gifts, and their abilities. The entry of women into the worlds of politics and commerce marked their corresponding desire for education and professional standards, and the Relief Society did its best to address those yearnings.

Although today's Relief Society leaders are careful to get priesthood authorization for anything they introduce into the church context, the education of women remains very important. Ward and stake Relief Societies have their own educational programs, writing contests, guest speakers, and homemaking programs. Every year, Brigham Young University gears up for Education Week, a full week of educational enrichment in a variety of areas. The two-day BYU Women's Conference held each spring also attracts huge participation. LDS women hunger for these programs. Today a woman might be asked to prepare curriculum for them. She might be informally invited by church leaders to study political science or education administration, or she might be "called" to run for the school board, or she might be encouraged to complete her education in history or family sciences so that she can influence the outside world or the saints with her gifts and talents.

In the early days, many of these educational callings were assigned by the church president. After Ellis Shipp received her call from Brigham Young, she completed her medical training and went on to do graduate work at the University of Michigan Medical School. She raised ten children with help from her sister-wives, delivered six thousand babies during sixty years of practice, trained many nurses and midwives, and served on the general board of the Relief Society. Other women who went east for college educations made similar contributions.

Utah's educational history is directly related to Relief Society. The leaders had been charged with educating young mothers about maternity and infant care, sound nutrition, and other important areas of family well-being. In the late 1800s and early 1900s, this sense of responsibility led to classes in maternal health, child development, and the beginnings of kindergarten. Brigham Young requested that various educators invest their talents in normal schools that Relief Society had already begun and he insisted that schools have at least one woman on the board of trustees. Martha Jane Coray was the first woman to serve in this capacity at Brigham Young Academy, the predecessor of BYU. She was the mother of twelve, an assayer, a teacher, an herbalist, and a writer. She represents scores of Utah women who have served in administrative and curriculum-shaping capacities, women whose names grace the halls of learning throughout Utah.

Spontaneous contributions from various sisters grew into prefabricated lessons that became written curriculum. Originally lessons designed by sisters in the various wards and stakes were presented to the general board and shared through *Woman's Exponent,* but interests varied from stake to stake; some sisters wanted to explore the cosmic spheres of their lives, while others wanted to share recipes and quilting patterns and tips for child care. By drawing on the breadth of lessons provided, Relief Society began to standardize a curriculum. The growing membership of the church demanded more formalized, systematic instruction.

By the early 1900s, the women who served as Relief Society general presidency were mostly college-educated, and they were sensitive to the desire of LDS women to connect with and reflect the trends of their American counterparts. As the older sisters who had come to the Salt Lake Valley with the first pioneers and those who dragged handcarts across the Great Plains went to their eternal reward, Relief Society became an organization envisioned by older women and expedited by middle-aged matrons. The issues and desires of younger women who were just beginning their adult lives and starting their own families needed attention, especially since they wanted to be progressive, making the most of new technologies and information. The Relief Society began to create a curriculum that blended earthly needs with spiritual ideals. As the church began to systematize, the brethren pressed the sisters to bring their conferences, curriculum, and meetings into alignment with the whole of the church. The Correlation Committee of 1913 requested that Relief Society cooperate in making conferences annual and in implementing a uniform course of study, and the sisterhood complied. From this time on, the lessons were handed down from the priesthood instead of being gleaned from the body of women. This shift became a source of concern to many LDS women since men don't always know what women need and want to know.

As the LDS Church grew exponentially in South America, the priesthood continued to streamline and coordinate church activities so that members would be adept in the modern world (without being "of the world"). In the 1970s, the Relief Society took a strong stand for all women to get an education, thus overthrowing centuries-old traditions in South America and in other parts of the world that had discouraged women from learning. Women were taught to organize their time and their tasks so that they could take classes while still being good wives and mothers. The Relief Society helped them find schools, supported them in organizing transportation, and celebrated with them when they graduated. Today, a significant number of LDS women go on to graduate study and are employed as professionals.[17]

How is it that LDS women, despite strong patriarchal influences, are actually afforded such support in educational autonomy and capability? Jesus Christ sat down with women, befriended them, and even pointed out to Martha, who was always doing traditional "women's work," that Mary, who sought instruction, had taken the better part. Spiritual and intellectual edification matters as much for young LDS women as for young LDS men. As those who have done it know, it is indeed possible and even necessary to be personally educated in the process of raising educated children. In most wards, LDS women support each other in their scholarly endeavors, taking turns with child care, preparing meals, and otherwise helping each other juggle domestic responsibilities.

With this in mind, it's interesting to note that women of LDS origin who are well educated are more likely to be highly active in the church. Generally speaking, LDS men also have no problem with being educated and also having a strong connection to the church, despite pressure in some universities to give up religious beliefs. During my graduate school years, a professor told me, tongue in cheek, that his greatest concern about dying from the cancer that consumed his lungs was that the Mormons might do work for the dead for him and he'd wake up in Mormon Heaven—no more drinking or smoking or womanizing forever! And that wasn't his version of Heaven, that was his version of Hell. I wasn't sure whether he was testing me, taunting me, or inviting me to express my sorrow about his deteriorating health. Perhaps to offer him some hope, I attempted to articulate my sense of the Gospel Plan, the grand design of repentance, redemption, atonement. I told him that reading Shakespeare and Emerson and Twain had enhanced the patterns of enlightenment I had learned in my religion and that this sense of order grew along with my education. As I gained knowledge, my ability to discern between useful, healthy habits of being and the life-denigrating evidence that consumes hope and inclines people toward cynicism improved.

Encouragement to get an education points up a radical difference between the official Church of Jesus Christ of Letter-day Saints and most fundamentalist groups. In polygamous circles, the less women and children know about the world, the more frightened they are and the less likely they are to rebel or leave the group. Due to the throwback nature of the polygamous subculture, fundamentalist leaders often discount education; their narrow theology might be overthrown as more choices become available to the educated man or woman.

So why did I, a child of polygamy, seek an education? My desire for knowledge sprouted from a yearning to validate myself, since I am illegitimate according to mainstream standards. Also, my father always reminded us that as "a righteous seed" sown by the Principle of Plural Marriage, we needed to be prime examples that "the glory of God is intelligence." Although my siblings felt a strong need to excel in public school as proof of that precept, most of them did not continue into college. My sisters went from high school into marriage, and I attended college without many blessings from my father, even though as a doctor he was college-educated himself. For me, getting a college education became part of my rebellion. I felt a huge desire to prove my credibility in the world beyond our polygamous group, perhaps because I didn't feel that I fully belonged. But then, I didn't fit all that well anywhere, and frequently lost and then found myself in books. I benefited hugely from scholarships and from the counsel of an older brother who told me that women have the right to make their dreams come true. By the time I graduated from high school, my father had warned his children that universities taught "the devil's doctrines" such as evolution, the Big Bang theory of creation, and other scientific theories that refuted Scripture. He worried that he would lose his children to advanced education. As indeed he did. My graduation from the University of Utah confirmed to my father that I had been lost to the world. Despite significant disagreements about education and marriage, we managed to continue our relationship on a ground of mutual respect and love. I am so grateful that before he died, we verbalized our unconditional love and acceptance for each other, and that he gave me his blessing.

Sweet Is the Work

Hand in hand with education, self-sufficiency has always been important in LDS culture. The pioneers who settled Utah bequeathed an industrious attitude on modern Latter-day Saints and an honest desire to establish a haven, a community based in love and commitment, ruled by the priesthood and patterned with Christian attitudes. Then, as today, Mormons were expected to provide for themselves and to give to the common good. The United Order, formed in 1874, detailed a communal economic system where church members in a ward or a community promised everything they harvested or made or could potentially create to the bishop to be redivided according to need, a way of life that exhorted the saints to work for "the kingdom of God" rather than for themselves. Early church leaders concluded that the cooperative system worked. Elder George Q. Cannon announced that a new order would fulfill the commandment given in the *Book of Mormon,* that the people of Zion could have "all things common among them; therefore there were not rich and poor, bond and free, but they were all made free, and partakers of the heavenly gift" (4 Nephi 1:3). Women proved their natural talent for making the United Order work; they devised many ways to meet the needs of their families (such as raising animals or fruit or vegetables to sell, or designing clothing and household goods, or crafting artwork) while contributing to the good of all.

Based on the Law of Consecration which had been practiced all along, the United Order assisted Utah Latter-day Saints in building a strong culture. The United Order thrived for a decade, and for longer in some parts of Zion. Fundamentalists have since attempted to practice the United Order with varying degrees of success and abuse. In some fundamentalist communities, the United Order and the Law of Consecration have been used as an excuse to strip members of all they earn and all they own, so that inevitably, the system fails. The Church of Jesus Christ of Latter-day Saints no longer actively practices the United Order and does not require members to turn over their assets.

During the early LDS Church's experiment in communal living, Brigham Young warned members of the church not to individually engage in commerce with "gentiles"—unbelievers—lest they undermine the emerging economy and put themselves at the mercy of their enemies. An astute entrepreneur, President Young appreciated the harmonious strength of the Relief Society and he did not underestimate the economic influence of the sisterhood—as manufacturers, marketers, and consumers. Eliza R. Snow complemented Brigham Young's abilities by being a visionary leader who illuminated the spiritual center of all efforts. Their cooperative leadership created a synchronicity between the Relief Society and the priesthood which resulted in cooperative merchandising. Early-day LDS women envisioned, stocked, and managed the first stores of Zion's Cooperative Mercantile Institute (which became department stores known as Z.C.M.I). Sarah Kimball initiated the buying of land and building of a Relief Society Hall, with the upstairs dedicated to arts and sciences, the downstairs to commerce. When her dream became real, Sister Kimball modestly called it a "stepping stone,"[18] but President Snow compared her to Eve, who with Adam lay a "foundation for Worlds."[19] Such visionary attitudes spawned economic prosperity along with abundant love, harmony, and spiritual edification.

As the Relief Society sisters prospered, priesthood leaders in various wards worried about who was in control and peevishly inquired why the men had not been given the charge of opening these cooperative stores. Brigham Young admonished them, saying he had repeatedly asked the brethren to open cooperatives but they hadn't done it; so he had asked the sisters, knowing that they would.

Young also instructed his members to stockpile wheat for times of need. The brethren, who sold their produce to the gentiles, could not seem to hold onto it, but the sisterhood displayed an admirable ability to plant, raise, and store wheat. Soon the stored grain could be sold at a profit to be replaced with fresh wheat. Through wheat storage alone, the Relief Society accumulated a substantial treasury. With funds and a broad overview of members' needs, the women's organization acquired a strong identity. Its leaders made plans to spend their money on education, cultural refinement, health care, and social improvement.

The charitable value of wheat storage proved itself during the San Francisco earthquake of 1906. The first railroad car of flour to aid the besieged city arrived compliments of the Relief Society, which sent a total of sixteen boxcars of flour plus other cars of clothing, quilts, and medicine. (Eighty-three years later, when another earthquake hit the area, the Relief Society repeated the performance when LDS ward and stake houses threw open their doors to offer relief to disaster victims.)

When parts of early Utah transformed from agricultural to industrial and issues shifted from rural to urban, the sisterhood stood with their church leaders to establish this phase of Zion. Each ward Relief Society decided what commerce to participate in, and each sister in the ward decided to what degree she would participate. To strengthen their ties with the rest of the nation, the people of the church sought transcontinental telegraph and railroad contracts. They also embraced the market that came with the locally garrisoned federal army and sought to supply the prospectors who established and worked in mines. In addition, LDS members utilized each other's goods and services. Even the church welfare system prospered, for people of abundance were encouraged to give liberally, and those in need contributed labor when possible.

For a time, the Relief Society itself incorporated, with officers and bylaws (in contradiction of the Prophet Joseph Smith's wishes). The federal encroachment on church assets catalyzed this change, for seizing property had proven to be the most effective means of discouraging polygamy. Although incorporating as a business made sense in this political climate, Relief Society President Zina Young worried that the worldly feel of being a corporation would undermine the spiritual center of the organization. So intent the sisterhood remained on their purpose of "charity never faileth" that the Relief Society continued without many changes and the bylaws and incorporated language faded away. By 1945, even the title of the corporation had been thoroughly eradicated from Relief Society.

In delivering charity, the Relief Society Social Service Department would study the family unit and then open doors to education and work opportunities. Among other services, this department placed girls and women in suitable homes where they could work as nannies and domestics. My great-grandmother Mary Catrina Rasmussen met my grandfather when she left the abusive influence of her stepfather to become a "mother's helper" for my great-grandfather's first wife, Helen. After a period of living and working together, Helen invited Mary Catrina to become Arthur Benjamin Clark's plural wife. The fine reputation of LDS-bred young women as nannies and au pairs continues worldwide, for they are well trained in their homes and by the church in raising children and caring for hearth and home. In modern times, a widowed or divorced father struggling to raise his children alone will sometimes marry his nanny; of course, polygamy is no longer an option.

The Relief Society Employment Bureau would assist women who needed or wanted to work outside the home in finding work as housekeepers, mother's helpers, laundresses, tutors, and practical nurses. The organization set standards and policies (although few legal employment guidelines existed at the time) to define the performance of employee and employer, including pre-employment interviews, requests for references, vocational guidance, and general counseling. The Society also provided retail outlets for homemade goods, an example of which survives to this day as Mormon Handicraft. The Work and Business Department gathered women for Relief Society workdays (now called homemaking days or evenings), where women learned new skills while serving the needy. Workdays allowed women to sew, to can fruit and vegetables, and to learn thrift, helping themselves and those in need while enjoying one another's company and exercising leadership within the group. Thus, through charitable service, many women were schooled in a variety of handicrafts as well as in social graces and management skills. "I learned to set a table for a formal banquet when I was about to graduate from the Young Women's program, and I was invited with the other girls in my class to attend a Relief Society social," my mother reminisced. "The evening had been created by the sisters during their workday, from the beautifully embroidered tablecloth and napkins to the roast beef and the raspberry sherbet. Relief Society provided entertainment for us as well, singing and playing musical instruments. As we dined, we received a brief lesson in table etiquette, learning which fork to use when, how to cut our meat, and that's when I learned to keep my elbows off the table!" She explained that afterward, the lovely tablecloth and napkins were donated to the ward kitchen and the leftovers were delivered to the sick or needy. She also told how one woman's performance on the piano deepened her own desire to master her musical talent. As the church has grown to include cultures throughout world, this tradition of meeting and sharing social skills and knowledge has become increasingly valuable.

A strong belief in tithing attends every economic act of the saints. The church and the membership practice this ancient law of increase to great advantage. Through tithes and fast offerings, many families survived crises that otherwise would have ruined them. Women of the Relief Society demonstrate ability, ingenuity, and leadership in this as in other areas. Even during the Great Depression, the sisterhood was able to serve its own as well as those beyond the church. By providing work for men and women, the holdings and capacities of the church and its membership grew exponentially and assisted Utah to rapidly recover from the dark years of the Depression. In fact, Latter-day Saints refer to this as another proof that the Lord takes the greatest darkness and turns it to light, transforming the worst evil to serve the good of all.

Paradoxically, the "Progressive Era" actually influenced the priesthood to take over the financial dealings of the Relief Society. As the brethren sought to make church systems more efficient, the bishops took over direct responsibility for ward Relief Society finances. As the Relief Society relinquished autonomy, LDS women experienced a subtle loss of personal power but everyone gained organizational consistency as the church grew. Standard policies and procedures were put in place, and the church organization hummed like the beehive that had become Utah's state symbol. But the more the church operated like a corporation, the less individuals were encouraged to be innovative. Even though women leaders had been called by priesthood authorities, female perspectives were often ignored or rejected outright. The fund raising bazaars, the dance festivals, and the theater projects that once inspired so much creativity became the province of a secular world or disappeared altogether.

But over the years, women have continued to be the chief consumers in the church. As a teen-ager, I went shopping with my devout LDS friend, Jeanne, and her mother at Z.C.M.I., where we engaged in a time-honored tradition of having lunch at the "Tea Room" (where no tea was served). Jeanne was the only person to whom I disclosed my background in polygamy during my young life; she told her mother, who expressed interest in my upbringing, having descended from polygamy herself. However, I did not reveal that my mother and I never shopped at Z.C.M.I. since it was too pricey for us. Instead, we shopped at "Desi's"—my mother's clever "dress shop" nickname for Deseret Industries, where well-to-do LDS members like my friend's mother made their cast-offs available to the poor while providing work for thousands of special needs employees.

Throughout the last century, LDS women have used their commercial influence and education in the larger world, reminding us that the children of the world are our children. They have shown us that by exercising our gifts and talents and sharing our increase, we can make a difference at home, in the halls of education, in the halls of government, and in the halls of healing throughout the world.

Sheri Dew, Chief Executive Officer of Deseret Books, has also served in the Relief Society general presidency and shares her significant gifts of writing, speaking, and administrating with the saints and with the world. She wrote biographies of LDS Church presidents Ezra Taft Benson and Gordon B. Hinckley and the biography of Miss America 1984, Sharlene Wells. Among many other accomplishments, she has expanded the body of acceptable literature for Latter-day Saints. She stands as a reminder to all LDS women of their individual significance and their power to make a difference. Dew always emphasizes the importance of motherhood, although she is single: "As daughters of our Heavenly Father and as daughters of Eve, we are all mothers and we have always been mothers. Like Eve, our motherhood began before we were born. Just as worthy men were foreordained to hold the priesthood in mortality, righteous women were endowed premortally with the privilege of motherhood. Motherhood is more than bearing children . . . it is the essence of who we are as women. We are all mothers in Israel, and our calling is to love and help lead the rising generation through the dangerous streets of mortality." She speaks of women's struggle to honor their calling as mothers: "For Satan has declared war on motherhood. He knows that those who rock the cradle can rock his earthly empire. And he knows that without righteous mothers loving and leading the next generation, the kingdom of God will fall."[20] A trip to Ghana made Dew aware of the plight of poor children who don't learn to read. Through her energy and resources, a shipment of 6,500 books was delivered to the children of Ghana and Fiji to begin a new humanitarian program for literacy in impoverished parts of the world. She exercises charity at home, as well. Dew's nieces and nephews benefit enormously from the understanding, cultivation, and unconditional love she brings to their lives. Many who have never met her have been touched by her words and her example, and claim her as a loving mother, sister, and magnanimous a soul as can be found in the family of man.

Sharlene Wells Hawkes, an LDS girl born in Paraguay, became the first foreign-born and bilingual Miss America. A gifted athlete, she used her magnetic screen presence and her love of sports to become an award winning ESPN reporter. After ten years, she scaled back to freelancing and local work so that she could focus on her four children and her husband. An LDS music Web site currently promotes religious songs that she has written and sung.[21]

Other LDS women inspire members of the sisterhood to make a difference through the example they set of applying their education in revolutionary ways. Carol Gerber Allred Fley developed Positive Action, a curriculum for preschool through adulthood to teach people how to feel good about themselves. Her program, well established in every state, is used abroad as well. Recently the Positive Action program received the highest ratings for character development programs from the U.S. Department of Health and Education.

In addition, several LDS women have capitalized on the special fashion needs of women in the church. Two LDS couples founded Mod Bod, a company that provides a lace-trimmed, long-line, cap-sleeved T-shirts designed to cover temple garments while making a fashion statement. Similarly, in working through some issues about her own body, Kathleen Williams (who happens to be my friend, Trudy Tracy's sister) had a great idea: She created two lines of tasteful and luxurious products for the enhancement of intimacy. *Anticipation* and *Just Between Us* offer creams, lubricants, and massage oils for women, as well as education for couples to assist them in truly enjoying connubial relationships without violating their sense that sex is private and sacred. The products can be purchased in top-line department stores and in such exclusive resorts as Bellagio in Las Vegas. In an expression of sisterhood, Trudy helps Kathleen advance her marketing plan.

LDS Women Keep on Giving

The saying goes that if you give a man a fish, he eats for a day, but if you teach a man to fish, he eats for a lifetime. The LDS Church practices genuine service and charity by "teaching men to fish," and the church welfare system has a worldwide reputation for effectiveness. People receive assistance when they need it, yet they are given the dignity of work, thus retaining self-respect while regaining their self-reliance. From there they are able to give others a hand up rather than a hand-out. Even today, Utah, with its primarily LDS population spends less on public welfare than any other state, thanks to the church's comprehensive welfare system. Wealthy church members also give a greater percentage of their income in charitable contributions than any other group.[22] Abundance results from this combination of charity and service so "well-fare" — faring well — becomes a reality.

The Church of Jesus Christ of Latter-day Saints is often held up as a model for other organizations by giving to those in need while organizing those in need to give in return when they are able. Through such synchronicity and reciprocity, we truly can take care of each other as brothers and sisters in a loving family are inclined to do. A generosity of spirit born of the faith that loving heavenly parents watch over us moves us to give more than we take wherever we live.

One woman from Denver who visited my ward the year after the Columbine High School massacre described how healing the experience had been for LDS women to gather together and make quilts for every student, teacher, and staff member undergoing Post Traumatic Stress therapy in that school. They called them comfort quilts, and the recipients took them to therapy, then carried the quilts home with them. These quilts made with love became a source of comfort during one of the bleakest hours of western civilization.

Similarly, I got involved with members of a Spanish-speaking ward when my son and others faced the tragedy of Hurricane Mitch in 1997. Women joined together to prepare relief packages—food, clothing, blankets and medicine—for the people of Guatemala and Honduras. Employees and graduates of our communication classes at Visionworks International contributed hugely, inspiring the Spanish-speaking ward to get an additional truck to deliver the relief packages. Assisting in that drive brought me more real comfort than anything else could have done at that time, especially since I knew I was reaching out to my son as I reached out to strangers.

The same phenomenon happened after Hurricane Katrina flooded New Orleans. According to the PBS special "The Mormons" (a four-part series aired in 2007), members of the LDS church showed up to help long before other relief workers. They not only brought supplies, they rolled up their sleeves and went to work, clearing away the wreckage and cleaning up alongside the victims of the storm. LDS wards worked with individuals to establish Louisiana families in Utah until their damaged homes could be rebuilt. So deep are the lessons on giving, so on-target in reaching the heart of who we are, even those who leave the LDS Church continue to practice charity. A friend of mine named Bea who has left the church personally supervised and subsidized the relocation of several families from New Orleans. She found housing, jobs, cars, and clothing for these people who needed a second chance at life and encouraged them to succeed, rather than continuing to be victimized by the storm. This type of work is essential to who we are as LDS women, and exemplifies the essence of charitable service

A leader of LDS humanitarian efforts says: "Modern-day humanitarian effort is a wonderful manifestation of the charity that burns within the souls of those whose hearts are tender and whose hands are willing to help. This selfless service truly demonstrates the pure love of Christ."[23] Recently-baptized Gladys Knight (of the singing group Gladys Knight and the Pips) joined in Mormon efforts to raise funds for Hurricane Katrina victims. Relief organizers pronounced the LDS Church a principal partner in delivering relief to tsunami victims. LDS humanitarian programs run welfare farms and canneries, help the unemployed to get work, provide child placement services, and offer goods through thrift stores to benefit the disadvantaged, among many other services. A Perpetual Education Fund provides low-interest loans to needy students in third world countries. Clean water, infant resuscitation systems, vision improvement, wheelchair procurement, and other programs raise the standard of living for our brothers and sisters everywhere, LDS or not.[24]

The desire of LDS women to be personally engaged in humanitarian service (rather than simply donating money, for instance) grows from the hands-on involvement of our grandmothers and great-grandmothers. Despite many changes over the years, the Relief Society has continued to reach out to communities beyond the LDS Church. For example, during the first half of the twentieth century, the sisterhood helped to establish a training school in American Fork, Utah, for the mentally disabled. The elderly of all denominations have benefited from Relief Society programs for 150 years. Maternity hospitals have been opened, nurses have been trained, and foster care programs have thrived. Community health clinics sponsored by Relief Society have arranged for tonsillectomies, eyeglasses, and other healthcare, generally promoting a healthier population in Utah than can be found most places in the United States.[25] This commitment to good health for our brothers and sisters expands every day. The LDS Church shares goodwill in many places where help is needed, reaching out in communities across the nation and abroad.

When Belle Spafford became Relief Society president in the 1940s she committed herself to making the Social Service and Child Welfare Department grow. To lay the groundwork for families to heal, she wanted to improve the personnel and procedures through professional direction. The areas that most concerned her were family welfare and care of unwed mothers. Sister Spafford succeeded so admirably that the Relief Society social work program became a big part of LDS Social Services, the church program that currently offers counseling, therapy, adoption, and foster care services. During Sister Spafford's term of service the Relief Society went through sweeping changes. Sisters no longer "joined" or paid dues. Visiting teachers went to sisters' homes as friends to promote spirituality and well-being rather than to ask for donations for the larger community. New systems of fundraising supplanted the door-to-door drives of yesteryear. *Relief Society Magazine* was subsumed into the new church magazine, the *Ensign*. During this era, the Relief Society lost any remaining autonomy, folded into the great body of the church and placed fully under the authority of the priesthood.

The church's humanitarian system continues to grow, as does its influence on international human services. The program has expanded to offer help to nonmembers who are refugees from political or geological disaster. The church initiates humanitarian missions across the globe, offering medical, social, or agricultural services. Retired couples frequently fulfill these humanitarian missions; my older sister Judy and her husband, a retired physician, fulfilled a mission in South America. The couples usually dedicate two years of their lives, sharing their area of expertise for the sake of the church and humanity. They receive many blessings for their unconditional service, including a broader global community and the experience of making a valued contribution, which is prerequisite to an abundant life.

As mentioned, the church has a highly successful adoption program.[26] The relatively small percentage of LDS girls who conceive out of wedlock are encouraged to have their babies (rather than aborting them) and to give them to parents who are temple-married. One particularly serendipitous story: A girl named Rosalind gave birth out of wedlock and, with church encouragement, gave up her daughter to an LDS couple. Rosalind recovered to some degree, finished high school and went on to college, then married in the temple and gave birth to three more children. Still troubled by her early experience, she went to her bishop. In astonishing synchronicity, the woman the bishop encouraged her to seek guidance from turned out to be the adoptive mother of her first baby. Rosalind got to meet her daughter and the two families began spending holidays together.

Of course, one distressing problem in Zion involves the welfare of polygamists. Despite its worldwide humanitarian relief efforts, the LDS Church traditionally does not assist polygamists, perhaps not wanting to encourage this illegal practice. In polygamous communities, very little exists in the way of welfare or social service programs. Fundamentalists are rarely willing to risk registering with the state and federal governments, for records could be used in court and put families in jeopardy. The little help available seems seem woefully inadequate. The insularity and poverty of polygamous groups exacerbate the situation, with many wives and many children totally dependent on one husband/father who in turn gives some or all of what he earns to "the prophet" or the fundamentalist priesthood organization. Many polygamists aren't prepared to make a living for themselves. Poorly educated, more often than not, and having grown up on the outskirts of mainstream society, the polygamous father may not be able to read or write and may not have viable skills to provide an income. For example, my aunt married a man who couldn't provide for one family, let alone his second wife's. He made his living gathering pine nuts, and would come home after months on the road with so little to show that my mother would weep for her sister, knowing that a poor harvest meant another year of wrenching poverty.

One year, near Christmas, I received a donation from an LDS family in my neighborhood for "people in need." They stated that the food and funds were intended for people who wouldn't be receiving welfare assistance from the state or the church and that "you would know those people." I took bushels of apples and oranges, canned yams and green beans, baskets of nuts in the shell, and several frozen turkeys and hams to a few of my sisters in the polygamous group. I knew that their husbands didn't make enough money to cover all their needs, and I wasn't sure how they were surviving. My heart broke when I saw bare refrigerators, bare cupboards, and bare houses without sofas or chairs or beds, without televisions or radios or reading lamps. The bottomless pit of need that opened before my eyes nearly swallowed the sweetness of being an agent of generosity.

Recently, a federally-funded advocacy organization called Utah Children formed a committee to change circumstances for polygamists in Utah. The committee was formed through the vision of a woman named Rhoda Thompson, who was born and raised in polygamy and who, after graduating from public high school as valedictorian of her class became a polygamist wife who bore ten children. During her fifties, she was overcome with dismay about the instances of physical and sexual abuse proliferating in too many polygamist homes. Having grown up and married in a fundamentalist community where fear and pride prevented mothers from asking for government assistance, she worried about unmet educational, medical, and mental health needs of polygamist families. With extraordinary initiative she returned to school to get her bachelor's degree in the hope that she'd be able to effect a change. Her studies combined with her unique experience led her to write a paper that reached the attention of Utah Children's director Roz McGee, (who since has become a Utah state legislator). Together the two women formed a committee to call for assistance from organizations and institutions in the larger community in bridging the gap between the "polygamist underground" and the mainstream culture. Women's shelters now are safe for polygamous wives looking for assistance in leaving abusive situations. Through this and other factors, including state and federal funds made available through growing consciousness and media exposure regarding abuse in polygamous communities, the Utah, Arizona Safety Net Committee was formed to ensure that the needs of children born in polygamy are met, domestic abuse curtailed, tyranny squelched, and medical, mental health, and educational needs of children (and their mothers) addressed. Those who perpetrate physical or sexual abuse on children, polygamist or not, are being aggressively prosecuted. Eventually, women who wish to defect may receive educational assistance as well as career counseling. A goal still in the works involves holding the polygamist patriarch legally and financially accountable for the children born into his family and into the fundamentalist group instead of drawing on state and federal programs. These men are breaking the law in the name of religion, so accountability must be focused on child welfare and their responsibilities as fathers. Holding them accountable for polygamy promises to be a complicated challenge, involving the Constitutional right to religious freedom. Many polygamous patriarchs are expert at hiding themselves and their assets, so it may take some time to fulfill the breadth of Thompson's vision. But I felt her commitment as she declared, "While reaching for this goal, the children's basic needs must be met."

LDS Women and Culture

Because girls are taught in their Young Women's programs to develop their talents and to achieve excellence, cultural refinements are found in most Latter-day Saint homes. When Elizabeth Smart disappeared, for example, videos of her playing the harp were highlighted to make people aware of her character as well as her countenance. Even in the most impoverished LDS homes, you often can find evidence of musical, dramatic, athletic, artistic, or writing talent. Respect for the arts invites masters into the home. My grandfather who started out as a dramatist and orator and became a teacher, an attorney, and a statesman, married Charlotte Pead, a woman who also loved oratory and literature; together they named their children for favored Shakespearean characters.

Some extraordinary cultural institutions have been born from the combined concerns for education, social health, and public welfare in the LDS Church and examples of this influence on the community are evident in Utah. Ballet West has been called the finest dance troupe between San Francisco and New York. Pioneer Theater hosts some of the best plays with world-class actors and directors. The Capitol Theater constructed by the pioneers currently houses the Utah Opera. The Utah Symphony now plays in the beautifully-architected Abravanel Hall.

Women have had everything to do with the genesis of this rich cultural life. In fact, the first state arts council in the nation was established by the Third Utah Legislature, midwifed into being by Representative Alice Merrill Horne. She had always been a patron and ran for political office specifically to advance the arts. The daughter of suffragette Bathsheba Smith, Alice followed in her mother's footsteps, representing the National Women's Relief Society and the United States at the International Congress of Women in Berlin, Germany, in 1904. Twice she addressed the United States Congress regarding the arts movement in Utah and on women in politics, drawing on her legislative experiences in enhancing community culture.

Ruth Draper, whose passion matches her regal presence, was appointed Director of the Utah Arts Council in 1974, and true to Alice Horne's legacy, she took the Utah State Arts Council to the next level. She found a real home for the Utah Arts Council, moving the organization from the carriage house behind the governor's mansion to the renovated James R. Glendenning home up the block. She inspired a community outreach program, established a tradition of performing arts exhibitions, and created a cooperative with the board of education to establish Arts in Education programs, the U.S. Film/Video Festival

(which became the Sundance Film Festival), the Utah Playwriting Conference, the Salt Lake City Arts Council and the Utah Arts Festival.
During her tenure, the nation's bicentennial celebration inspired fund-
ing for Symphony (now Abravanel) Hall and the Salt Lake Arts Center as
well as the renovation of the historic Capitol Theatre. Demonstrating
the thrift and practicality for which women are famous, Draper also
made sure that the discarded copper from the renovation of the Utah
State Capitol dome was given to a sculptor for the creation of Utah's
own Vietnam Veterans' Memorial.

Janice Kapp Perry has carried on in the spirit of pioneer women,
writing songs, as did her predecessors Eliza R. Snow, Emily H. Woodmansee, and others. A prolific composer of more than fifty albums,
Perry's work carries enthusiasm and energy combined with deep spiritual sensibility. Her background as a recreational educator combines
with her music to involve the whole of a person's being in song. "As Sisters in Zion" puts the words of pioneer poet Emily Woodmansee to
Kapp's effulgent music, and may be the song that best represents the
Relief Society today; anyone can witness the joy that claiming sisterhood brings to women as they sing this song.

Today, LDS women share their talents, many of them working from
their homes, and around their family schedules. Marie Osmond has
been a significant stage presence while bearing and raising a family. She
has used her public persona and her personal experience to assist women
suffering from postpartum depression, and invests herself hugely in the
Children's Miracle Network. Every year she pays tribute to the Savior
through her Christmas music special. In addition to making public appearances on behalf of women, children, and family, she quietly shares
the advantage of her fame to promote the gifts and talents of other
women, such as Liz Lemon Swindle whose "Son of Man" paintings invite
viewers to claim a personal relationship with the Savior. Shown from a
woman's point of view Swindle's work opens new dimensions of heart
and mind concerning the passion of Christ.

Religious beliefs have tethered the LDS people to natural law and
women have reinforced it. Emma Smith catalyzed the Word of Wisdom
and established a foundation for women to remind men that we must respect the physical body and the physical world. This foundation held

firm as the saints made their way west. Brigham Young saw the land as Zion, the place for saints to dwell, the earthly equivalent of the kingdom of God. Eliza R. Snow and Zina Young reminded him that education, social welfare and culture are components to build a heaven on earth. Many LDS have been true to that ethic, emphasizing healthy living, seeking homeopathic treatments, and finding sustainable solutions to land use.

In *A New Genesis: A Mormon Reader on Land and Community,* co-editor Terry Tempest Williams and her fellow-editors, Bill Smart and Gibbs Smith state: "In our compassion toward all living things, we bow to the imagination, intelligence and great love of God. Our stewardship toward the earth becomes our humility. Quite simply, through responsible actions toward the land, we return our love to the Creator and the Creation."[27] Somewhere along the line, greed has taken over for too many Americans, including some members of the church. People have sold out again and again, allowing all sorts of things to happen in our beloved Zion. Dugway Proving Ground in the Utah desert has seen one too many nerve-gas experiments and now the company, Energy Solutions has established a facility for toxic waste management.

Williams's mother and Terry herself were exposed to atomic fallout blowing from the nuclear testing ground in the Nevada desert into nearby St. George, Utah. Her mother contracted cancer, likely as a result of "downwinder's syndrome". In *Refuge: An Unnatural History of Family and Place,* Williams parallels the rising of the Great Salt Lake with her mother's dying. As the birds lose their habitat to the rising flood, Terry loses a habitat for innocence. The only refuge, at last, is the "healing grace of the Earth":

> Most of the women in my family are dead. Cancer. At thirty-four I became the matriarch of my family . . . .
>
> In Mormon culture, authority is respected, obedience is revered, and independent thinking is not. I was taught as a young girl not to "make waves" or "rock the boat . . . .
>
> For many years, I have done just that—listened, observed, and quietly formed my own opinions, in a culture that rarely asks questions because it has all the answers. But one by one, I have watched the

women in my family die common, heroic deaths. . . . I witnessed their
last peaceful breaths, becoming a midwife to the rebirth of their souls.
The price of obedience has become too high.[28]

Williams suggests that human beings must tell the truth in order to
establish authentic and healthy relationships with self and nature. She
reminds us that our role as stewards of the earth requires great respect
for all that lives and the humility to honor our place in the grand design.
And she has lived true to her standard.

I'm not sure how the present-day patriarchs of her native religion
feel about Terry Tempest Williams's autonomy, her insistence on personal responsibility and independence of thought. But I know that
Brigham Young would be pleased that she has carried the ecological vision of her ancestors forward through her writing and her activism. In
1996, the night before the United States Congress was to vote on
whether to open the Grand Staircase in Escalante, Utah to private use,
or to make this stunning pastel rock formation into a National Monument, Terry distributed the pamphlet she had put together, *Testimony:
Writers Speak On Behalf of Utah Wilderness,* a collection which offered an experience of the place, and gave our legislators reason to preserve this jewel of nature for our progeny. In *The Open Space of
Democracy,* she says, "I do not think we can look for leadership beyond
ourselves. I do not think we can wait for someone or something to save
us from our global predicaments and obligations. I need to look in the
mirror and ask this of myself: If I am committed to seeing the direction
of our country change, how must I change myself?" She has called us to
account for our abuse of Mother Earth, and referred us to our own belief
systems to consider the magnitude of our actions.[29]

All in all, the sisters of Zion have functioned in their communities
as women function everywhere. We preserve and honor the life around
us. We conceive life, with the help of man and God. We gestate, holding
the new life in our bodies, feeding it with our own substance. Then we
deliver the life into the world, where we continue to nurture, using every
resource to sustain this new life. Then we cultivate it, deliberately teaching life skills and wisdoms, survival skills and cultural refinements. Then
we send it forth into the world where it may do good. As we do with our

children, women of the LDS Church have gestated and sent forth education, commerce, welfare, social work, artistry, and ecological responsibility to enhance the life of the planet as well as the lives of our brothers and sisters in the family of man. Every woman is indeed a mother, each in her own way.

7

What Would Jesus Do?

People want you to choose sides. When I was a child my mother told me that the Lord had no patience for people who sit on the fence. I don't know what kind of ambivalence I could have been expressing at the age of four, but she wanted me to choose—something, I don't know what, perhaps promise that I would marry into polygamy. I grew up with many black-or-white dialogues, people quoting third LDS President John Taylor (the one who refused to abolish polygamy) every time I didn't wholly agree with them: "You are either for us or you are against us." they would say. In my experience, this either/or thinking, besides being primitive, can be dangerous, provoking resistance, fanaticism, and encouraging people to play the destructive game of "be right and make others wrong." In the world, such black-and-white scenarios have galvanized massacres, jihads, and genocide. In my father's case, this thinking led to our exile and his assassination. Forced dilemmas create an environment for race and gender discrimination that is out of alignment with the basic context of a gospel that promises all God's children a legacy of joyous fulfillment.

In the fundamentalist group, I also grew up with a lot of talk about our elite status in the eyes of God, about being "chosen" and "saints".

After I started to attend the official Church of Jesus Christ of Latter-day Saints when I was eight years old, I heard people declare that we belonged to "the only true church on the face of the earth." In our culture all non-Mormons were regarded as gentiles, and when I read about the Holocaust and the history of the Jewish people I felt sick that, even with our history of persecution, we could apply the term "gentile" to them because our religious beliefs differed. A superior attitude toward those of other religions contradicts the even-handedness of Christ's commandment: "That ye love one another; as I have loved you, that ye also love one another"(John 13:34). Hauteur toward others can create insularity that eclipses the Thirteenth Article of Faith: "We believe in being honest, true, chaste, benevolent, virtuous, and in doing good to all men; indeed, we may say that we follow the admonition of Paul—We believe all things, we hope all things, we have endured many things, and hope to be able to endure all things. If there is anything virtuous, lovely, or of good report or praiseworthy, we seek after these things" (The Articles of Faith: 13, *Pearl of Great Price*). I asked myself, if we Mormons think we are better than everyone else, how can we regard others as valuable? How can we look at life beyond the LDS Church and find anything "virtuous, lovely or of good report"? Not until I was grown, with my family and my future happiness at stake, did I realize that needing to be right is not the same as being righteous. At about the same time, I realized the difference between taking a position and taking a stand.

In March of 2006, when I attended the fiftieth session of the United Nations Commission on the Status of Women, I had the opportunity to observe the difference between taking a position and taking a stand when the "right to life" group and the "right to choose" group stalemated, one taking a position against elective abortion and the other taking a position for elective abortion. At some point a group of women (some were LDS) realized that the issue that held everyone's concern was women's health and they took steps to focus everyone on this common ground. Had it happened earlier, the tide would have turned in time to create unilateral agreement. But because a cohesive stand for women's health had not been taken in time, no clinics were funded, and no comprehensive health initiative was achieved. The losers, of course, were women. I'm not suggesting that anyone should sell out their ethics: a compromise is not a stand for life. But if either group had begun with a stand for women's health, instead of a position representing their own agenda (for or against abortion) the outcome might have been different. With the stalemate of right/wrong, our common ground disappears; then it is almost impossible to create a life-enhancing result.

As the world's fastest-growing American religion, on a planet ever-more enamored of democracy, the LDS Church has become a growing international influence. In taking a position with other "right to life" groups, LDS women at the UN conference found themselves allied with representatives of regimes we Americans generally protest. With our roots in democracy and individual freedom, any alliance with govern-ments that regularly violate human rights poses a disturbing paradox. This paradox points up subtle cultural similarities, since they are gov-erned by patriarchs. It invites comparison of the gentle but conservative patriarchy of the LDS culture with harsher systems of patriarchy that value sexual morality (for females, at least) but oppress human rights. All suppressed groups develop rebellions and communication systems to create loopholes for freedom. Some of these communication systems are happening among LDS women today, in book groups and study cir-cles, in retreats and symposiums, at Internet sites and small publishing houses: gatherings where women discuss what's really going on in their world.

In *Reading Lolita in Tehran,* memoirist Azar Nafisi leads her most committed female students in a secret study of forbidden classics. As Nafisi explores the dynamics of tyrannical relationship, seeing *Lolita* through the eyes of women in the Islamic Republic of Iran, she's con-cerned about her youngest student, Yassi, who has been denied the nor-mal pleasures of life because of a repressive religion, a repressive regime, and a repressive patriarchy. Nasifi tells her students: "The desperate truth of *Lolita*'s story is *not* the rape of a twelve-year-old girl by a dirty old man, but *the confiscation of one individual's life by another.* We don't know what Lolita would have become if Humbert had not en-gulfed her." Then Nafisi declares the victory of enlightenment: "Yassi . . . could be whatever she wanted to be . . . What mattered was for her to know what she wanted."[1]

Knowing what we want. This is Everywoman's challenge, whether mainstream LDS, polygamist wife, Baptist, Catholic, Jewish, Moslem, Buddhist, or nondenominational. Education sheds light on what we want, and LDS leaders have encouraged this, urging young women to choose an area of interest and get an education. And we obey. LDS women surpass those of Protestant faith and nearly parallel Jewish and secular women in acquiring college degrees and in holding professional occupations.[2] This education produces its own set of problems: As scholars, teachers, historians, entrepreneurs, and healers, we are thinking women who usually heed our leaders' encouragement to stay home and raise our children. We can take classes online or in the evenings, and we can be in charge of our own schedule for learning. But the commitment required to take on a career that makes a difference would contradict our commitment to the hearth. We prepare out minds, but we have limited ways of exercising what we learn. Essentially, for the first twenty or thirty years of our adult lives, we are all dressed up with nowhere to go.

Christian in origin and American in impetus, The Church of Jesus Christ arose in a democracy. People are "called" to positions in the church, but members still vote for or against that person filling that position. Democracy and Christianity combine respect for freedom with faith in personal exaltation. In the LDS religion, the worth of the individual soul dovetails neatly with the "all is one and one is all" consciousness of eastern theologies represented by the pluralistic aspects of early Mormonism such as the United Order and the Principle of Plural Marriage. Remember that the Prophet Joseph Smith and other leaders have said, in essence, that when The Church of Jesus Christ was restored, all things were restored with it, including: priesthood authority as held by Peter, James, and John, plural marriage as practiced by Abraham, Isaac and Jacob, and women established in their full potential with the "curse of Eve" lifted once and for all. Basic to the restoration, the doctrine of free agency insists that everyone, man or woman, has the right to choose. Although some of the pluralism of the early church has been lost, some remains. The belief that we are all brothers and sisters, children of a loving Heavenly Father, and that we share the great work of building the kingdom of God on this earth creates unity among Latterday Saints and connection with the human family

Second LDS Church President Brigham Young said, "We believe that women are useful, not only to sweep houses, wash dishes, make beds and raise babies, but they should stand behind the counter, study law or physic, or become good bookkeepers and be able to do the business in any counting house, and all this to enlarge their sphere of usefulness for the fit of society at large. In following these things they but answer the design of their creation."[3]

Present-day LDS Church President Gordon B. Hinckley has echoed those sentiments in speaking to young women in the church: "The whole gamut of human endeavor is now open to women . . . . You are creatures of divinity, for you are daughters of the Almighty. Limitless is your potential. Magnificent is your future, if you will take control of it."[4]

The radical history of Mormon women indicates that well-educated and intelligent leaders were supported by the brethren in taking a stand for women's rights and drawing up an initiative that allowed Utah women the franchise well ahead of the nation. Remember that LDS women once had the authority to publish their own newspaper, develop their own lessons, design their own service projects, and officiate in their own organizations. They elected their own leaders, made their own money and executed their own budget. They conducted washing and anointing, and practiced "laying on of hands" for the purpose of healing, prophesying and blessing. Gradually these points of authority were stripped away as the established church became more and more conservative. What remains of this power in LDS women, what courses in our blood and stands recorded in our DNA, is the indomitable dignity with which Eliza R. Snow spoke at the "Great Indignation Meeting" of the Relief Society in 1870: "Were we the stupid, degraded, heartbroken beings that we have been represented, silence might better become us; but as women of God, women who stand not as dictators, but as counselors to their husbands, and who, in the purest, noblest sense of refined womanhood, being truly their helpmates, we not only speak because we have the right, but justice and humanity demand that we should."[5]

In those days, the voices of LDS women were heard by people throughout the church and throughout the nation. Today, all organizations and all people in the LDS church operate under priesthood direction and women don't speak officially without specific permission. We believe that Jesus Christ stands at the head of The Church of Jesus Christ of Latter-day Saints. As long as people down the chain of hierarchy are doing what Jesus would do, it works. But people being people, not everyone offers the trust and respect to women that Jesus did. And women can be just as undermining to their sisters as men.

The men who drew up the Declaration of Independence forgot to mention women and others as equal beings, but in the spirit of the document, Americans are beginning to rectify this. The Equal Rights Amendment, like the Civil Rights Act, attempted to restore some of the withheld freedoms, but as we know, the LDS Church used tithes (many of them paid by women) to mount a campaign to stop the ERA.

Indignation from some LDS women escalated when Sonia Johnson was excommunicated after mounting a Mormons for ERA campaign. Women who nursed grudges because they hadn't been given priesthood authority came to the pulpit. Women who resented the mystery surrounding the female deity and wanted to pray to a Mother in Heaven were told they could not. Women who wanted to work outside the home received clear direction that their most important work was in the home. Contention mounted. More women stood in danger of being excommunicated. Since excommunication involves being cast into "outer darkness"—beyond the light of the Gospel—many fear it is like being thrown into prison, or buried alive, and gradually outbursts faded.

Somehow, order had to be restored, for according to scripture, God's house is a house of order. Setting the stage for peace fell to LDS leaders. One way to stop contention (at least temporarily) is to send it away. Many Mormon women cannot understand what the brethren had in mind in wanting to stop the ERA. (Were they concerned women might go out and seek elective abortions? Were they concerned that women would be forced to work outside the home? Were they concerned that children would be abandoned as their mothers marched into freedom, like the children of the suffragette mother in *Mary Poppins?* Were they concerned that the way would be opened for same-sex marriages?) Whether we are pleased with the result or not, when women choose to be members of the LDS Church, they also choose to trust the Living Prophet and to follow the counsel of church leaders.

To those who grow up in The Church of Jesus Christ of Latter-day Saints the right to choose membership comes when we're eight years old, the Age of Accountability. As children, however, we don't always realize how much we're choosing. I've never met a child who balked at being baptized; most approach the experience with joy and excitement, even if they're afraid of being immersed in water. Those who are converts to the church usually make a choice from a mature perspective and when they are baptized accountability begins. Accountability opens the door to free agency, which is basic to the Restored Gospel of Jesus Christ. But whenever a person crosses the line of commitment and chooses to be baptized into the LDS Church, many other choices are implicit, such as how she will behave and what she will do with her life.

Say a woman has an unwanted pregnancy: If she has been baptized into the LDS Church, the choice about what she can do has already been made unless certain exacerbating circumstances such as rape or threat to life surround the conception. Because she is accountable for her behavior, if she chooses to have sex and conceives a child, she will not terminate a healthy pregnancy. She still has choices even then: She can choose to keep the child, or she can offer the child for adoption. She can also choose her attitude about the pregnancy. If she chooses to terminate the pregnancy anyway, she has demonstrated unbelief or an unwillingness to follow the guidance of church leaders. Knowing that the consequences of disobedience can include excommunication, many women stop taking responsibility for their own choices and simply do whatever men tell them to do. When women forget that they have free agency and that ultimately they are accountable for their own lives, they set themselves up for frustrating and resentful experiences. Being accountable makes all the difference between rejoicing in a pregnancy and resenting it. Likewise, women who take responsibility for the choice they made when they were baptized are much more likely to live their religion wholeheartedly. Such women are also more likely to get on their knees and seek confirmation of the prophet's guidance through prayer, taking personal responsibility for their own behavior.

In the early days of the LDS Church, a commitment to baptism might subsequently require that the woman would be called upon to enter polygamy. She might be required to live in a communal society (the United

Order) where she'd have to survive in an economy managed by religious leaders. Her goings and comings would be ruled by the priesthood. And she might be required to experience various hardships and to endure losses impelled by religious persecution and forced emigration. If we, their progeny, could ask these women whether it was worth it, what would they say?

In the modern church, some of the experiences that follow the choice to be baptized are different but similarly difficult to endure. Imagine, for instance, finding out after you've married a man in the temple that he has a pornography addiction that precludes genuine intimacy. Although you have a right to sever the relationship on moral grounds, suppose your bishop reminds you that you have married for time and all eternity, and asks you to be patient, for the Lord can make even the most loathsome thing into light. Meanwhile your life ticks by.

Imagine marrying a man whose priority is to make so much money that his tithing would be "a significant contribution to church coffers." His marriage becomes a means to an end, his wife an obligatory accessory. His wife, like Isabel Archer in Henry James's *Portrait of a Lady* finds that she has made a marital choice founded on appearances and that she is little more than a lovely bird in a gilded cage. When everything that matters lies outside the marriage, then home becomes insignificant too, regardless of church encouragement to put priority on family.

Imagine having a gift of healing, knowing that you were born to be a vessel for the spirit of God to heal your brothers and sisters. When you are baptized, you agree that as a woman you will honor the priesthood, the men who have been given specific permission to heal through laying on hands, while you have not. What happens to your God-given gift, then, if the church doesn't condone the practice? What happens when you face God to explain what you did with your talent?

Imagine being held at arms' length by all the traditional women in your ward who are bothered by your unique approach to the Gospel, then being pitied by all other educated, intelligent women on the planet because you choose to obey your religious leaders and exercise your freedom in unpopular ways, such as staying home and raising your children? This is a lonely way to live. Being so consistently misunderstood can result in feeling, as one LDS woman put it, "as if the skin of her body had been rubbed raw by sandpaper."[6]

Compromised or not, a woman is accountable for her wins and her losses, her mistakes and her feats of heroism, her blindness and her vision. Ultimately, she must take responsibility for the life created through her choices, as Isabel Archer does. But doing this requires moral courage, support, and a willingness to confront the contradictions. Some overwhelming questions arise, such as the one raised by writer Claudia Bushman: "Just where do the women of the Church stand, those self-sacrificing purveyors of service, that silent majority . . . that crowd that can never be considered a quorum. Is there a female LDS world?"[7] Growing up in an environment where women consistently defer to men, we women are not always well prepared to make our own decisions. In childhood, many girls in the LDS Church assume that they won't be making decisions beyond how to decorate their homes, what food to fix and what clothes to wear. But even when it comes to dress, men influence our choices. In 1912, President Joseph F. Smith requested that the Relief Society general presidency (headed by a woman president called by the priesthood) set a standard of modesty, which they did "by refusing to wear short-sleeved or low-necked dresses"[8] The priesthood also influenced female tastes in music, books, magazines, and films, suggesting that LDS homes be filled with love and light and cleanliness, rather than bad language, unsavory relationships, and violence. The priesthood disseminated the standard through Relief Society leaders, who readily obeyed. I wonder if we women would have taken initiative to dress modestly without priesthood guidance. Perhaps. But perhaps we would have succumbed to our immediate desires or to the influence of fashion or to the appetites of the men in our lives.

Many of us struggle with whether to own our power as a daughter of God or to defer to the men in our lives. Even with our college educations, we don't always learn how to negotiate a real estate deal or buy a car—often we leave that to our fathers or our husbands or our sons. Sometimes we forget that it was a woman who initiated many of the rules for clean living in the Church. Emma Smith's complaints about tobacco stains on her floor and the reek of pipe smoke moved Joseph Smith, Jr. to pray and receive the revelation called the Word of Wisdom.[9] Yet today some sisters smoke cigarettes, drink on the sly, or consume a quart of ice cream at a sitting as a form of rebellion against the brethren. We may be listening to our inner wisdom, headed in a good direction, but a little push from behind will make us balk and refuse to go forward. In doing so, we abandon our sensibilities, our intelligent bodies, our enlightened beings—all in the name of resistance and "independence."

Being brothers and sisters in the Gospel encourages us to call forth the best in ourselves and others. Men who righteously exercise their priesthood authority set the stage for women to excel, and women in turn will encourage their sisters, their children, and the men in their lives to do their best. But when we women don't feel safe and honored, when we are required to renounce our native gifts in order to please the men in our lives, sometimes we thwart each other's growth. I think of the Chinese girls whose mothers bound their feet and then forced them to walk, the bones breaking, so that they could please men with their "golden lilies." I pray I haven't pushed my daughters to be something they are not in the name of pleasing men. I pray that I have not been one of those crabs who pulls her sisters back into the community pot where they'll be boiled alive.

When women collude against each other, we collude against ourselves. In the polygamous group where I grew up, during the times we lived in one house or one compound and even during the times we lived in widely spread homes, the collusion between wives and children took the form of competing for my father's attention. Generally the women assisted each other with childbearing and rearing, housecleaning, holiday preparations, and so on. But occasionally one or the other of the mothers would feel lonely or overlooked. "Choose me!" she seemed to be saying through her behavior, and soon the other wives and the daughters followed suit. One would get sick, then others would also require my father's services as a physician. One would be in torment, requiring a priesthood blessing, and suddenly another was set upon by dark spirits. One mother would thrust her golden child in front of my father, and another would whisper undermining facts about the child. One would perform her talent of piano-playing or singing, and another would step up and insist on doing the same. The competition wasn't all bad, as it promoted high-spirited competition among the women in regard to housekeeping, appearance, and development of artistic gifts. But the contest became destructive when women vied to be the wife who could bear the most children at the expense of their physical and psychological health.

Women who are afraid to make their own decisions seem boxed in a predetermined domain, an exclusive and cramped arena that precludes original thought. Critical thinking requires the ability to consider all the facts, to weigh them and form opinions based on all the information available. Original thought requires the ability to "think outside the box" in the realm of creativity. When preconception and dogma proscribe some of the necessary or available information, arriving at authentic and meaningful conclusions becomes next to impossible. So women avoid making decisions both because the process is unfamiliar and because they are constrained in the activity. A woman I know inherited a "nest egg" from her father, but she had never handled money. She didn't want to turn it over to her husband, knowing it would quickly disappear, so she simply left it unaddressed. She could have protected it in a variety of ways but this didn't occur to her, and she didn't dare reach out for advice for fear that her husband would find out. She lost the whole thing to taxes.

Women who forgo their personal power and abdicate their choices operate under a canopy of belief determined by those in authority. But men in the church run a similar risk of foregoing their autonomy and ability to think for themselves. Even though personal revelation remains the right of every member of the church, not everyone takes responsibility for praying or pondering the words of the prophets. Although church leaders encourage us to exercise this right, not everyone wants to be accountable for his or her choices. And sometimes it's hard to distinguish the voices of dogma from the voice of the Holy Spirit.

I have a friend named Crystal who has heard (as many Mormon women have heard) that she should stay at home and raise her children rather than go to work. In the days before she became a mother, Crystal demonstrated her gifts as a manager in the workplace, and she has more than her share of energy. Now that she is a stay-at-home mom, she visits all her managerial talent on her little children, and they show all the signs of being over-controlled: rebellion for the boy, blind obedience for the girl. Crystal knows she's obsessive about her children; she knows they need more room to be spontaneous, to play, to be children. Occasionally she considers returning to the workplace, where she felt valid and challenged and happy. But the admonition of the brethren to stay at home and raise her children echoes in her mind and heart. When she prays about the issue—usually after she's been on one of her tirades to make her children walk the line—all she can hear are rote words.

Like Crystal, Joyce brings a strong, energetic presence wherever she goes. She had taught school since before she married but when she gave birth to three children in seven years, she had very little energy for her students. She wanted to quit and turn her attention fully to her children while they were young, but her family counted on her income. She reminded her husband what the brethren have said about mothers staying at home with their children. He agreed; what else could he do? But his covert resentment that he worked away from home all day and she didn't began to corrode their relationship. Every day things got a little worse, and the receptionist in the office where he worked looked better and better. Both Joyce and her husband knew what was wrong—that he blamed Joyce because he had to work overtime with no money for movies or dining out or going on vacation—but they still don't talk about it. How can they talk about it? The people they're blaming for their life decisions aren't in the room with them.

We are introduced to the concept of accountability before we're baptized, but LDS women don't always embrace it. People in The Church of Jesus Christ of Latter-day Saints spend enormous amounts of energy perpetuating the illusion that everything is working fine. Our preoccupation with image involves our desire to gain the approval of religious leaders and also our fear that our imperfections may become someone else's stumbling block. (The assignment from church leaders of "every member a missionary" reminds us that our example is a powerful influence for good or ill.) When things don't work, we're not practiced at facing hardcore realities. Women aren't always used to solving problems, whatever they may be, so we go to our husband or our son or the bishop and ask for a solution. This process, besides being unwieldy, doesn't work. If we are faced with an unpleasant reality and we can blame someone else for it, we will. And if we can avoid dealing with it at all, we will. Either way, the problem remains unresolved, and we women remain unempowered.

Complaining about the choices men force on us becomes one way to avoid accountability. Women who want to blame the church or the priesthood for their unhappy lives find many willing ears. One woman shared a list of expectations imposed on her in her LDS marriage.

1. Make sure his clothing was clean and ready to wear each day.
2. Offer three hot meals each day, along with delectable, homemade snacks.
3. Take care of the children and make sure they are quiet.
4. Ask before you spend any money.
5. Ask before you plan outings with sisters or girlfriends.
6. Get permission before cutting your hair.
7. Do not complain.
8. Don't disagree with him, especially not in front of others.
9. Allow him to make every major decision.
10. Be continually available to have sex.[10]

Even on the typewritten page, the tone of victimization comes through. Many of us know how easy it is to turn our lives over to someone when we've been trained to do that through our mother's and grandmothers' examples. But when we consciously choose stifling parameters, it isn't fair to blame the church for our unhappiness.

Provo, Utah, home of Brigham Young University stands in the shadow of magnificent Mount Timpanogas. I suspect the valley is known as Happy Valley because everyone smiles so much. Ask Marie Osmond, who lived there. Her book *Behind the Smile* shows how difficult it can be to appear to be joyous when your heart is breaking, your soul weighted with depression, your future bleak. Marie realized that no matter how successfully you magnify your talents, no matter how obediently and faithfully you live the Gospel, you must deal with reality— dark and unappealing as it might be at the moment. Facing the truth about factors that contributed to her postpartum depression allowed her to work through it[11]

Those who refuse to be accountable, those who defer their power of choice tend to repress their talents and succumb to boredom. And there are prices to pay. Recently the Utah media took on a new subject—drugs in Happy Valley. Not that drugs are entirely new, but that their use has taken a quantum leap in popularity. It seems that high school kids and their friends—some of them LDS—are shooting up and snorting heroin in their clean kitchens while mom is at the grocery store or upstairs nursing the baby.[12]

Some professionals believe that the kids are following examples from the adult community and hold the culture accountable for the high rate of drug use. Some studies indicate that Mormon women tend to abuse prescription drugs such as pain relievers more often and with greater recidivism than other groups of women in America. Some studies indicate higher-than-average use of psychoactive drugs such as antidepressants, mood elevators, muscle relaxants, and so on.[13] This has led researchers to broadcast epidemic depression in LDS circles. More than once, the subject has been the focus of media articles and specials. But other studies indicate that women inside Mormonism are actually happier than the average woman, with lower frequency and shorter durations of depression than non-Mormon women, but that LDS women who are depressed suffer from lower self-esteem.[14] In other words, Mormon women are happier than the average woman, but we feel worse about ourselves when we are depressed. I've heard more than one woman say that she feels guilty for being down "when I have so much to be grateful for." Ultimately, the gap between ideal and real exacerbates the issue, and in order to alleviate bad feelings, we need to resolve the contradiction. Mostly likely we could close the gap by facing what is real, then working toward improvement without judging or making ourselves and each other wrong.

In the late 1970s, when I did research for an article about child abuse, I was puzzled and distressed to learn that Utah held the number one spot for child abuse per capita in the United States. Since then, Utah's child abuse statistics have improved significantly, but any amount of child abuse requires our consideration. It's tempting to distort the principle of obedience into a façade that we maintain even when something is wrong. Sometimes the whole family joins in perpetuating an illusion that everything is perfect. This pattern of sustaining a façade is common among all people, but is exacerbated by the church's past, when members had to lie to keep their beloved patriarchs out of prison. We have inherited subliminal permission to forgo "lesser laws" in order to keep "laws of God." Such habitual justifications encourage a strange, sliding-scale morality and a form of rationalization known in Utah as Mormon logic, which was practiced during the polygamy trials of the late 1800s and early 1900s. The trick was for anyone testifying to protect polygamists by thinking of something else when answering—so the answer wouldn't be a lie. For instance, if a wife or a child was asked, "Does your husband (or your father) have more than one wife?" the wife or child would imagine being asked if they hated the Gospel of Jesus Christ, so of course the answer would be an emphatic "No!" Mormon logic makes it possible to engage in denial, to misrepresent all kinds of things, and may be responsible for Utah's unofficial reputation as a scam capitol as well as some instances of child abuse.

That some Mormons are proprietary about their large families may increase instances of child abuse. However, it's encouraging to note that according to the 1996 rankings by the Children's Right's Council, Utah was considered "the number one place to raise children."[15] Besides having low infant mortality rates, Utah has a small percentage of single-parent families due to the low divorce rate. In addition, a small percentage of Utah children live in low-income families. In a later national study, Utah ranked third as a desirable place for children according to ten categories that included death rates, poverty and education.[16] Clearly, we're making progress.

Almost everything in Zion seems wonderfully safe, and the future looks even brighter as more wards and temples are built, more members are baptized, more understanding is reached. But we house our share of wolves in sheep's clothing, those who use religion to perpetrate evil. The widely reported kidnapping of Elizabeth Smart was another violent expression of fanaticism in a long list emanating from our underground culture. Through enormous faith and ingenuity, the Smart family brought Elizabeth home again, but we were all startled to learn that she had been forced to lead an alternative life in the vicinity of her own home. Perhaps our cultural tendency to look for perpetrators who are not religious created a blind spot so that everyone focused on the wrong suspect. Anyone familiar with the tactics employed in brainwashing understands that control is easy to accomplish when you add the threat of damnation, with scriptural rhetoric and hellfire preaching. Cities, like people, carry the seeds of their own destruction, but it is too easy to blame the culture for this crime. Informed Mormon women disagree with the media-bred notion that Elizabeth's acceptance of her situation can be blamed on a male-dominated culture. As Andrea Radke has said, "While these reports may feed into readers' desires for anti-Mormon sensationalism, they do not speak to the complete picture of practicing and believing Mormon women's experiences."[17]

The failure to distinguish between members of the mainstream LDS Church and underground polygamist cultures continues to create a lot of misunderstanding, judgment, and suspicion about the official Church of Jesus Christ of Latter-day Saints. This may be because women in both cultures face disapprobation if they stand up for themselves and voice their opinions. But in fundamentalist cultures, going along to get along can subject a woman to an intolerable life.

In fundamentalist groups, fourteen-year-old girls are sometimes promised to men five times their age, and the girls believe that it is the will of God because someone who says they have priesthood authority announces it is so. If you have been raised in a fundamentalist community, taking that first step to claim independence and make your own decisions even knowing that you might lose everyone you love is a lot like standing at the edge of Dead Horse Point near Moab, overlooking the Colorado River basin. Like the horses, you must either jump or succumb to lifelong captivity. Women faced with polygamy consign themselves to subjugation. Women who leave polygamy face the challenge of beginning a new life without any knowledge of how to function in it. Many know little about their legal rights and responsibilities, having grown up and married in a community where the only law was "God's law"—whatever their husbands or the "priesthood council" decided was law. Since the polygamous community refuses to comply with the law of the land (regarding plural marriage, and other laws and taboos as well), for those who leave it is like arriving in a foreign country. So it was for Tamar's mother, who left the polygamous group for fear that her daughter would marry the head of the religious group, a man she regarded as a tyrant. Warren Jeffs not only knew how to strip people of their money and property, he knew how to strip them of their daughters.

Tamar, one of several girls "betrothed" to Warren Jeffs, liked the idea of being married to "the prophet" and was furious with her mother for packing up the family and "running away without telling Father." If she had been raised in the LDS Church, Tamar might have received an excellent education, for she was very bright. She might have focused on slumber parties and exercise sessions and deciding what to wear to the combined Young Men's and Young Women's events. Instead, she was embroidering pillowcases for her wedding night with fifty-year-old Jeffs. Women who had already escaped the fundamentalist community reached out to free Tamar of her illusions; they could see what would serve her better. But Tamar dreamed of returning to Colorado City to take her place as the youngest of Warren Jeffs's more than one hundred wives. Her dream was shattered when he was arrested in 2006.[18]

People marvel that otherwise ordinary men seem to commandeer the lives of many lovely women through the religious rhetoric surrounding polygamy. Alex Joseph came into my father's polygamist group after converting to the LDS Church. He had been a Marine, he was obviously looking for something with more potential for sovereignty than he found in the LDS Church, and he moved right into the role of polygamous patriarch. He didn't have the looks to explain his sudden success in recruiting coeds from the University of Montana at Missoula to become his plural wives. Was it his charisma or the idea of communal living that attracted these young women during the experimental 1970s? The girls' parents were livid and called the police to find out what was happening to their well-educated daughters. When my father instructed him to desist, Alex laughed, saying, "You did it, so why shouldn't I do it too?" The women drifted into each other's slipstreams and followed Alex dreamily, as if they were about to embark on a peculiar ecclesiastical spring break. They left their solid, middle-class families and my father's group to homestead in the desert of the Four Corners area, trading in their comfortable lives for the idea of celestial glory.

Whether we come from fundamentalist quarters or the legitimate Church of Jesus Christ of Latter-day Saints, many members of the sisterhood admit that we crave the strong definitions imposed by men. We treasure the gender-based friendships and affiliations that prosper when women don't struggle for the top office because it is already filled. Some of us believe that because men hold the priesthood, women are liberated from men's excessive behaviors: freedom from an alcoholic reprobate who refuses to make a living, freedom from a philandering spouse who might bring home a social disease, freedom from a football fanatic who watches games all day Sunday while his wife herds the children to church and home again. By encouraging men to hold their priesthood, the thought goes, we improve our own lot and the lot of our children.

Some of us believe that because men must contend with the outside world, we get to cultivate the hearth, the home, the arts, the soul. But sometimes men try to commandeer even these arenas, which are traditionally women's domains. When this happens, many women rise up to defend their border.

In the late 1990s Gloria Steinem came to town to read and sign her new book, *Moving Beyond Words* [19] and to remind us that in order to create change, we've got to take some risks. Many LDS women who actively participated in the women's movement in the 1970s, recalling our great-great-grandmothers who fought for women's rights in the 1870s are grateful to women like Steinem. We relate to her passion on behalf of women who are abused or underpaid or overworked or marginalized. That day we talked about what women can do that men cannot: carry life in their bodies. From this came recognition of the mystery, the awe, the enormous and unreplicated power of womanhood. Steinem suggested that many religions were designed to usurp women's rightful domain.

When my husband and I were dating and I talked with him about how helpless and small I often felt in the eyes of my father and the men in the church, he spoke with a touch of envy about women's power: "All men get to do is plant the seed. Or we can take life. But we can't really give life. We don't get to hold it and grow it inside our bodies." Would men really go so far as to commandeer a woman's power just to ensure that they would be in charge of everything, as Steinem suggested? I've always been sure that Jesus did not want our lives to be appropriated. He came to earth and made His sacrifice so that we could reclaim our agency, so that we could be free from bondage. But maybe He's the only man magnanimous enough to honor our wholeness. Was it possible that people would try to keep us from our native gifts, our God-endowed powers? And would women do this as well as men?

LDS women often discuss their frustration about a larger societal viewpoint that LDS women live in effect of patriarchy. Some women are defiant in attitude, like one who said at a recent gathering: "As I see it, no person can deny a person a gift of the spirit—only God can allow or deny such a gift!" Another woman asked, "How can women be empowered if we don't consider what we can do instead of being seen as victims?" Still another woman observed, "Even with the social changes in the larger world, some woman still seem committed to being victims."

Someone asked, "Have women's lives have become more complex in the wake of the Women's Movement?" As we looked at the women around us, we saw that women with careers are still doing most of the work—at the office, at home, with the children, at the school, at the church. Men delegate to their secretaries, come home from their jobs and wait for dinner, watching TV or reading the paper the way they've always done. Women executives don't want to heap more work on their secretaries, so they stay late, then go home from work and make dinner, wash dishes, help the kids with their homework, tuck them into bed, and wash and iron their clothes for the next day. If it is Saturday night, they stay up late to prepare a lesson for Sunday school, then fall into bed beside a sulky husband who's waited too long for some hot romance.

We wondered if maybe Gloria Steinem and other outspoken feminists have called us into waters we can't navigate. We wondered if we would be better off staying near the harbor. Regardless of what the outside world says, perhaps the brethren in the LDS Church truly have the best interests of women and children in mind. By encouraging women to stay home and urging men to be good providers, women get a share of life's burdens they can actually shoulder, instead of an impossibly huge task.

Women have so much responsibility for the home, the raising of children and teenagers, functions within the church, compassionate interaction with community, yet they have no genuine *authority* in the LDS Church. As Claudia Bushman, author of *Mormon Sisters: Women in Early Utah,* points out, "Men hold priesthood, while women do not. Women, even those in high leadership, ultimately answer to men while Protestant Churches . . . level gender differences."[20] When we have no authority, we have difficulty being empowered in our daily lives.

One woman described her experience as a visiting teacher, going to see a single mother and finding that she and her children had come down with the flu. Their fevers raged, they hadn't kept food or drink down for two days, and they writhed with muscle pain. In the middle of the workday in the semi-rural community, all the men were at work, including the bishop and his counselors. The single mother begged the visiting teacher not to call an ambulance or a doctor—she had no insurance and had a hard enough time making ends meet. "We just need a blessing," the woman begged, licking her dry lips. The visiting teacher hesitated. She knew that priesthood holders could provide healing blessings, and she also knew that no priesthood holders were around. She remembered hearing that in the early days of the church, women had given blessings to one another as requested, with the full endorsement of Prophet Joseph Smith. She took the woman's hands in hers and asked God to bless her with health and strength to care for her children. Within ten minutes, the woman was able to keep water down, and her fever was gone. She rose and stood over her children and gave them a mother's blessing, promising them rapid and full recovery. Then the visiting teacher made soup. The mother fed herself and her children while the visiting teacher changed the sheets and tucked everyone in for a restorative rest. She left with tears in her eyes—tears of gratitude that she had been able to act as an agent of God's love and tears of sorrow that she would have to keep this event quiet, as if she should be ashamed of acting with authority on her sense of responsibility.

The gap between responsibility and authority seems to generate a good deal of the controversy that runs through the female sector of the LDS Church. Those who feel adamantly about the rift seem to attract trouble, like Maxine Hanks and Courtney Black who responded in the *Boston Globe* to the current LDS Church President Gordon B. Hinckley, who had said in an interview, "I haven't found any complaint among our women." Hanks and Black printed their response in the *Boston Globe*, signed by fifty Mormon women from around the world. "Mormon women are in a bind," the letter said. "If we disagree, we reap trouble; if we relent, we lose our voice." It went on: "[I]in our church today, all women's programs, leaders, and texts—even the leading women's speeches—are designed and governed by men. All church doctrine, theology, and policy are created by men. While women may be included in 'discussion' about issues and policy, the 'decisions' are still made by men."[21]

The repercussions of this action, if any, are not clear. Maxine Hanks has said, "My feminist views were never welcome in the church . . . Excommunication was a small price to pay for my voice. It didn't take away my theology or my spirituality."[22] Apparently she had been excommunicated before she wrote her letter to President Hinckley.

Among LDS women, feminism provokes controversy. Elizabeth Dionne, another self-described Mormon feminist, answered Hanks and Black, saying that in a church of "11 million, 50 signatures 'from around the world' . . . is an underwhelming show of support." Dionne also suggested that she'd be surprised if more than one in 50 agreed with Hanks and Black.[23]

While having no formal authority constrains our lives in some ways, most of us don't complain about barriers to our growth, nor have we been pining to hold the priesthood. Some women are vocal about perceived restrictions, but as a whole LDS women seem to feel that they have plenty of opportunity for growth and plenty of responsibility. As far as I'm concerned, I have all the authority I need, having "authored" with God and my husband our children, and having authored the life I live through choices I have made or abdicated. Most LDS women bear testimony to some kind of spiritual authority, having seen and felt the power of a healing prayer as we put our hands on the head or heart of a sick child. We have had predictive dreams that have illuminated and perhaps saved lives. We have calmed another's panic with gentle words and warm hands. We have felt truth work through us that is more dynamic and encompassing than our own perceptions and being. We have an experience of the power of God to serve and minister to our fellow beings.

Still, our self-perceptions are at stake. How do we interact with each other within the faith? Do we walk on eggshells, avoid difficult topics, pretend that everything is all right? Do we walk around the elephant in our livingroom, pretend that we don't know it's there? Or do we delve into the dilemma and preoccupy ourselves with it, to the neglect of everything else that matters—such as our children?

If we roll over and play dead, we might survive unscathed. But then we are cowards, and our self-esteem takes a terrible beating. Hiding or keeping quiet might allow us to survive as wives, mothers, members of our faith, but after a few sell-outs, we don't like ourselves and then we don't want to be alive. If we seek to rectify the situation, if we stand up for truth and fair play or even if we complain, we are seen as "troublemakers" and our loyalty is questioned. What is at stake is our faith—genuine belief in the Gospel of Jesus Christ—and our way of life, a lifestyle that puts priority on the family in a world that seems intent on undermining the home.

But such controversies are not new. Women historically have found themselves in these situations. In the gap between what has been and what is now, electricity shoots back and forth, a heated dialogue between those who agree with the status quo and those who don't. The debate emerges in a variety of ways as people seek to be right and make others wrong. Often the issue surfaces as male versus female, patriarchy versus matriarchy (even though a man may be arguing the female point of view and a woman arguing on behalf of the priesthood). But it isn't a matter of who is right and who is wrong. It's a problem of what works and what doesn't work, what serves life and what works against life. Oppressing people simply doesn't work. People tend to fight back, even if the "oppressors" are kind, even if the "oppression" comes from a pair of loving hands that also deliver blessings.

Generally speaking, people do the best they can. LDS men struggle to be humble. LDS women struggle to be accountable. We are grateful for the knowledge and special blessings that come with our testimonies. We are thankful to have, as the hymn says, "a prophet to guide us in these latter days." We are thankful to have been sent "the Gospel, to enlighten our minds with its rays."[24] We are glad to participate in the body of the church. We do our best to be loyal and true followers of Christ. We are grateful to women like writer Linda H. Kimball, who reach out to offer a hand of friendship and understanding when we feel we don't belong, pleading with us "Don't go. If for no other reason than that I need you."[25]

A good many educated, well-spoken, and faithful Mormon women contribute to various periodicals and Web sites, speaking for themselves as they take on and enlighten us about the gamut of LDS women's issues. They gather evidence to prove their opinions about the value and validity of the church and they share it with the discontented. One comprehensive document by Andrea G. Radke manages to handle the most pressing issues in 23 pages of carefully researched, lucid prose.[26]

One "hush up and be happy" argument that caught my attention is perhaps the most practical, offered by Elizabeth Dionne, who sees the church as an inherently "feminist organization" for women of the international LDS Church because progress for them "means teaching men to stop drinking, to become industrious, and to treat their wives and children with love and respect." Her argument for women's liberation extends to teenage girls who are given community protection from "sexual predation until they have the maturity to make self-realizing decisions."[27]

Various women have addressed the pressure on Mormon women concerning perception both inside and outside the church: "One is the constant need to defend themselves from outsiders' criticism of their place in the Church and the second is seeking ways to bring greater gendered awareness and progress within their own culture, especially where some unrighteous traditions and practices have perpetrated gender inequality."[28] Then there's the universal dilemma of listening to one's own spirit, of receiving promptings from the Holy Spirit that do not correlate with what's going on outside.

Some of the brethren have assured us that we will be rewarded in the hereafter for the injustices we've suffered on this earth. I confess that I don't believe that anyone can afford to forgo the learning and initiative that needs to happen here on this earth in the hope that things will be taken care of in eternity, work for the dead notwithstanding. To postpone living stands contrary to everything I've been taught in the Gospel that encourages me to make the most of this life. I wouldn't want to face the Creator and confess that I waited to use my talents instead of investing them. The burden of awareness is also the burden of responsibility—we must exercise our ability to respond.

The dialogue about Mormon women—between men and women, between women and women, between members and non-members—attempts to separate wheat from chaff, discerning what's true and letting the husks of lies and denial fall to the threshing floor. The problem is that whenever there's controversy, both sides think that they have the wheat and that the other side has chaff. Given that women in The Church of Jesus Christ of Latter-day Saints are members by birth or by choice or both, we're back to the basic question: What would Jesus do?

How would Jesus reconcile living in a religion that offers so much yet reduces the vistas of feminine life to tunnel vision? What advice would he give on how to wear blinders and simultaneously speak what is true in our own minds and hearts?

Talents of writing or speaking truly are not the only gifts women have felt compelled to hide or diminish. I took some of these gifts for granted in my fundamentalist household. I still remember a day when I was five and I came home early from the spinach fields where we worked for twenty-five cents an hour. My mother and her twin sister stood in the living room, clothed all in white. They hovered over a woman draped in a white sheet, seated in a chair. The woman's face, almost as white as the sheet, grimaced with pain; I knew she was pregnant because her belly made the sheet bulge, but also from the energy of impending birth that I had come to recognize. I watched as the mothers—my mother and her twin—dabbed the woman's head and body with water and with oil, saying sacred prayers they'd probably said a thousand times before. Each body part had a sacred prayer for strength, for health, for functionality. My mother and her twin wore identical clothing and identical smiles, beatific as twin angels murmuring together in the afternoon sunlight, the pale woman letting the pain go, releasing the worry until her face was smooth and a radiant smile. Washing and anointing, the mothers called it. Every pregnant woman in our religious group requested it so that she would be ready for birth. They made the request of my mother and her twin, who performed this sacred ceremony that only women could give to women. At one time women of the Relief Society in the LDS church conducted this ritual for expectant mothers. During the early 1900s, this practice was gradually taken from women by priesthood leaders and no replacement ritual has been offered.

Women have protested this change, especially since it often falls to them to take care of the sick, and since only women can really comprehend the valley of shadow they must travel in order to give birth. This dilemma about healing through the laying on of hands has confronted midwives in particular, of whom there are many in the LDS Church. Most midwives have wholesome but independent personalities. They work closely with creative forces and, having seen the results of patriarchal abuse (men who insist that their wives have more babies than they can physically bear, men who want to have sex before their wives have healed from childbirth, men who lose their tempers and beat wives who are too sick to get up) and they aren't inclined to give their power away to men. One midwife I know, a woman named Layne, carries a small vial of oil consecrated by her priesthood-bearing husband for blessing the sick. If a need for blessing presents itself, and a priesthood holder isn't available she has no compunction about giving a blessing herself, sharing in her husband's priesthood as her right in his absence, an action with a strong history of church leaders' support. As a healer, exercising priesthood isn't a matter of hierarchy or gender for Layne; it's about the power of God and the sanctity of life.

Layne has the most angelic manner of any human being I've met. She looks angelic—golden-haired and beautiful, with clear blue eyes and a serene countenance. Her gentle attitude creates an immediate sense of well-being and safety, no matter what is going on. When I was expecting my fourth child, she was apprenticing to the woman who agreed to deliver my baby at home. I had been born at home, as were my brothers and sisters. Most of my sisters gave birth at home. I had given birth in hospitals to my first three children. Every time, the doctors got upset with me because I wanted a natural birth. Every time I left feeling that hospital personnel had ruined one of the most beautiful moments of family life. My children weren't permitted anywhere near the delivery room. My husband could watch but wasn't allowed to participate. Besides, I had conceived this baby under mystical circumstances. My husband and I were having the same dream when we conceived. When I was fully awake and realized that I was likely pregnant, I began to worry: We had just started our own business, we had no health insurance, and we were utterly unprepared for this new little blessing in our life. None of my forty-seven brothers and sisters had died during natural childbirth at home. It seemed like a requirement of my tribe that I give birth at home at least once; otherwise I wasn't worthy of the family legacy—whatever it may be.

Everything around this birth seemed different. I woke up at 3 A.M. with contractions. It started to snow, and by the time the contractions came close and quickly, the phones didn't work. The roads were terrible, visibility was poor. We weren't sure the midwives would arrive in time.

But Layne arrived and I relaxed, her angelic countenance all I needed to reassure me that everything would be all right. Then we learned that the baby was breech and the cord had prolapsed. With the weather, the usual thirty-minute ride to the hospital might take an hour or longer. We wouldn't get there in time, so we had to make it work. I was terrified for my baby, though we did not speak of the danger. Every contraction sent the cord pulsing into the air, cutting off the baby's oxygen supply. At last she was out, a tiny white being. Not purple. Not a blue baby, as my mother had been with her congenital heart defect. White white. The white of death. Layne passed her hands over the baby's body, which was limp as a dead fish; she patted her and spoke to her. Long moments went by with no change. Then she prayed over her. Layne produced her vial of oil and my husband anointed our tiny daughter and said a prayer for healing, for life. I said aloud, "God, please bless this baby." Layne told her to breathe, then commanded her to breathe, and she did, a little sucking sound that ended in a sigh. I knew that I had witnessed a miracle and that I had been part of that miracle. I knew I had a living child, my beautiful Laurie, because of the faith and the healing power in that room.

Layne still carries her little vial of consecrated oil. One afternoon as she returned from a baby case, she saw a ten-year-old girl get hit by a car. She jumped out and joined the others who bent over her. The girl wasn't breathing. Layne glanced around and saw women and children, tearful and aghast. She had her car keys with the little vial of consecrated oil in her hands. She cradled the girl's head in her lap and surreptitiously let one, two drops of oil fall on her head. Layne put her palm over the oily patch on the girl's head and prayed that she would have the faith to return to her body, to live out her life, to be there for her parents and to fulfill her purpose on earth. The girl's chest heaved and she coughed, her eyes fluttering open.

Layne tells me not to reveal her real name, for she could get in a lot of trouble for her practice of anointing the sick and afflicted when necessary. Something inside me groans at this knowledge. Layne loves the church, loves Jesus, loves Heavenly Father. She loves people. She's about as far from radical as a human being can get—except when it comes to fulfilling her calling. I am reminded that Jesus was criticized for healing on the Sabbath. I pray that we as a congregation have not become whited sepulchers, reducing those filled with spirit and faith to letter-of-the-law smallness, cast out by those in positions of stature.

Midwives have a long history of being seen as a threat to patriarchy, as historians of witch trials and inquisitions can testify. Midwives know a lot about double standards and female exploitation. They know about a woman's use of seduction and emotional blackmail and intentional pregnancy to get what they want. They know about men's insensitivity and lack of commitment and the violent desire that culminates in rape. Midwives will show a woman how to reclaim her autonomy and her choices. They will prescribe herbs and practices for conceiving. They will also teach women how to avoid pregnancy and prescribe various natural methods of birth control. They will advise women whose bodies have been ravaged by too many births to outright refuse their husbands if nothing else avails.

As men have become increasingly involved in birthing practices, the systems have become more bureaucratic, and caesarean sections have increased exponentially. The move in the twentieth century to edge out midwives and establish maternity care in hospitals jeopardizes women's authority in administering to other women. Paradoxically, women are reclaiming it through education, by taking on careers in nursing and medicine. It seems we women will not be denied.

Several LDS women have taken on the challenge of shoring up women's power by telling women's stories. For example, an LDS woman Laurel Thatcher Ulrich, wrote *A Midwife's Tale* which won the Pulitzer Prize and was later developed into a documentary film for PBS. To possess the vision to record the history of a midwife requires open-mindedness, and the willingness to acknowledge the dynamics of a patriarchal society and to deal unflinchingly with truth. It took Ulrich many years to achieve her education, which she did while raising her family. Add to this her MacArthur Foundation Fellowship, her appointment to Harvard University, and her recent appointment as the 300th Anniversary University Professor and you see a woman of extraordinary talent, discipline, and wholeness. A proposed invitation for Thatcher to speak at the annual BYU Women's Conference in 1992 was vetoed without comment. That she was subsequently invited to offer an address at BYU in 2004 and that she accepted indicates in Ulrich a persistent dignity that would make Eliza R. Snow proud. Perhaps it also indicates a warming trend in the politics of the LDS Church correlation committee making these decisions.

In writing the 2002 Utah Book Award-winning *Red Water,* about the 1857 Mountain Meadows massacre, LDS-born writer Judith Freeman draws on the journals and the fictionalized points of view of three of John D. Lee's plural wives. Lee was the only person held accountable for the murder of one hundred and twenty Arkansas pioneers bound for California, seated upon his coffin to face his firing squad at the site of the massacre. Through her writing, Freeman exhumed two skeletons from church closets: the church's early-day practice of polygamy and the massacre, which President Hinckley had tried to put to rest in 1999, when the construction of a new monument to honor the victims uncovered the bones of twenty-eight adults whose skulls bore bullet holes clearly implicating Mormons, rather than the Indians who historically had been blamed for the massacre. Freeman is a lovely woman—graceful as her sentences, beautiful as the words she chooses, yet relentlessly honest. She wonders if she'll be excommunicated now that she's shared the fruits of her creativity and research with the world. In speaking with a reporter, Judith said that a proposed meeting with her bishop to discuss her membership "brought up a lot of feelings. One of the feelings was 'I'm about to be ejected from my tribe,' a tribe my ancestors had served for generations."[29] Certainly it's uncomfortable to have someone talking about things we'd rather forget. But I'd like to be able to reassure Judith Freeman that the church doesn't want to get rid of members for telling the truth unless those members are looking to get rid of the church.

I can relate to Judith Freeman's situation. At the time I wrote my previous books, LDS writers who had brought up polygamy and feminism and other touchy subjects were being called into their bishop's offices to have their loyalty questioned. I didn't want to follow in the footsteps of women who had been excommunicated for speaking their minds. I didn't want to follow in the footsteps of my grandfather, who was excommunicated for writing a defense of polygamy called *A Leaf in*

Review, nor in the footsteps of my father, who was excommunicated for writing articles in defense of polygamy for *The Star of Truth.* I have no desire to live polygamy. I love the church. I love the prophet. And I love the truth. Straddling controversy exacts a price, however, so I worried and prayed. Imagine how astonished I was when, instead of being invited into my bishop's office to be upbraided, church leaders invited to me speak at wards and at stake conferences. Imagine how deeply I was touched when my own ward Relief Society read my books and invited me to speak at a mixed-gender meeting. Members of that ward healed many of my childhood wounds of exile and persecution by the church and its agents. I felt I had been welcomed home.

My daughter Layla has a horse named Cedar Fox that she loves so much, but it's a high-spirited beast, inclined to decide when and if he should be ridden. Layla is likewise high-spirited, and she likes to make her own decisions, too. Among other things I have told Layla since she was tiny is that free agency is her birthright, that she gets to decide what she does with her life. Layla is a diligent and practiced rider, but one day Fox threw her into the fence, broke her finger, cracked her tailbone, and generally left her feeling skittish. She considered selling the horse. Then she went to get help from an LDS woman who trains horses—a Mormon female horse whisperer, if you will. The woman looked at Layla and said, "You're afraid, and you get to break through this fear. You can't wait for the perfect horse to come along. You get to ride your horse and you get to do it now."

Sometimes that's how I feel about the church. From what other LDS women have told me, I suspect they have similar feelings. I could avoid telling the truth. I could spend the rest of my life looking for a perfect fit. But this religion is mine, and I believe it is the truest representation of Christ on this earth. I get to be part of it, even if it tries to throw me. The Gospel is something no one can take away from me as long as I honor the covenants I have made.

What if it's a scam? my skeptical friends and loved ones ask. I know they care about me, that they don't want me to waste my life in the Emerald City. They list many points of evidence and insist that the foundations of the church are lunatic and full of lies. When you're gathering evidence to prove any point, you can usually find it.

I'm willing to follow the recommendation of my literature professors, to suspend disbelief until I reach the end. When I reach the other side, if I find out the whole thing is a scam, well . . . if I discover that I was fooled, yet my family is bonded by love, our optimism strong, our health good, our finances stable, and we live in a community of neighbors who love and care about us and we about them, and we come to each other's aid in times of need, and we go to funerals and experience the reassurance that we will join departed loved one in the next life, and our hearts are comforted and our lives are full . . . well, then it's okay because I will have lived a better life. It's true that it is a confined life where certain behaviors are not acceptable: murder, infidelity, promiscuity, smoking, drinking, eating too much or too little, getting into unnecessary debt, lying, cheating, stealing. I'm expected to live the Golden Rule and to give of my substance unconditionally and to be willing to receive the blessings of living this way. But that's *why* it's worth it—as long as I don't have to give up who I am. Worth it as long as I get to exercise my gifts, my voice, and my vote. Worth it as long as I get to be who God created me to be.

What would Jesus do? Well, if we take the Bible at its word, we know what Jesus did. He faced down a culture when the woman taken in adultery was about to be stoned. When the mob prodded him to either keep the law (condone death by stoning) or contradict the law (make "the wrong statement"), Jesus knelt and wrote in the dust, then held them accountable: "He that is without sin among you, let him first cast a stone at her." When they were "convicted by their own conscience" Jesus did not condemn her either, but told her to "go and sin no more" (John 8: 3–11). This reveals His commitment to an equal playing field where women have the right to lead lives of repentance, redemption, and integrity just as men do. It also reveals unfathomable reservoirs of forgiveness and love. Jesus seems to have regarded women as friends. He urged them to sit with him, encouraged them to study and look within rather than to be caught up in the "many cares" of the world.

In the ground-breaking anthropological study of female and male dynamics, *The Chalice and the Blade,* Riane Eisler makes a recommendation for "actualization power" rather than "domination power."[30] In the light cast by her vision, I gather that the challenge of gender isn't male versus female, patriarchy versus matriarchy. It's about sharing power and respecting each other's power. It's about sharing responsibility and honoring the other's ability to do the same. It's about being accountable for the lives we lead, making our own decisions and bearing our own consequences. I suspect that this is what Jesus wanted—the kingdom of Heaven on earth, where we don't have to worry who is in charge because we know that God is in Heaven, counting on us to do our part. In the meantime, we have that saying to guide us from Matthew 7:20: "By their fruits ye shall know them." I look up and see the love among members of my ward, among members of my family, among the sisterhood, and I know something life-enhancing happens here. I see the kindness and integrity of the brethren as ministers and witnesses to Jesus Christ. I can see the commitment and generosity of my sisters in Zion. Certainly the LDS Church has dealt with destructive influences, perhaps even has generated some. But for the biggest part, life for LDS people is good and The Church of Jesus Christ of Latter-day Saints emanates a highly constructive force. You can sit in our meetings and feel the Spirit coursing through them, and you'll remember that life is a precious gift. Despite the terrifying world in which we live, LDS women are "anxiously engaged in a good cause" (Doctrine and Covenants 58:27) and LDS people are "preparing the way of the Lord" (Doctrine and Covenants 34:6). We know that a day is dawning when love will rule and peace will prevail.

8

The Sisterhood

I live in a Motherless house
A broken home.
How it happened I cannot learn.
When I had words enough to ask
"Where is my mother?"
No one seemed to know
And no one thought it strange
That no one else knew either.
I live in a Motherless house.
They are good to me here
But I find that no kindly
Patriarchal care cases the pain.
I yearn for the day
Someone will look at me and say,
"You certainly do look like your Mother."
I walk the rooms
Search the closets
Look for something that might
Have belonged to her—
A letter, a dress, a chair,
Would she not have left a note?
I close my eyes
And work to bring back her touch, her face.
Surely there must have been
A Motherly embrace
I can call back for comfort.
I live in a Motherless house,

Motherless and without a trace.
Who could have done this?
Who would tear an unweaned infant
From its Mother's arms
And clear the place of every souvenir?
I live in a Motherless house.
I lie awake and listen always for the word that never comes, but might.
I bury my face
In something soft as a breast.
I am a child
Crying for my mother in the night.[1]

As Carol Lynn Pearson states in her poem, members of the Church of Jesus Christ of Latter-day Saints live in a Motherless house. Well . . . not exactly Motherless. We just don't know Her. It's as though She's gone on an extended journey, or She's sick or tired or She's done something wrong and has been sequestered in another room. We know She's somewhere, but we don't get to meet Her. I think of the few times my children have been separated from me—when I've gone to the hospital to give birth, or when I was working, or too sick to lift my head—I remember how hurt they were, how anxious to bridge the gap, how desperate to reconnect. I remember times when my little ones wouldn't let me take an afternoon nap, so painful was the idea of being separated from me. "Don't go away, Mommy," they'd say, patting my face to keep me there, with them. Sometimes I think we should have been this insistent with Our Heavenly Mother.

I think of our restiveness as a world, a nation, a people, our violent, needy, and dismal ways, our constant button-pushing, computer-searching, remote-control flipping. I think of our frenzies of buying and selling, a new car every two or three years, a new house every ten or twelve, and new toys or things to eat or movies to watch every day. I think of us speeding everywhere, skipping from job to job, from relationship to relationship, from interest to interest, and I know it has something to do with growing up without the conscious influence of Mother. We suffer for the lack of Mother's cooling touch. We need to be grounded in Her lap, embraced by Her arms, brought back to reality with a firm grasp and an urging to meet those divine feminine eyes and tell Her the truth. We yearn to reconnect with female magnetism. We ache for Heaven, for Home.

It's hard for men to be without Mother. But they have their wives and their daughters and their biological mothers—and they have themselves, in league with Father in Heaven. Someone up there who actively shows them how to be a man. Someone who helps them see what to do. We women have a tough time finding a divine corollary. It's not that we don't love Father in Heaven—oh, we do. But He spends a lot of his words and directions on the men. Heaven knows they need it. But so do we. And we don't get to go to Mother for the inside scoop on how to be a woman.

We look curiously at other religions, where people pray to androgynous deities, where the female divine is acknowledged alongside the male divine. We feel brief pangs of envy, even jealousy that we, who thought we were geared up to have it all—the Restored Church of Christ, never again to be taken from the earth—are obviously going without knowledge regarding our Divine Mother.

In the absence of Mother in Heaven, we women in the LDS Church have turned to each other for a reflection of the feminine divine. Poet and dramatist Carol Lynn Pearson created a beautiful one-woman play called *Mother Wove the Morning,* tracing the experience of sixteen women from Scripture. In this play much of Mother's grief comes from being suppressed, denigrated, hidden, and misunderstood. Pearson comments on historical attitudes toward the feminine divine:

> Images of the powerful divine female were turned upside down to become dark and negative images, including "the mother of harlots," "the Abomination," "the mother of abominations," and "whore of all the earth" in the Bible and Book of Mormon. Negative female images we have. But where are the images of our powerful and magnificent Mother who bore and sustains us all? Where are the female images which girls and women can relate to, which validate rather than belittle our femaleness? Having a wonderful father does not preclude the need

for a mother. The absence of the Mother inevitably demeans the daughters and deprives the sons. No matter how many good men are kind to their wives or how many women say they have never felt less important than a man, in a Motherless house, we are all wounded children."[2]

Women in the church do their best to be the embodiment of Mother, healing God's wounded children as best they can. When we reach out to each other, we transform our relationship; beyond being a union of mothers calling on the Mother, we establish a sisterhood, a union of women dedicated to woman. This sisterhood sometimes involves mothering each other and teaching each other to mother ourselves. Sometimes the sisterhood involves being a sister, standing at someone's side and cheering her on or helping her do what must be done. Sometimes sisterhood means being a great friend, a sounding board or a shoulder to cry on. Sometimes sisterhood involves having fun together, making the tasks of raising children and homemaking pleasant and convivial. Sometimes sisterhood means rolling up your sleeves and diving into an unpleasant task together, whether it's cleaning up a flooded basement or a swamped marriage or a runaway teen. Sisterhood means exercising your gifts of the spirit even if they are strange and incomprehensible.

This sisterhood has been meeting each other's needs for a long time, since the days when Eliza R. Snow and her sisters met to pray together and bless one another. During the winter of 1846–47, after the Mormon Battalion of 500 men left their stranded wives and children in the care of church leaders and marched off to fight for the United States in the Mexican War, the exiled saints waited for spring to arrive at the way station known as Winter Quarters on the west bank of the Missouri River. Despite the careful organization of wards and stakes and the United Order, the saints struggled to survive. Insufficient provisions, destructive storms, inadequate shelter, and the malarial diseases of the riverside took a huge toll, depleting morale and touching every family with sickness and death. The saints drew on their faith, in twice-weekly congregational meetings, in weekly family meetings, and in occasional dances and feasts. The women gathered to quilt, to braid straw for burning and basket-making, to wash and mend clothing, to groom one another, and especially to entertain and uplift one another. During this time, Eliza met with Patty Sessions, Lucy Young, Emmeline Wells, Zina Young, and others, the women rejoicing in the gifts of the spirit that poured out on them as if to compensate for their hardships. The Mormons were a record-keeping people even then, and the women's diaries bear this out. One entry after another refers to blessings given by women to women, women speaking in tongues with other women receiving the interpretations, women prophesying and declaring their knowledge, women healing the sick, women testifying of the truthfulness of the Gospel. Often this knowledge included the recognition of a spiritual gift in another sister or one of her children and the women would prophesy of a great works to be performed, such as the prophecy by Snow, who spoke in tongues, and of Zina Young, who gave the interpretation that the child playing on the floor would grow up to be an apostle of the Lord Jesus Christ. That child was Heber J. Grant, who would become the seventh president of the LDS Church.[3]

Patty Sessions, one of the most beloved and respected midwives of the early church, conferred physical and spiritual healing on her sisters and her patients. On Wednesday, March 17, 1847, she attended the funeral of one sister, then visited the sick and went with her husband to bless "the widow Holman's daughter," who was healed. On another day, she recounts a meeting only of women where "it [the Holy Spirit] was got by E.R. Snow. They spoke in tongues. I interpreted and some prophesied."[4]

Lucy B. Young, one of Brigham Young's wives, and a constant companion of Zina Young and Eliza R. Snow acquired a reputation for healing. The tales of her healing influence abound:

> One sister who had not walked for twelve years was brought, and under the cheering faith of Sister Young she went through the day's ordinance and was perfectly healed of her affliction. Numbers of times childless women have sought the prayers and faith of Sister Young in her temple duties, and have afterwards turned, as Hannah of old, to bring up their promised child to receive further blessings in the temple. Volumes would not contain the myriad instances of cases of illness and disease healed by the power of God under Sister Young's hands. No one was too high, none too low, no one too poor, no one too sick for her faith to reach.[5]

Revelation, meaning "to uncover or reveal," may be one of the greatest of all spiritual gifts for it allows us to know what God intends. For a woman, the gift of revelation often pertains to the safety, well-being, and mission of family members, or to comfort them when grief-stricken or overcome with troubles. Eliza R. Snow had been married to Joseph Smith Jr. only two years when he was assassinated. She was bereft. For hours on end, lying in the darkness of her room, she begged the Lord to take her from this dark world. Finally, Joseph appeared to her and in this visitation told her that her work in mortality was not yet completed and that she must throw off her sorrow and comfort others.[6]

Often someone doing genealogical research receives a revelation. The Pearys were traveling for the husband's work in an eastern seaboard city in 1980. For some time they had struggled to find a family line that seemed to dead-end in England, where some ancestors had been subject to severe religious persecution. Both husband and wife felt strongly that the family members were calling to them from "the other side," begging that their work be done. The wife had a dream that they were walking through a graveyard and that they came upon a headstone engraved with the name of the person they had been re-searching. The next day, after visiting some historical sites, they came upon an old cemetery. "This is it!" she exclaimed, and ran to the grave-stone she remembered from her dream. Her husband followed her, his brow knitted in perplexity, for he knew nothing of her dream. When he read the name, his mouth fell open and he pointed at his wife. "You knew. You knew it was here." She smiled softly. "It was revealed to me in a dream."

Doing genealogical research and doing "work for the dead" in the temple are inextricably linked, and women often undertake this chal-lenge during the day while their husbands work. The flexible nature of mothering allows a woman to put her children in school for the day or get a babysitter or use nap-time to research family history. The sis-terhood can plan temple days together, completing three or four proxy sessions in one visit. Although most non-Mormons are mysti-fied by the phenomenon of gathering names of ancestors and then performing ordinances for them, the concept and the experience are beautiful. Through revelation, Elijah "committed the keys of this dispensation" to Joseph Smith for performing work for the dead, "to turn the hearts of the fathers to their children and the children to the fathers" (Doctrine and Covenants 110:13–16). By doing baptisms, initiatory and endowment sessions, and sealing ceremonies, departed ancestors on "the other side" are given the blessings of eternal family and personal exaltation:

> The Prophet Elijah was to plant in the hearts of the children the promises made to their fathers, [f]oreshadowing the great work to be done in the temples of the Lord in the dispensation of the fullness of times, for the redemption of the dead, and the sealing of the children to their parents, lest the whole world be smitten with a curse and utterly wasted at his coming. (Doctrine and Covenants 138:47–48)

When our ancestors are at peace, some of the negative patterns we carry in this life disappear. If they are not literally expunged from our DNA systems, at the least we are psychologically and spiritually relieved. One day I was driving to work, and even though I was running late, I had a sudden, overwhelming urge to return home. Thinking that I had left a pot boiling on the stove or the iron turned on, I hurried into the house where the phone was ringing insistently. I picked it up to hear the voice of a friend who'd been stricken with a serious illness, saying that he had "died" on the operating table, that while he was on the other side he met members of my family who were longing for their "work to be done." Two days later I received an invitation to go to the temple to participate in marriage and family sealings for people in my genealogical line, and of course I accepted. Many LDS women have shared similar experiences, including the impression, after doing work for the dead, of rejoicing and happiness from people on the other side.

Sometimes revelations are given to children. My daughter Denise, besides being born with healing hands, has also demonstrated a gift for receiving and understanding revelations. When my cousin's two-year-old, David, drowned in a swimming pool, our family was devastated. Eight-year-old Denise awakened the next morning and told me that her guardian angel had come to show her that David was needed to do some missionary work in other worlds.

When my father died, my mother spent most of her time and energy comforting others—her children, her sister-wives, my father's followers and patients. But she, of course, felt the loss excruciatingly. Denise, who was nine at the time, wrote my mother a letter in the loopy cursive of a child and left it on the kitchen counter, saying "Dear Grandma, Grandpa has asked me to deliver this message: 'In all you have lost, think of what you still have.'" My mother kept the comfort of my father's message from beyond the grave close to her heart for the rest of her life.

My father seems to have appeared to a number of people in this world after crossing over. My cousin's youngest child disappeared not long after my father had died. No one knew what had happened to him. Was he lost in the mountains behind his parents' home? Had he been attacked by a coyote or a black bear? The boy's mother kept saying that she knew he was all right, and she held faith that he would be found alive. Three days later, the rescue crews were about to give up the search when the mother came and said that, as she prayed, she'd seen a hole in the ground at the edge of their property. The searchers followed her instructions and found the boy in an abandoned root cellar, at the site of a burnt-out homestead. He'd been playing and had fallen in the hole too deep to scale. As they gave him water and food, his mother said, "You must have been so lonely down there all this time." The little boy shook his head. "I wasn't alone. Uncle Rulon [my father] stayed with me the whole time." The mother's faith for her child had been well founded.

Sometimes a woman stands alone, unrecognized in her vision, and only the sisterhood will support her in developing her gifts and talents and fulfilling her purpose. When Juanita Brooks began writing her landmark book, *Mountain Meadows Massacre,* she spent long, lonely hours in the St. George Library surreptitiously conducting research that she knew that various parties wouldn't like. For three-quarters of a century, the church and the state had been silent about events surrounding the slaughter. After John D. Lee's execution, a few surviving children had been returned to relatives in the east: all else had been buried. But for Brooks, the subject wouldn't die. My grandmother, Etta Josephine Finlayson, was the St. George librarian in those days, and she observed Brooks as she did her research, marveling at the questions raised by this sister in The Church of Jesus Christ of Latter-day Saints. Grandmother Etta noticed Brooks's frustration as she tried to locate information that had been misplaced or hidden or perhaps didn't exist; and yearned to help her. My grandmother was a brave woman. Her husband had died of congestive heart failure when they were in their early forties, and her only son died the following year, thrown from the back of a pickup truck as they returned from a Young Men's church activity. All four of her daughters had married into controversial polygamous marriages, sacrificing their membership in the mainstream church, and now people in Grandmother's ward treated her like a pariah. After a lifetime of caring for her family and being active in the official church, she was utterly isolated. As Grandmother Etta watched Brooks struggling, she identified with her lonely quest to wring some sense and order from the deaths up in the Mountain Meadows above St. George, Utah. She prayed that she might know how to help the truth come out. After that prayer, she received various promptings of the Spirit. Somehow she knew where to look, whom to call, which door or drawer or cabinet to open. As she came to understand Brooks's project, she took notes, found hidden documents, and stayed late at the library to accommodate the writer's schedule. When the book was finally published in 1950, Grandmother Etta was as proud as if she'd written it herself.

Friends I regard as sisters showed up in my life to support me as I wrote my first book. They continually reassured me that I had reason to complete the work. Some of them read it a chapter at a time, lending me the benefit of training in literature or sensibilities as avid readers. Once the manuscript was finished, I had a battered box of pages with lines scratched out and scribbled margins complete with asterisks and footnotes and inserted pages—a confusing mess, really. I was pregnant, due to deliver on Valentine's Day, and I desperately wanted to get the manuscript out of the house. I needed to make room in my life for a new baby. One night I dreamed that I was holding a baby and another lay at my feet, crying to be held. I dreamed that I gave the baby in my arms to Gayle, my sister in the Gospel. The next morning Gayle called and said she had dreamed that she'd taken my manuscript and typed it up, put it in a new box, and tied it with ribbon. Would she permit her to do that for me? Tears of relief and gratitude rolled down my cheeks that day as I accepted her offer of assistance. Gayle took the manuscript and typed a clean copy for submission, using her expertise as an English teacher to make sure that everything was correct. She wouldn't allow me to compensate her in any way. I hope that I would have the generosity of spirit to do the same for my sisters if given the opportunity.

One of the beautiful things about sisterhood is that we don't need to be anything we are not in order to fulfill what is needed in the relationship. In fact, one woman's weakness creates a need for another's strength, and vice versa. One woman I know, I'll call her Norah, had come on hard times with her family. Her husband had been laid off and they'd sold their house to make ends meet. They had been staying with relatives, but the welcome had worn thin and following some cool words between Norah and her brother-in-law, none of them wanted to spend another night there. They drove aimlessly for a while, then stopped at a wedding reception where they ran into some people, the Shafers, from a ward where they had previously lived. Norah and Helen Shafer sat nibbling brownies and chatting, watching their children chase each other around the recreation hall, when Helen put her hand on Norah's. "Tell me what's wrong," she said. Norah burst into tears; the story came pouring out. Norah blew her nose on her napkin. "So that's it. Thanks for listening. I feel better, just having talked about it." Helen lifted an eyebrow. "You won't feel better until your family is safe under a roof you can call your own. But first things first. You'll come home with us tonight, and we'll move your things tomorrow. Then we'll start looking for a job and a house."

Norah protested, but Helen wouldn't listen. "You're coming home with us. That's all there is to it." Indeed, as we are told in Scripture, "the people of the church should impart of their substance, every one according to that which he had; if he have more abundantly, he should impart more abundantly; and of him that had but little, but little should be required; and to him that had not should be given" (Mosiah 18:27).

Five years later, when Norah's husband had his dream job and Norah was decorating her dream house, she recalled what Helen had done for her. "I'll be forever in your debt," she said. "I don't know how I'll ever repay you." A week later, Helen's daughter died in a car crash. Norah was there to hold her through ordeal. She was there to help with arrangements for the funeral and to clean up after all the mourners had departed. Over the next year, she helped Helen get through the worst of the pain, talking on the phone, sometimes driving over to hold her while she cried, once finding her parked on a hill overlooking the city, another time finding her parked at the site of the crash, kneeling on the roadside. Even the promise of eternal bonding cannot allay the anguish of death, and there are times when only a pair of loving arms can help. Over the next years, Norah helped Helen pick up the pieces and glue them back together. She helped her get her back on her feet so that she could show up for her other children and her husband.

Sisterhood is all about reaching out to each other in times of need, regardless of age or social strata. A group of women of various ages and incomes reach out to pregnant teenagers. They volunteer their help, giving the girls room to talk about their fears, their hopes, and their dreams without judging them. Each older woman chooses a young woman to mentor, promising their commitment over the long haul—and they mean it. This is not a utilitarian relationship; it's all about serving the highest good of all concerned. This is a bond for life, or for as long as the teen wants to keep it going. The older women support the younger women who experience pain when boyfriends leave them to fend for themselves, or when outraged parents kick them out. They befriend and nurture and sometimes simply wrap their arms around the teens and let them sob. They support the teens with complicated situations at home and help them get maternity care. The older women provide teens with scriptural passages and quotes from the First Presidency underscoring the preciousness of all life, the value of every soul, and they will ask the teens to ponder and pray about them. More often than not, the teen will carry the baby to full term and give it up for adoption to a temple-worthy couple. Everyone wins in this situation, for one young woman's mistake becomes the answer to a childless woman's prayer. The change happens through the transforming love of sisters who give of their time and love to make sure that confused, abandoned, rejected girls get the guidance they need so that everyone has enough light to find their way home.

Women also heal each other when it comes to their marriages. There are so many people out there who are willing to commiserate with someone in an unhappy marriage: All you have to do is list your husband's faults, and you have half a dozen people, men or women, advising you to give the jerk the boot. People with their own list of failed relationships are eager to tell you that you don't deserve to be treated poorly, that there are other fish in the sea, that you and the kids would be better off without him. My friends and I have observed that most people encouraging someone to leave a relationship have been through their own disappointing marriages, usually ending in divorce, or they wish they were divorced and they're indulging in some wishful thinking, or they haven't been married at all. At least half of the marriages in America don't make it, and those statistics include Mormons, if you count those who only have civil ceremonies and have not married in the temple. Only a tiny percentage of those who have gone through the temple actually seek a divorce. Why? In addition to the reinforcing power of eternal commitment, they have friends who stand up for eternal marriage as an institution worth preserving, friends who support them in keeping their covenants. Women who are married in the temple know something about commitment, about the hard parts of showing up day after day, of building relationships valuable and durable enough to last through the eternities. They'll appear out of the blue and be there for their sisters during their darkest times. Sometimes they'll advise the woman under duress to leave for a while or they'll tell her that she needs to tell her husband to leave for awhile—especially if the offense has been dire. They keep their heads. They don't advise upset wives to go on the warpath or to hire a divorce lawyer unless it's a matter of life and death. They encourage their woman friends to stand up for themselves the way only another strong woman can.

Corinne married Seth, the smartest boy in her high school, caught him with her pretty eyes and smile, and she was glad for that. Her father had made all the family decisions and her mother had simply nodded her agreement throughout Corinne's young life, so of course she didn't expect anything to be different in her own marriage. Both Corinne and Seth met the most important criteria, to be "temple worthy," having followed the rules and fulfilled the commandments to receive their temple recommends. Corinne's cousin, Sheila, was happy for her, but she warned Corinne to wait awhile. "Find out what this guy is really like; see how he'll treat you when all the masks are gone." But Corinne was eager, and so was Seth, so Sheila contented herself with having shared her concerns and being the maid of honor. Seth had already completed his mission and a year of college; in another a two years, he graduated from premed, and then specialized in anesthesiology. They soon acquired a home much nicer than those of other couples their age. Their children had all the right clothes and toys. Corinne should have been happy. But at home, in their marriage, Seth was a cold fish. The only time he emerged from his cool way of being was when he was angry with her, and then she'd duck and run for cover. Soon their affluence and Seth's flexible schedule caught the attention of church authorities, and they asked him to be on the bishopric. He humbly agreed. With the members of the ward, Seth was incredibly loving and kind. He was literally generous to a fault, giving to people when they'd have been better off creating what they needed themselves. Ironically, the kinder he was in the ward, the crueler he was to Corinne. She began to gain weight, trying to buffer herself against his cold or brutal words. The more weight she gained, the more Seth diminished her. By the time he was promoted to another important ecclesiastical position, she had gained one hundred pounds and a personality disorder. One night, while considering whether to swallow all her sleeping pills at once, she knew she had to talk to someone, and she didn't know if the bishop would take her part when her husband was so beloved in the ward. . . ."He doesn't hit me," she told Sheila, her cousin. "I guess I should be grateful for that." Sheila raised her eyebrows. "Corrie, you need to do something. What he's doing is out of alignment with the Gospel and with his calling." By then, fifteen years into the marriage, Corinne had grown accustomed to mistreatment and she didn't quite believe—if she ever had believed—that she deserved to be treated better. But through Sheila's constant coaching Corinne stood up for herself. She went to Weight Watchers. She bought a new wardrobe. She enrolled in graduate school. She told Seth to be respectful or move out. The cold fish became a raging bull and then a sulky puppy. Corinne stood her ground. "I'm tired of living a lie, Seth."

Before Seth discovered true humility, he pulled some legal stunts, got her evicted from the house, had the kids asking what happened to Mom. Then something in him clicked, and he wanted Corinne to come home. When he realized he might lose her forever, he knew that whatever he'd been doing was wrong. First he had to find her; she was staying with Sheila, who advised him that he didn't even get to talk to Corinne until he'd changed his stripes. After he spent some time praying, attending temple, confessing to his priesthood leaders, he engaged in a courtship to get Corinne to come home again. At a party thrown by their friends for their wedding anniversary, Seth publicly recommitted to Corinne. He acknowledged the ways in which he'd met the letter of the law, but not the spirit. He acknowledged his pride, his egotism, his unkindness. He made new promises and assured Corinne that he fully intended to keep them . . . in addition to the covenants he'd made in the temple. As Corinne received his words, she looked over his shoulder at her cousin, her sister in the Gospel, Sheila, and she knew that she would never have made it to this day without her help.

The strong emphasis on following the example of the Savior and leading a perfect life weighs heavily on LDS women, especially when they are trying to do it alone. Married life, staying home with the little ones all day, sending the older ones off to school and being there when they get home, helping with homework, doing housework, shopping, preparing meals, making sure everybody goes to music and dance lessons and that team sports are coached and that everybody practices every day, then getting dinner on the table, herding everyone to sit down, making sure the blessing is said, that everyone eats their vegetables first, that the dishes are cleared and washed and the counters sponged off and the baths taken and the Scriptures read and the prayers said . . . it requires extraordinary strength and focus to make home a "heaven on earth." Talking to people under the age of ten all day long can make a woman with a masters' degree in business or a PhD in history or a bachelor's in biology feel like she's on the wrong planet. My daughter and her friends have decided to do something about that. One night every month, they gather at a restaurant while their husbands fill in, serving dinner, being the homework police, making sure the necks and ears are scrubbed and that the clothes and wet towels make it into the hamper, that the bedtime stories are read and the lullabies sung. Meanwhile the wives are having a long, slow dinner together, telling jokes, sharing a Girls' Night Out. Sometimes they have a theme and bring articles or snippets from the newspaper they've gathered over the month. Some-times they all read the same book and spend dinner discussing it. And sometimes they take turns talking about their lives, what is working and what is not working, and what needs to change so that they're looking forward to tomorrow or next month or next year. That's when they set personal goals, and somebody writes what they'll do by when. And they support each other in attaining them. When a goal has been reached, Girls' Night Out becomes a celebration. It works like nothing else. Al-most as if Mother were there, cheering you on.

Sometimes I think that the sisterhood sustains the gifts of the spirit so well because we haven't been given explicit support from the men in exercising them. If it were institutionalized, if we were encouraged to give blessings or to prophesy, we might resent being told to do it, or it might become so commonplace we'd cease to yearn after these gifts, and they would become another item on a long list of responsibilities. One sister complained about her husband, who had given a woman he'd never met before a blessing while visiting a friend in the hospital, and when they encountered the woman in another setting, he didn't remember her. "I worry that he does it automatically, that it means nothing to him. He doesn't even get to know the people he's blessing." We pointed out that the power of God doesn't require that the vessel be perfect or even fully conscious. But still his wife worried. "How can he have such incred-ible power entrusted to him and then take it for granted?"

We all knew that her husband was frequently asked to give blessings because people had so much confidence in him; everyone placed this ex-pectation on him. People took for granted that he would share his priesthood authority in this way. I have to admit, I take cooking for granted. I expect to do it regularly, and others expect it of me, too, and I don't always get excited about it. Perhaps that's how it would be if I were expected to exercise spiritual authority on cue.

As it is now, however, any woman who demonstrates gifts of the spirit often receives a cool reception, both inside and outside the church. People in general seem wary of women who have obvious spiri-tual gifts. I have one friend with amazing spiritual prowess who has raised people's eyebrows as long as I've known her. Even though she's a luscious blonde, men don't know what to do with her and they keep her at arms' length if they're not up to dealing with her power. She calls or e-mails every time she has a dream about me. Born and raised LDS, she was trained in Jungian psychology, so she gives me these amazing run-downs on the symbols and meanings in her dreams. They're almost like a map to a certain problem I'm struggling to resolve or an obstacle course I'm negotiating. Sometimes her dreams about me surpass my own dreams in usefulness. She also interprets my dreams, from the most straightforward to the most cryptic, showing me the potent symbols, helping me to uncover the meanings. It's a rich and lovely friendship that I've had since high school. We've seen each other through babies and broken hearts, through illnesses and injuries and triumphs and tor-ments. We are each other's cheerleaders and confidantes. And we offer a shoulder to cry on when necessary.

I have another friend who grew up in the church, but what drew us together was our mutual love of literature. From there, we found much in common. Many LDS women have the experience of "knowing" some-one the first time they meet them, and we reason that perhaps we knew each other in the Pre-existence, before we came to this earth, and that we made promises to each other there. We know them. We just can't re-member how. That's how it was when I met Sally. I knew I'd always known her and that I'd be seeing her forever. Sally is the friend who told me that I don't need to dress up reality to make it look good. "You can be honest with me. You are my friend. And because you are my friend, I also know when you're lying . . . so don't do it." I was twenty-two years old at the time and I had not fully emerged from the history of lying to protect my polygamous family. I didn't know yet how important honesty is to keeping a relationship healthy. Sally taught me about the enormous practical value of truth, not by going to church with me but while giving me a ride home from the school where we both taught hormone-crazed junior high students. It was Sally who showed up for me when I came down with a kidney infection that almost killed me. First, she called my husband and told him to get me to a doctor. She made an hour-long drive to bring a crockpot of soup, a loaf of homemade bread and Toni Morri-son's *Beloved* to read while I was recovering. Then she sat on the edge of the bed to talk with me. "The kidneys cleanse the blood," she said. "And blood is always about family. So what kind of poison is running through your family?" And so we talked, because this made sense to me and to her, even if it made no sense to anyone else. And I realized that I needed to do something about the family problem that had been keeping me awake at night.

Janie came to take care of me after my youngest baby was born and I developed mastitis. We had no insurance, the baby had thrush, my toddler had a terrible diaper rash, and my other two had to go to school. Janie came with her toddler and set her to play with mine. She fed the baby a bottle, washed her mouth with saline solution, and then gave me hot packs to put on my swollen, tender breast. The baby slept, I slept, my fever broke, the angry red lump dissolved, and I awakened to my milk flowing freely again. Janie had prepared lasagna and garlic bread and salad, my girls were home from school and she was tiptoeing out of the bedroom. "I just wanted to make sure you're still alive before I go." She smiled, her dark almond eyes tilting; she looks more like a fashion model than somebody's sister. "How can I ever thank you?" I said. She tilted her head. "You know you already have. You've done the same for me on some other plane. Or you will . . . ." I nodded. She knows about déjà vu, too.

Dee Dee is one of the most passionately LDS people I've ever met. Her testimony burns strong and bright and true. She's always converting people or attending the baptism of someone she's brought into the church. In addition to her gift for sharing the Gospel, she was born with an enormous gift for healing and she's not sure how to live with it. As a child she'd get impressions about people, predicting heart trouble before it overcame her father, cancer in her grandmother before it manifested, diagnosing broken bones on the playground. People laughed at her, brushed off her predilections, asked why she had to be so dramatic—until the prediction materialized, and then they'd keep her at bay, perhaps resentful that she'd known, perhaps suspecting that like a voodoo child, she'd had something to do with the illness. In the church, she wasn't supposed to use the healing gift because she didn't hold the priesthood. The man she married wasn't a member, so she didn't feel that she had access to priesthood power. Still, she found herself putting her hands on people, touching where it hurt, letting the warm energy that coursed into her from above flow through her fingertips, and people would sigh and stretch and say thank you. Once in a while people would look at her coldly, making her step back, sending her away. Then she would try to suppress the gift, fit in, be like anyone else.

After years of wondering what to do with her healing touch, she became a massage therapist. Through her gift many gained relief and occasionally she was recompensed for what she gave. While doing massage therapy, she discovered that she could tell exactly what was wrong with someone. She knew which muscles were knotted, which vertebrae were out of alignment, which nerves were pinched. But she didn't know how to apply this knowledge. She wasn't a chiropractor or a medical doctor. And she wasn't a priesthood holder. It was like having a terribly powerful secret without having the authority to reveal it or the license to use it. Sometimes she literally knew secrets—the things people thought or did that made them sick. They didn't always like it when she rifled through their psyches and came up with truths they'd rather not confront.After one particularly angry person told her off, she again tried to suppress her gift, which resulted in some health problems for her. Her attendance at the LDS temple brought her enormous peace and a sense of direction that allowed her to trust her gift, to stop suppressing it. She discovered that by using aromatic oils she could use her knowledge to heal and could do it with some legitimacy. (Although medicine doesn't fully acknowledge the power of herbs to heal, a body of respectable research supports the viability of homeopathic remedies.) As a massage therapist and an herbalist she could touch people with the intention of healing and could call forth their faith without having to directly hold the priesthood. Human energy became a map, and by pressing here and there, she could get the electricity flowing everywhere it needed to go. She began to respect her gift, and her own health improved dramatically. With encouragement from her women friends (who had long been recipients of her healing touch) and a new husband who was kind and supportive while honoring his priesthood, she made the decision to go to college and become a homeopathic physician. By then her children were grown and the coast was clear—she had an open road to follow for the rest of her life.

Within polygamy, women often talk about the sisterhood. Sometimes the sharing is acerbic, as with one woman who had left polygamy, who said, "My sister-wife and I were closer to each other in many ways than either of us were to our husband. We shared a lot of things: children, financial troubles, vaginitis . . . ." But others sincerely celebrate the sharing, such as this woman who said, "My sisterwife and I are the best of friends. We share a bond with each other that could not be there if we were not sisterwives. I would not trade our relationship in order to be the only wife."[7]

Growing up in polygamy made me wary of other women although I knew that my mother and her sister-wives loved each other. They celebrated each other's birthdays; they even celebrated each other's wedding anniversaries! They tended each other's children and cared for each other when they were sick. They helped each other shoulder life's burdens, and once I was married in monogamy, I longed for someone like my mothers to share my life—someone to talk to, someone who shared my values, someone who shared my future. As many women have said, I wouldn't mind having a wife, someone who shared my values and my interests, someone who loves the same people I love, someone to support me with the housework and the children while I followed my dreams. I just didn't want her to sleep with my husband. I always felt guilty because I didn't want to share my husband. I had single women friends who wanted to get into a committed relationship where they could have a family, and I felt like the most selfish woman in the world. Plus, I knew about the pecking order. I had watched my mother and her sister-wives struggle for position. The strongest always stayed on top. Those at the bottom were so henpecked they could hardly scratch out a life. I knew that there were beautiful elements to the Principle of Plural Marriage, the times the wives showed up at each other's bedsides when one of them was sick or giving birth, the times they worked to surprise each other with a dress or a homemade knickknack or an apple pie. But in my estimation, the cruel, emotionally debilitating realities often outweighed the beauties. I hurt for the wife who was least educated, the one who was younger than the others, the one who didn't know how to assert herself. These women suffered torments of self-doubt and self-abnegation. And the women whose prodigious energy eclipsed them didn't know how to pull their sister-wives up and out of the pit. Marrying into polygamy seemed to me like it would be a leap into Hell—for me, and for anybody who went there with me.

But then I wasn't altogether committed to monogamy either, and I got cold feet about marriage more than once. When I was trying to get past all my fears about taking out my endowments and getting married in the temple, I identified inconsistencies and contradictions, any reason to postpone the temple date. Support came from an unlikely source. I had a writing student who went jogging with me three or four times a week. She was the stuff of a novel—dreamy and fragile—but she always showed up to jog, and her presence got me out of the house and down the road. With each stretch we took on another of my concerns about temple marriage, and she pondered it with me, turning it so that I answered my own questions. After six weeks of this, I had run out of excuses. It was time to commit. Needless to say, she accompanied me to the temple and attended me as my escort.

Jogging and hiking with sisters has taught me about my place on the earth, including occupying my body respectfully and respecting the life around me. Women in the Gospel of Jesus Christ know that He created this beautiful world and that it runs by the same natural laws we do. By going into nature, we remember who we really are, and we learn from the trees, the streams, the wildlife, about our significance on the earth. We are told in Doctrine and Covenants, 88:45–47:

> The earth rolls upon her wings, and the sun giveth his light by day, and the moon giveth her light by night and the stars also give their light, as they roll upon their wings in their glory in the midst and power of God. Unto what shall I liken these kingdoms that ye may understand? Behold all these are kingdoms and any man who hath seen any or the least of these hath seen God moving in his majesty and power.

The knowledge and desire to care for this kingdom on earth that God has given us comes under fire as greed tempts us to build at the expense of wilderness. In the area surrounding Park City, where my husband and I moved so that our children would know the natural world, wildlife refuges have become little more than isolated parks as long-time landowners—many of them sons and daughters of Mormon pioneers—seek to cash in on ski-resort real estate prices. In my ward, a group of women met once a week to hike the beautiful mountains around Park City and to pray for the land where they'd chosen to raise their children. The seasons changed the mountains, but the group was consistent, spring, summer, winter, fall, showing up with their cameras and their backpacks and their enthusiasm. They helped to preserve the sandhill crane and red fox habitat, the wetlands known as the Swanner Nature Preserve. And they preserved something inside themselves. When we walk, we talk, and we pace our talk to the rhythm of our lives. Keeping these actions together—walking and talking in the presence of other women and nature—may be one of the most powerful bonding experiences we can have as a sisterhood. More than once on such walks I have learned precious truths from nature—or from a sister who walked beside me in the wilderness, celebrating Mother Earth.

My sister-in-law, whom I regard as my angel, would take me for hikes when I visited her in California, sharing with me the same path she walked in her meditations. I knew that these meditations had yielded up answers to prayers and concerns about herself, about me, and about others in our family. She stopped before a thistle bush and said, "When you are not here, this is my friend. The thistle bush lets me know what God wants." I looked at her, half smiling, then back at the bush. It was a magnificent Russian thistle, tall as manzanita, decked with large purple blossoms. But it was a thistle bush, after all. Then I realized that she wasn't kidding. Somehow the bush mirrored or relayed to her what she needed to know; it was her own bush without the burning. This orientation to nature helped me as I took walks of my own. Once, when faced with a life-changing decision, two eagles flew overhead and each dropped a feather at my feet. I took it as a sign. Later I learned that this is the Native American manifestation of having chosen your correct life path.

Another group of women east of Salt Lake City meets once a week to drink Postum and eat coffee cake and discuss whom they should serve. In the spirit of the Relief Society sisters of the early church, they want to be "anxiously engaged in a good cause" (Doctrine and Covenants 58:27). Their husbands thrive in their professions, their children are launched, and the sisters want to do something more meaningful than going shopping or baking casseroles or getting their nails done. So once a week they gather and eat and chat and then they pray. Each woman has substantial spiritual gifts, and they open themselves to being useful. Sometimes they receive no sense of direction, and so they read

Scripture and talk and wait. Sometimes they get a very clear sense of what needs to happen and who needs their ministrations. They go as a sisterhood, taking the rest of the cake, and they do what the Spirit dictates. Once they arrive at their destination sometimes it's a matter of talking and reading Scripture and saying a prayer, as a visiting teacher would do. Sometimes they suggest a song to sing or that a poem is read aloud, or they simply wait for the woman to talk or cry, and then they hold her and comfort and devise ways to help her.

RaNelle Wallace, author of *The Burning Within* was horribly burned when the light plane in which she and her husband flew back from an LDS Church conference crashed into the side of a mountain and burst into flames.[8] Burned everywhere except where her temple garments covered her skin, RaNelle climbed down the mountain to get help for her husband, and only when the paramedics arrived and took over did she let go. She went into cardiac arrest and had a near-death experience where she met her deceased grandmother and her unborn son. She knew she had to return to this earth and undergo the pain of healing so that she could give birth to this child, even though she deeply regretted leaving this beautiful, enlightened place and reentering her burned, disfigured body. For a year she had to wear neoprene bandages to help her skin heal without the ridges and wrinkles generally associated with burn scars. The year in bandages had not yet ended when, one afternoon, her neighbor's house burst into flame. She had spoken to her neighbor only half an hour before and RaNelle knew that the woman and her baby were taking a nap together. Despite the pain of the being horribly burned still fresh in her memory, she raced into the burning house and saved her neighbors' lives. RaNelle was given the California "Woman of the Year" title and other awards for her heroism. But the most precious outcome was the sisterhood that was formed—relationships that would follow her and sustain her through all the years of healing, of writing, of touring, of working out the pain that had the Wallace family still had to deal with, an eternal sisterhood founded in gratitude.[9]

My friend Rachel has taught me a deeper meaning of sisterhood. Rachel is busy and popular with many women in the circle of sisterhood, and her friendship is always impeccable, extensive, embracing. She was diagnosed with breast cancer ten years ago, and she caught it early enough to keep it from spreading. But it makes her nervous. When her sister-in-law's sister came down with breast cancer that soon became terminal, Rachel took the challenge of flying to another city and caring for this woman who was related to her through family ties but not by blood, because, as she said, "She's one of my sisters. I'd want her to do this for me." Even though Rachel still quaked at the thought of breast cancer, even though this mother leaving her children embodied Rachel's worst nightmare for herself, she faced the fear and did what needed to be done anyway. She helped her with the bedpan, she changed her sheets, and she gave her sponge baths. She did the laundry and made dinner and helped the sad children with their homework and found ways to make them smile. And when it was almost over, she made a commitment to this dying mother that she would watch out for her children. She came home and resumed her busy life. But she's not so afraid of the cancer. And she watches out for those children, albeit from a distance.

Through the sisterhood, we can acknowledge the bittersweetness in life as well as death. At fast and testimony meeting, the sacrament meeting where we are allowed to speak to the congregation, a woman I have not met stands at the microphone. She gives thanks through tears. She is grateful to have sent two sons on missions in the past two years, grateful to have a daughter recently marry in the temple, grateful to have another engaged to be married. Soon her nest will be empty—and here she breaks down and has to pause to regain composure. "I can do this," she says. She quotes Sister Tanner, president of the Young Women's organization: "We can do hard things with the help of the Lord." She says she is grateful that her husband will be there with her. Most of all, she says, she is grateful to the women who have helped her in the flurry of the past eighteen months, the sisters in the ward who helped her with food and decorations for a wedding, two farewell parties, and an engagement soiree. Grateful that they comfort her, grateful that they reassure her when she wonders if she has outlived her usefulness. Grateful for the lessons they prepare for Relief Society, for the visits they make as visiting teachers, for the kindness and caring and service they've always extended from the days when she was recovering from the births of these children she's now seeing out the door. "Thank you, God, for my sisters in Zion."

Listening, I know that whatever challenge we've embraced can be done because "we can do hard things with the help of the Lord." We have enough—enough power, enough authority, enough challenge, and enough spirit to keep ourselves and our daughters and granddaughters growing for years to come. Indeed, the women of The Church of Jesus Christ of Latter-day Saints prove their purpose: "men [and women] are that they might have joy" (2 Nephi 2:25).

The joy is in the partnership. We women have learned about partnering from our mothers and our sisters and our children. And we have learned it by embracing our men and including them in a world of blessed partnership. After all, we women bit the apple first.

In Moses 5:10–11, in *The Pearl of Great Price,* we discover:

> And in that day Adam blessed God and was filled, and began to prophesy concerning all the families of the earth, saying: Blessed be the name of God, for because of my transgression my eyes are opened, and in this life I shall have joy, and again in the flesh I shall see God.
>
> And Eve, his wife, heard all these things and was glad, saying: Were it not for our transgression we never should have had seed, and never should have known good and evil, and the joy of our redemption, and the eternal life which God giveth unto all the obedient.

We are all, men and women alike, living witnesses of God's promise to the human family. Perhaps our Heavenly Mother is purposefully vague, deliberately inscrutable. Perhaps by not imposing Her version of the rules and Her book of doctrines, She has spared us another detailed map of prescribed behaviors, allowed us a plot of wilderness and bestowed freedom that only She can ordain: the freedom to create.

Linda Sillitoe, a writer of LDS background who has long stood for life, gives us her version in "Song of Creation":

> Who made the world, my child?
> Father made the rain
> silver and forever.
> Mother's hand
> drew riverbeds and hollowed seas,
> drew riverbeds and hollowed seas
> to bring the rain home.

Father bridled winds, my child,
to keep the world new.
Mother clashed
fire free from stones
and breathed it strong and dancing
and breathed it strong and dancing
the color of her hair.

He armed the thunderclouds
rolled out of heaven;
Her fingers flickered
hummingbirds
weaving the delicate white snow,
weaving the delicate white snow,
a waterfall of flowers.

And if you live long, my child,
you'll see snow burst
from thunderclouds
and lightning in the snow;
listen to Mother and Father laughing,
listen to Mother and Father laughing
behind the locked door.[10]

Mother and Father are there together, a partnership. And the door won't be locked forever. As we've been told, all we need to do is knock, and it will be opened. "For behold, this is my work and my glory—to bring to pass the immortality and eternal life of man [and woman]" (Moses 1:39).

Certainly, our Mother in Heaven found joy in partnership, gestated this process, and celebrates as we, in turn, give birth to the universe.

Glossary of LDS/ Mormon Terms

Aaronic Priesthood　　Known as "the lesser priesthood," this includes deacons, teachers, and priests, all of them accountable to the bishop, who is their priesthood head. Faithful young men become eligible to hold the Aaronic Priesthood at age 12, and their authority increases through age and faithfulness.

Adversary　　This usually means Satan or Lucifer or the Devil, but can mean anything or anyone working against good, the Gospel and God; anything that has been sent forth to do evil.

Apostate　　This refers to an individual or a group of people who have at one time been members of The Church of Jesus Christ of Latter-day Saints who have abandoned the faith. This happens by sinning, then refusing to repent, by breaking covenants and sometimes by reviling the church and its leaders.

Apostle　　This lifelong calling to be a special witness for Jesus Christ throughout the world is the high office of the Melchizedek priesthood. Along with the First Presidency of The Church of Jesus Christ of Latter-day Saints, the Twelve Apostles are regarded as Prophets, Seers, and Revelators.

Articles of Faith　　Drafted by Joseph Smith, Jr. in 1842 in a letter to "Long" John Wentworth, editor of the *Chicago Democrat*, these thirteen articles profess the general principles or doctrines of The Church of Jesus Christ of Latter-day Saints.

Atonement　　This refers to the sacrifice made by Jesus Christ so that all mankind may be redeemed of sin and granted eternal life.

Baptism　　Children are eligible for baptism at age 8, the Age of Accountability, or whenever they are prepared to take upon them the name of Christ and become a member of The Church of Jesus Christ of Latter-day Saints. Baptism by immersion is followed by Confirmation.

Bishop　　This refers to the leader of a ward, or local congregation. As the president of the Aaronic priesthood in the ward, the bishop's duties are similar to those of pastor, priest, minister, or rabbi. As with other clergy in The Church of Jesus Christ of Latter-day Saints, the bishop gives his time and devotion as a service; the position is not paid.

Book of Mormon   Subtitled *Another Testament of Jesus Christ,* the *Book of Mormon* tells of the ancient inhabitants of North, Central, and South America who were visited by Jesus Christ after his crucifixion and resurrection. The record containing the Gospel as taught by Christ and the history of these ancient peoples was inscribed on metal plates buried in the Hill Cumorah and revealed to Joseph Smith, Jr. by a heavenly messenger. The *Book of Mormon* contains several books named after their principle authors: First Nephi, Second Nephi, Jacob, Enos, Jarom, Omni, Mormon, Mosiah, Alma, Helaman, Third Nephi, Fourth Nephi, Mormon, Ether, Moroni.

Brethren   This refers to all male members of the Church, but can also describe how Latter-day Saints regard all mankind. "The Brethren" often refers to the General Authorities, including the First Presidency, the Twelve Apostles, the Seventy, and the Presiding Bishopric of the LDS Church.

Calling   This refers to an assignment or opportunity to serve in the LDS Church or to serve the larger community, usually delivered by the bishop or the stake president. Typically, once a person agrees to accept a calling, he or she is set apart by the bishop or appropriate priesthood leader. A calling can also refer to a strong sense of purpose in one's life, especially when combined with a spiritual gift.

Chapel   This is the specific room in a church building where members congregate on Sunday to worship through prayer, speech, and song. The chapel is a place where members exhibit reverence, but is not to be confused with the temple.

Confirmation   This priesthood ordinance confers the Holy Ghost to be a companion and guide to a newly baptized individual, and confirms him or her as a member of The Church of Jesus Christ of Latter-day Saints along with other blessings pronounced by the ordinance-giver.

Convert   This is a person who chooses to join The Church of Jesus Christ of Latter-day Saints by being baptized and confirmed. Usually the term refers to someone who has not grown up with the influence of the church.

Covenant   This refers to a sacred agreement between a person and God, each making promises to the other. Covenants are binding, and there are blessings for keeping them, and consequences for breaking them.

Deacon   This is the first office in the Aaronic priesthood conferred on worthy males beginning at age 12, which includes the authority to prepare and offer the sacrament to church members, and to visit members and collect fast offerings and other contributions for the poor.

Doctrine and Covenants   A text regarded as scripture by The Church of Jesus Christ of Latter-day Saints, originally called the *Book of Commandments,* and containing revelations given to the Prophet Joseph Smith and subsequent presidents and prophets of the church.

Elder   This is the first office in the Melchizedek or higher priesthood to which worthy young men are ordained before fulfilling a mission for the church, and other worthy men as well. "Elder" is a general title designating missionaries, General Authorities, and other men of the church who hold the Melchizedek priesthood.

Endowments   The process of receiving endowments happens in LDS temples. Endowments involve deepening commitment to principles of the Gospel and certain blessings bestowed by making covenants with God.

Eternal Progression   This refers to the belief that we can grow continually, infinitely and eternally, creating more life and greater joy through exaltation.

Exaltation   This refers to being lifted up and dwelling in Zion, or in Celestial Glory, a state of enhanced being that includes eternal progression.

Family Home Evening   Also called Family Night, this regular family meeting occurs weekly, usually on Monday evening, and involves scripture study, spiritual lessons, exercise of leadership, sharing of individual talents, and family unity. The meeting usually begins and ends with prayer, may include a song, a treat and fun activities inside or outside the home.

Family Search   This computer system assists church members as well as non-members with family research and genealogical pursuits. The system can be accessed at the Website: www.familysearch.org.

Fast Sunday   The first Sunday of each month is usually designated Fast Sunday, when church members abstain from food and drink for two meals, then donate at least the cost to assist the poor and those in need. While fasting, members also have the opportunity to stand in the special sacrament meeting—called Fast and Testimony meeting—to bear their testimony of Christ, the Gospel and the Church.

Fireside   Once called "cottage meetings," these informal gatherings of church members usually occur in homes and feature speakers or study focused on spiritual matters. Some firesides occur in the chapel. Occasionally they are held by the First Presidency, and can be broadcast by satellite.

First Presidency   This term is used to describe the current prophet and president of The Church of Jesus Christ of Latter-day Saints and his two counselors.

Garments   These articles of clothing are given to worthy members (those who have received a "temple recommend" signed by the bishop and stake president following an extensive interview) as part of a ceremony of purification and promise in the LDS temple before endowments are received. These white undergarments are regarded as sacred, and remind members of the covenants they have made in the temple.

General Authorities   These are the leaders who serve the entire Church of Jesus Christ of Latter-day Saints in a general capacity, including members of the First Presidency, the Quorum of the Twelve Apostles, the Quorums of the Seventy, and the Presiding Bishopric.

Gentile   Those who are not members of The Church of Jesus Christ of Latter-day Saints have sometimes been referred to as "gentiles". Used more commonly in the early days of the church when Latter-day Saints experienced persecution, forced emigration, and prosecution, the term has lost favor as the church has grown internationally.

Golden Plates   These metal plates containing the history of the ancient peoples of the Western Hemisphere were hidden in the Hill Cumorah in upstate New York, a portion of which were translated by Joseph Smith, Jr. and became the *Book of Mormon*.

Home Teachers   Two priesthood holders are assigned to visit each family in a ward on a monthly basis, where they offer prayer, a brief lesson or scripture reading, and see to the family's well being.

Investigator   This refers to a person investigating the church who is earnestly concerned with knowing the truth. Missionaries answer questions and otherwise assist in the inquiry of investigators.

Latter Days   This refers to the last dispensation of time upon the earth before the Second Coming of the Savior, Jesus Christ. Also known as the Last Days, this period includes the time of the Restoration of the Gospel and reestablishment of the original Church of Jesus Christ.

Latter-day Saints (LDS)   This refers to members of The Church of Jesus Christ of Latter-day Saints and emphasizes the earnest engagement of members to prepare the earth and all mankind for the Second Coming of Christ.

Law of Chastity   In the LDS Church this refers to chastity before marriage and sexual fidelity in a monogamous relationship. In some polygamous communities, the Law of Chastity refers to the commitment to have sex only if you intend to conceive a child. Women who are pregnant, nursing, or post-menopausal, or couples who are not interested in conceiving would abstain from sex under this rule.

Law of Consecration   Based on the concept described in Psalms 24:1 that the earth and everything on it belongs to God and that man is merely a steward of the earth, the Law of Consecration invites each member to dedicate property, time and talent to building up the kingdom of God. In the United Order, members in the early church were encouraged to hold all things in common with their brothers and sisters. The Law of Conservation involves taking care of the poor and giving unconditionally to the church, thus eliminating greed and poverty while serving the highest good. While the spirit of this law is still in force, it isn't literally practiced in the LDS Church as a whole today. Fundamentalist leaders sometimes use the law as a means of exploiting the members of their polygamous communities.

Laying on of Hands   This refers to a priesthood holder putting hands on someone's head for the purpose of blessing. When the blessing is for healing, the head is anointed with consecrated oil.

Manifesto of 1890   This refers to the revelation and ensuing declaration that ended the practice of polygamy for members of The Church of Jesus Christ of Latter-day Saints.

Melchizedek Priesthood   This refers to the offices of higher priesthood, which can be conferred on worthy males from the age of eighteen upward. This priesthood includes the offices of elder, high priest, patriarch, seventy, apostle, and prophet, and includes the authority to lay on hands for the gift of the Holy Ghost, for the healing of the sick, and to fulfill assignments in the church. Although the office of bishop is technically a function of the Aaronic priesthood, the bishop is virtually always a Melchizedek priesthood holder.

Mission   This formal period of voluntary service may range from six to twenty-four months during which time members devote themselves wholly to proselytizing, strengthening, and serving. Young men over the age of eighteen, women over the age of twenty-one, and retired members, including couples who are worthy and willing, put in "papers" or applications before being called to fulfill missions. Individuals and couples are also called to be ward and stake missionaries, to assist full-time missionaries in their work. In addition to proselytizing missions, there are also humanitarian, welfare and building missions. A mission may also refer to an area where missionary work is performed.

Missionary Training Center   Known as the MTC, missionaries are given Gospel and language instruction and otherwise trained in facilities throughout the world before departing on the missions to which they've been called.

Mormon   This informal term is used synonymously with Latter-day Saint to describe members of The Church of Jesus Christ of Latter-day Saints, the famous Mormon Tabernacle Choir, and anything pertaining to the church. The name is actually taken from a fourth century prophet who abridged the historical and spiritual records contained in the golden plates, which became the *Book of Mormon.*

Moroni   This is the name of the son of Mormon, who buried the plates inscribed by his father. In 1827, the resurrected, or "Angel" Moroni delivered the plates to Joseph Smith, Jr. A statue of the Angel Moroni usually is found on top of LDS temples.

Ordinance   This includes blessings or covenants such as baptism, confirmation, marriage, etc. which must be performed by one ordained with priesthood authority.

Patriarchal Blessing   This blessing, requested by worthy individuals is given by a designated patriarch, a high priest who receives this calling for life. A patriarchal blessing involves the pronouncement of lineage and special blessings as well as guidance to serve individuals throughout their lives. Every stake has a patriarch called to serve in this capacity.

Pearl of Great Price   This LDS scripture includes translations and additions to the writings of Abraham and Moses and the History of the Prophet Joseph Smith plus thirteen Articles of Faith.

Personal Revelation   The belief in revelation is contained in the Seventh Article of Faith. Personal revelation refers to a belief that in addition to the power of revelation given to prophets of The Church of Jesus Christ of Latter-day Saints and to other priesthood holders in their callings, each member of the church may receive revelation through the Holy Spirit for his or her own life and stewardship.

Pre-existence   This refers to the belief that we lived together as a family of spirits created by our Heavenly Parents, and that we made certain choices in communion with God that determined some of the challenges of our earthly state.

Presidency   This refers to the president of any church organization and his or her two counselors, who make decisions and act as a unit.

Priesthood   The priesthood is the power to act in the name of God. The office and authority to act in God's name is bestowed on worthy LDS men as part of their growth and spiritual development, so that each may become a "minister and witness" of Jesus Christ. Priesthood also refers to the body of priesthood-bearing men in the LDS Church.

Primary   This is the religious education and activities program for children ages three to eleven in the LDS Church. Children enter Primary from the nursery to become "Sunbeams" and continue through CTR (for "Choose the Right") at age 11.

Prophet   This refers to a person authorized to speak for God, particularly the president of The Church of Jesus Christ of Latter-day Saints. Joseph Smith, Jr. was the first LDS prophet. As of this writing, President Gordon B. Hinckley is the Living Prophet of the LDS Church.

Quorum   A Quorum is a group of priesthood holders.

Region   For purposes of administration, the earth is divided into regions in The Church of Jesus Christ of Latter-day Saints, each of which includes several stakes.

Relief Society   This is the adult women's organization in the church, whose purpose is contained in the organization's motto: "Charity never faileth."

Restoration   This refers to the return of all aspects of the original Gospel of Jesus Christ and His Church as established while He was on this earth. Joseph Smith, Jr. was the emissary of this restoration.

Returned Missionary   This usually refers to a young man who has recently completed a full-time mission for the church (sometimes affectionately referred to as an RM) who is now ready to return to school and/or marry. Women and couples are also returned missionaries but the distinction seems less marked in those instances.

Sacrament   This is the ordinance of blessing and administering bread and water, emblematic of the body and blood of Jesus Christ in a weekly sacrament meeting, to members of The Church of Jesus Christ of Latter-day Saints to remind them of their covenants.

Sacrament Meeting   This weekly meeting happens during the three-hour block when members of the ward gather to pray, sing hymns, partake of the sacrament, and listen to talks given from the pulpit. Usually, the speakers are members of the congregation who have been invited to prepare speeches, sometimes on an assigned topic.

Saints   One way of referring to devout members of The Church of Jesus Christ of Latter-day, this term reflects the strong encouragement to members to be obedient to the commandments of God and to lead exemplary lives.

Sealing   A sealing is an ordinance performed only in the temple to bind couples in marriage and families together "for time and all eternity."

Set apart   When people receive callings, they are "set apart" through a priesthood blessing to perform their responsibilities with guidance from the Holy Ghost.

Stake   This is an area made up of several wards and/or branches (neighborhood congregations). The stake president and his counselors and the stake high council administrate affairs at the stake level. A chapel in most areas is designated as the stake center.

Temple   Temples are "the house of the Lord". In these beautifully appointed buildings sacred ordinances of the Gospel are performed, including endowments, marriages, sealings for the living and the dead as well as vicarious baptisms and confirmations. Only people who hold temple "recommends" may attend. The sacred nature of these ordinances gives rise to the inaccurate notion that secretive, cultish practices go on inside LDS temples.

Temple "recommend"   This is a certificate granted to a member in good standing following an interview between a member and his or her bishop and stake president. The interview determines the worthiness of the member to attend the temple, and once it is signed, the bearer is eligible to attend any LDS temple in the world.

Testimony   A testimony is a personal experience of the truthfulness of the Gospel and the doctrines of the church. When a person expresses such personal belief, this is called "bearing your testimony."

Tithing   The Law of Tithing requires that members pay one-tenth of their income to The Church of Jesus Christ of Latter-day Saints.

United Order   This economic system draws on the Law of Consecration and was formed through revelation by the Prophet Joseph Smith and is elaborated in the Doctrine and Covenants: 104, along with the Law of Consecration. Early attempts were made to live the United Order during the disruptions and forced emigrations of the 1840s. The economic system was firmly established in Utah Territory, known then as the "state of Deseret." It involved giving all income and harvest to the bishop, to be redivided according to need so that the order "in heaven will be practiced and enjoyed by men on the earth." According to Elder George Q. Cannon, the purpose was to introduce a time "when there shall be no rich and no poor among the Latter-day Saints, when wealth will not be a temptation; when every man will love his neighbor as he does himself; when every man and woman will labor for the good of all as much as for self." The system was very successful in establishing cooperative institutions in the early church. The human foibles of selfishness and mismanagement combined with political pressure put an end to the various United Orders in the LDS Church by 1880. Some fundamentalists have attempted the practice, with varied results. Most modern attempts at the United Order in fundamentalist communities result in the poor being egregiously exploited by the leaders.

Visiting Teacher   This calling assigns a pair of women to visit other women in the ward. The visitors offer a lesson, pray with the sister, and assure her overall well-being. Visiting teachers often become good friends.

Ward　　A ward is a congregation from a geographical area or neighborhood, and can include several hundred members presided over by the bishop and his counselors.

Word of Wisdom　　Based on the Doctrine and Covenants 89 which presents "the order and will of God in the temporal salvation of all saints in the last days," the Word of Wisdom was given to Joseph Smith, Jr. by way of revelation in 1833, proscribing alcohol, tobacco, tea, coffee, and encouraging good health habits and promising blessings for observing the revelation.

Work for the Dead　　Baptisms, endowments, and sealings are among the work performed by proxy for our deceased ancestors. When this work is performed, spirits on the other side can progress further in their spiritual lives.

Zion　　This refers to a paradisiacal idea as well as a literal place (such as Salt Lake City and Jackson County, Missouri) where the righteous saints gather through obedience to the Gospel.

For Further Reading

Ballard, M. Russell. *Our Search for Happiness,* Salt Lake City, Deseret Book, 1995

Batchelor, Mary, Marianne Watson, and Anne Wilde, eds. *Voices in Harmony.* Salt Lake City: Principle Voices, 2000.

Beecher, Maureen Ursenbach, and Lavina Fielding Anderson. *Sisters in Spirit: Mormon Women in Historical and Cultural Perspective.* Urbana: University of Illinois Press, 1987.

Benedict, Jeff. *The Mormon Way of Doing Business: Leadership and Success Through Faith and Family.* New York: Warner Books, 2007.

Bradley, Martha Sonntag. *Kidnapped from That Land.* Salt Lake City: University of Utah Press, 1993.

Brooks, Juanita. *Mountain Meadows Massacre.* Oklahoma City: University of Oklahoma Press, 1991 (first published 1950).

Brody, Fawn. *No Man Knows My History.* New York: Alfred A. Knopf, 1945.

Church History in the Fullness of Times: Student Manual, Salt Lake City: The Church of Jesus Christ of Latter-day Saints, 1989.

Bushman, Claudia. *Mormon Sisters: Women in Early Utah.* Salt Lake City: Olympus Publishing Co., 1976.

Compton, Todd. *In Sacred Loneliness: The Plural Wives of Joseph Smith.* Salt Lake City: Signature Books, 1997.

Derr, Jill Mulvay. *Women's Voices: An Untold History of the Latter-day Saints 1830–1900.* Salt Lake City: Deseret Book Co., 1982.

Derr, Jill Mulvay, Janath Russell Cannon, and Maureen Ursenbach Beecher. *Women of Covenant: The Story of Relief Society.* Salt Lake City: Deseret Book Co., 1992.

Dew, Sheri L. *Go Forward with Faith: The Biography of Gordon B. Hinckley.* Salt Lake City: Deseret Book Co., 1996.

Dew, Sheri. *No Doubt about It.* Salt Lake City: Deseret Book Co., 2006.

Diamant, Anita. *The Red Tent.* New York: Picador, 1998.

Eisler, Riane. *The Chalice and the Blade.* San Francisco: Harper & Row, 1987.

Hanks, Maxine, ed. *Women and Authority.* Salt Lake City: Signature Books, 1992.

Hill, Donna. *Joseph Smith: The First Mormon.* Garden City, NY: Doubleday, 1977.

Hinckley, Gordon B, *Standing for Something: 10 Neglected Virtues That Will Heal our Hearts and Homes.* New York: Three Rivers Press, 2000.

Hinckley, Gordon B. *The Teachings of Gordon B. Hinckley.* Salt Lake City: Deseret Book, 1997.

Johnson, Sonia. *From Housewife to Heretic.* Garden City, NY: Doubleday, 1981.

Kaufman, Debra. *Rachel's Daughters.* New Brunswick, NJ: Rutgers University Press, 1991.

Krakauer, Jon. *Under the Banner of Heaven.* New York: Doubleday, 2003.

Lyon, Tom, and Terry Tempest Williams. *A Great and Peculiar Beauty.* Salt Lake City: Gibbs Smith, Publisher, 1990.

Madsen, Carol Cornwall. *Sisters and Little Saints,* Salt Lake City: Deseret Book Co., 1978.

Nafisi, Azar. *Reading Lolita in Tehran: A Memoir in Books.* New York: Random House, 2003.

Newell, Linda King, and Valeen Tippetts Avery. *Mormon Enigma: Emma Hale Smith.* Garden City, NY: Doubleday, 1984.

Osaka, Chieko. *Lighten Up!* Salt Lake City: Deseret Book Co., 1993.

Osmond, Marie. *Behind the Smile,* New York: Warner Books, 2001.

Pearson, Carol Lynn. *Daughters of Light.* Salt Lake City: Bookcraft, 1973.

Pearson, Carol Lynn. *Good-bye, I Love You.* New York: Random House, 1986.

Pearson, Carol Lynn, and Emily Pearson. *Fuzzy Red Bathrobe.* Salt Lake City: Gibbs Smith, Publisher, 2000.

Perera, Sylvia Brinton. *Descent of the Goddess.* Toronto: Inner City Books, 1981.

Schow, Ron, Wayne Schow, and Marybeth Raynes. *Peculiar People: Mormons and Same-Sex Orientation.* Salt Lake City: Signature Books, 2006.

Snow, Eliza R. *The Life and Labors of Eliza R. Snow.* Heber City, UT: Archive Publishers, 1999; reprint of 1888 edition.

See, Lisa. *Snow Flower and the Secret Fan.* New York: Random House, 2006.

Shipps, Jan. *Mormonism: The Story of a New Religious Tradition.* Urbana: University of Illinois Press, 1987.

Solomon, Dorothy Allred. *In My Father's House,* New York: Franklin-Watts, 1984.

Solomon, Dorothy Allred. *Predators, Prey, and Other Kinfolk,* New York: W. W. Norton, 2003.

Solomon, Dorothy Allred. *Daughter of the Saints,* New York: W. W. Norton, 2004.

Steinem, Gloria. *Revolution from Within,* Boston: Little, Brown, 1992.

Steinem, Gloria. *Moving Beyond Words,* New York: Simon and Schuster, 1994.

The Book of Mormon: Another Testament to Jesus Christ, Salt Lake City: The Church of Jesus Christ of Latter-day Saints, 1981 (first edition in 1830).

The Doctrine and Covenants of The Church of Jesus Christ of Latter-day Saints, Salt Lake City: The Church of Jesus Christ of Latter-day Saints, 1986.

The Holy Bible, King James version

The Pearl of Great Price, Salt Lake City: The Church of Jesus Christ of Latter-day Saints, 1986.

Ulrich, Laurel Thatcher. *A Midwife's Tale: The Life of Martha Ballard, Based on Her Diary, 1785–1812.* New York: Alfred A. Knopf, 1990.

Van Wagoner, Richard. *Mormon Polygamy: A History.* Salt Lake City: Signature Books, 1986.

Wallace, RaNelle and Curtis Taylor, *The Burning Within* Carson City, NV: Gold Leaf Press, 1994.

Wilcox, S. Michael. *Daughters of God: Scriptural Portraits.* Salt Lake City: Deseret Book Co., 1998.

Williams, Terry Tempest. *Refuge: An Unnatural History of Family and Place.* New York: Pantheon Books, 1991.

Williams, Terry Tempest. *Desert Quartet: An Erotic Landscape* New York: Pantheon Books, 1995.

Williams, Terry Tempest. *An Unspoken Hunger,* New York: Pantheon Books, 1994.

Williams, Terry Tempest. *Leap,* New York: Pantheon Books, 2000.

Williams, Terry Tempest. *Red: Patience and Passion in the Desert,* New York: Pantheon Books, 2001.

Williams, Terry Tempest, William B. Smart, and Gibbs M. Smith, eds. *A New Genesis: A Mormon Reader on Land and Community.* Salt Lake City: Gibbs Smith, Publisher, 1998.

Women and Christ: Living the Abundant Life: Talks Selected from the 1992 Women's Conference Sponsored by Brigham Young University and the Relief Society. Salt Lake City: Deseret Book Co., 1993.

Other Reading
and Viewing

"Articles of Faith," *The Pearl of Great Price*. Salt Lake City: The Church of Jesus Christ of Latter-day Saints, 1989, pp. 60–61.

Bushman, Claudia. "The Lives of Mormon Women." FAIR (The Foundation for Apologetic Information and Research) Publications, August 31, 2006, www.fairlds.org.

Church Educational System. *Church History in the Fullness of Times: Student Manual*. Salt Lake City: Church of Jesus Christ of Latter-day Saints, 1989.

"Church Welfare Resources." Salt Lake City: Intellectual Reserve, 2005.

Dionne, Elizabeth. "Latter-day Saints' Feminism Is Much Strong than Many Want to Acknowledge or Believe," *Salt Lake Tribune*, 22 October 2000, AA6.

Degn, Louise. "Mormon Women and Depression," KSL Television, 1979.

Evergreen International, www.evergreeninternational.org/how_many.htm.

"Facts Regarding the LDS Humanitarian Program," www.mormonwiki.com/mormonism/Humanitarian_Efforts.

The Family: A Proclamation to the World. The First Presidency and Council of the Twelve Apostles of The Church of Jesus Christ of Latter-day Saints, September 23, 1995.

The Latter-day Saint Woman, Part A and Part B. Intellectual Reserve, Church of Jesus Christ of Latter-day Saints, 1979, revised 2000.

LDS Church Distribution Services. Various educational videos and literature about the Gospel of Jesus Christ.

LDS Family Services, Provident Living, "It's About Love," www.providentliving.org.

Lindsay, Jeff. "Mormon Answers: Love, Dating and Marriage and Morality: The Latter-day Saint Way," www.jefflinsay.com/LDSFAQ/love.shtml.

Marriage and Family Relations. Salt Lake City: Church of Jesus Christ of Latter-day Saints, 2000.

"Mormon Women and Ritual Healing: A Gift of the Spirit That Might Be Restored." *Exponent II*, July 26, 2006, http://exponentblog.blogspot.com/2006/07/mormon-women-and-ritual-healing-gift.html.

Pearson, Carol Lynn. "Mother Wove the Morning" (a monologue of 16 women from Scripture on DVD and video), www.clpearson.com.

Pearson, Carol Lynn. "News and Views" www.nomoregoodbyes.com

Ponder, Kent. "Mormon Women, Prozac, and Therapy," 2003, http://home.teleport.com/-packham/prozac.htm

Radke, Andrea G. "The Place of Mormon Women: Perceptions, Prozac, Polygamy, Priesthood, Patriarchy, and Peace." FAIR Publications, www.fairlds.org/FAIRConferences/2004_Place_of_Mormon_Women.html.

"Sampling of Latter-day Saint/Utah Demographics and Social Statistics from National Sources," www.adherents.com/largecom/lds_dem.html.

"Ten Ways to Improve Family Communication." Church of Jesus Christ of Latter-day Saints, 1996.

The Church of Jesus Christ of Lattery-day Saints website. www. LDS.org

"The Testaments" www.LDS.org Distribution Services, 2005 Intellectual Reserve, Inc.

Utah Child and Family Services (DCFS). www.hsdcfs.utah.gov/statistics.htm/www.providentliving.orgsesbirthmother/wecanhelp/0,12266,2181.

Notes

Chapter I

1. Emily Woodmansee, printed in *Women's Exponent* and cited in Janice Kapp Perry, *Songs from My Heart* (Salt Lake City: Sounds of Zion, 2000) pp.77–78.
2. "Brigham Young: Letters to His Sons" cited in Jill Mulvay Derr, Janath Russell Cannon, and Maureen Ursenbach Beecher, *Women of Covenant: The Story of Relief Society* (Salt Lake City: Deseret Book,1992) Pay specific attention to endnote 94 on p. 113. Many claim that the first legal votes were cast in Wyoming territory in September of 1870, questioning the legality of all things Mormon during this time of legislation and prosecution aimed at polygamy.
3. Relief Society Minutes, March 24, 1842, Archives of the Church of Jesus Christ of Latter-day Saints, 18–19, cited in Kathleen Hughes, "That We May All Sit Down in Heaven Together" General Relief Society Meeting, LDS Church Conference, October, 2005.
4. For extensive treatment of this theme, read Jolene Edmunds Rockwood, "The Redemption of Eve," in *Sisters in Spirit*, ed. Maureen Ursenbach Beecher and Lavina Fielding Anderson (Urbana: University of Illinois Press, 1987).
5. Wallace Stegner, "At Home in the Fields of the Lord," *The Sound of Mountain Water,* Doubleday and Company, 1969. Included in *Great and Peculiar Beauty,* ed. Thomas Lyons and Terry Tempest Williams (Salt Lake City: Gibbs Smith 1995) p. 236.
6. Sam Walter Foss, "The Coming American" in Hazel Fentleman, *The Best Loved Poems of the American People,* Garden City, NY: Garden City Books, 1936, pp. 107–108.
7. Wallace Stegner.
8. President Lorenzo Snow, *Millennial Star,* vol. 54 (Liverpool, England: Thomas Ward,): 404.
9. "Sampling of Latter-day Saint/Utah Demographics and Social Statistics from National Sources" www.adherents.com/largecom/lds_dem.html, accessed 11 November 2006.
10. This statement, which I heard from early childhood seems to have been drawn from Doctrine and Covenants 100:16: "For I will raise unto myself a pure people that will serve me in righteousness."
11. "Fifteenth Ward Relief Society Minutes" February 19, 1870, cited in Derr, Cannon and Beecher, *Women of Covenant,* p. 112.
12. Eliza R. Snow, "O My Father" *Hymns of the Church of Jesus Christ of Latter-day Saints* (Salt Lake City, the Church of Jesus Christ of Latter-day Saints, 1948) p. 134.
13. Laura Vance, "Evolution of Ideals for Women in Mormon Periodicals, 1897–1999," *Sociology of Religion* (Spring 2002) at http://findarticles.com/p/articles/mi_moSOR/is_1_63/ai_84396060.
14. Oscar W. McConkie, *She Shall be Called Woman* (Salt Lake City, Bookcraft, 1979) p.124, cited in "Gifts of the Spirit" by Linda King Newell, in *Sisters in Spirit,* ed. Beecher and Anderson.

Chapter 2

1. "Fall: Benefits of the Fall," LDS.org—Topic Definition, www. lds.org/portal/site/LDSorg/ menvitem.3933737
2. Todd Compton, *In Sacred Loneliness: The Plural Wives of Joseph Smith* (Salt Lake City, Signature Books, 2001) p. 27.
3. Ibid. pp. 32-35; p. 6.
4. Ibid. pp. 312, 313.
5. Ibid. pp. 314, 315. Despite rumors and reports, Eliza, who kept a journal and penned an autobiography, only mentions her move from the Smith residence, and writes nothing about an altercation with Emma. Biographers of Emma Hale Smith, Valeen Tippets Avery and Linda King Newell indicate that Eliza would not have been permitted to act as governess to the Smith children if she had been "great with child."
6. Ibid. pp. 78–86.
7. Brigham Young, "Plurality of Wives: Remarks Made in the Bowery," Provo, Utah, July 14, 1855, *Journal of Discourses* 3:264, at http://www.mormonpolygamy.org/brigham_young_1855.html.
8. Richard Van Wagoner, *Mormon Polygamy: A History* (Salt Lake City, Signature Books, 1986) p. 89.
9. Jill Mulvay Derr, Janath Russell Cannon, and Maureen Ursenbach Beecher, *Women of Covenant: The Story of Relief Society* (Salt Lake City, Deseret Book Company, 1992) pp.110,111.
10. Ibid., pp.111, 112.
11. John Kincaid, "Smashing the Twin Relics of Barbarism—Slavery and Barbarism: Rejecting Territorial Multiculturalism in American Federalism" *Comparative Federalism Newsletter,* 2002, vol. 17 (2).
12. T.B.H. Stenhouse, *Rocky Mountain Saints,* cited in Samuel W. Taylor, *The Kingdom or Nothing* (New York, MacMillan, 1976).
13. Mary Batchelor, Marianne Watson, Anne Wilde, editors, *Voices in Harmony* (Salt Lake City, Principle Voices, 2000) p.205
14. *The Pearl of Great Price,* p. 60
15. Derr, Cannon, and Beecher, *Women of Covenant, p. 112*
16. Rianne Eisler, *The Chalice and the Blade: Our History, Our Future* (San Francisco, Harper and Row, 1987) pp.120–134.
17. *Autobiography of Parley P. Pratt,* (Salt Lake City, Russell Brothers, 1874) p. 52.
18. President Spencer W. Kimball, *The Teachings of Spencer W. Kimball* (Salt Lake City, Bookcraft, 1982) p. 311.
19. Peter Gardella, *Innocent Ecstasy: How Christianity Gave America an Ethic of Sexual Pleasure* (New York, Oxford University Press, 1985).

Chapter 3

1. "Let the Little Children Come" words by Emily Hill Woodmansee, in *The Children Sing* (Salt Lake City: Deseret Book, 1951) p.184
2. The First Presidency and Council of the Twelve Apostles of the Church of Jesus Christ of Latter-day Saints *The Family: A Proclamation to the World,* September 23, 1995.
3. From "Autumn Day" by A. B. Ponsonby, in *The Children Sing* (Salt Lake City: Deseret Book, 1951) p.179
4. From "Pioneer Children," Elizabeth Fetzer Bates, *The Children's Songbook,* (Salt Lake City: The Church of Jesus Christ of Latter-day Saints, 1989) p. 214
5. Quoted in Julie A. Dockstader, "Limitless Is Your Potential, Magnificent Is Your Future." *Church News,* March 31, 2001.

6. "For the Strength of the Youth," Salt Lake City: Intellectual Reserve, 1995.

7. *Teachings of the Prophet Joseph Smith,* selected by Joseph Fielding Smith (Salt Lake City: The Church of Jesus Christ of Latter-day Saints, 1976).

8. Dorothy Allred Solomon, "Suffer the Little Children" *Utah Holiday Magazine,* April, 1979.

9. Jane Chen, "Writer Rose Beecham Goes Undercover in a Polygamous Cult," September 13, 2006, p. 3 http://www.afterellen.com/Print/2006/9beecham.html,.

10. "The Articles of Faith," *The Pearl Of Great Price,* (Salt Lake City: The Church of Jesus Christ of Latter-day Saints) p. 60.

11. Jill Mulvay Derr, Janath Russell Cannon, and Marueen Ursenbach Beecher, *Women of Covenant: The Story of Relief Society* (Salt Lake City: Deseret Book Company, 1992) pp 107, 149.

12. Gordon B. Hinckley, "Cornerstones of a Happy Home" (pamphlet, Salt Lake City: The Church of Jesus Christ of Latter-day Saints, 1984).

13. "Statement Issued on Abortion," *Church News,* January 19, 1991, p. 5.

14. Angela Lafranchi, M.D., F.A.C.S., "Coalition on Abortion and Breast Cancer," www.abortionbreastcancer.com.

15. *Statistical Abstract of the United States: 1997: National Data Book* (Washington, D.C.: Census Bureau, U.S Department of Commerce, 1997).

16. Provident Living, LDS Family Services.

17. "The Articles of Faith," *The Pearl of Great Price,* p. 60.

18. Derr, Cannon, and Beecher, *Women of Covenant,* p.121.

19. Derr, Cannon, and Beecher, *Women of Covenant,* p. 167.

20. Derr, Cannon, and Beecher, *Women of Covenant,* pp. 227–232.

21. Naomi Randall, "I Am a Child of God," *Hymns of the Church of Jesus Christ of Latter Day Saints,* (Salt Lake City: The Church of Jesus Christ of Latter Day Saints, 1985), p. 301.

22. Rabbi Harold Kushner, "The Human Soul's Quest for God," *BYU Magazine,* February, 1995, issue 22, p.29.

Chapter 4

1. President Gordon B. Hinckley, "The Women in Our Lives," *Ensign* (November 2004) p. 83.

2. LDS Church Conference, October 2001, www.lds.org/conference/display.

3. Gordon B. Hinckley, *Teachings of Gordon B. Hinckley* (Salt Lake City: Deseret Book, 1997) p.8.

4. President Gordon B. Hinckley, LDS General Conference Talk, (October, 1998.) www.lds.org/conference/display.

5. President Gordon B. Hinckley, "What Are People Asking About Us?" *Ensign* (Nov. 1998) p. 71.

6. Carol Lynn Pearson, *Good-bye, I Love You* (New York: Random House, 1986).

7. Andrea Radke, *The Place of Mormon Women: Perceptions, Prozac, Polygamy, Priesthood, Patriarchy, and Peace* (Redding, California, FAIR Publications, 2004) p. 20

Chapter 5

1. The First Presidency and Council of the Twelve Apostles of The Church of Jesus Christ of Latter-day Saints, *The Family: A Proclamation to the World,* September 23, 1995.

2. Ibid.

3. "Love at Home" by John Hugh McNaughton, *Hymns: The Church of Jesus Christ of Latter-day Saints,* (Salt Lake City: The Deseret News Press, 1948) p. 383.

4. LDS Conference Report, 1942; found in "The Message of the First Presidency to the Church" *Improvement Era,* Nov. 1942, 761.
5. Boyd K. Packer, LDS General Conference Report, 1993.
6. Lee Davidson, "Utah's Birthrate Is Highest in the Nation: But Out-of-Wedlock Birthrate Is Lowest" April 18, 2001, citing data from the National Center for Health Statistics in *Sampling of Latter-day Saint/Utah Demographics and Social Statistics from National Sources* at , accessed November 28, 2006.

Chapter 6
1. S. Michael Wilcox, *Daughters of God: Scriptural Portraits* (Salt Lake City: Deseret Book Company, 1998), pp. 273–289.
2. Jill Mulvay Derr, Janath Russell Cannon, and Maureen Ursenbach Beecher, *Women of Covenant: The Story of Relief Society* (Salt Lake City: Deseret Book Company, 1992), p 28.
3. From *The New York Herald,* cited in ibid., p. 111.
4. "Fifteenth Ward Relief Society Minutes, February 19, 1870, cited in ibid., p. 112.
5. "The Woman Suffrage Bill," *Deseret News,* February 12, 1870.
6. Brigham Young to Heber Young, February 16, 1870, cited in Derr, Cannon and Beecher, *Women of Covenant,* p. 113.
7. Ibid., pp 137,138. Although no clear statement is made here regarding the reasons for the Relief Society's relinquishment of membership in national and international women's groups, the increasingly conservative trends of the LDS Church and the increasingly liberal trends of most women's organizations have made it difficult for Relief Society leaders to find common ground with their counterparts in the world.
8. From *Emily Dow Partridge Young,* p. 48, cited in Donna Hill, *Joseph Smith: The First Mormon* (Garden City, N.Y.: Doubleday, 1977), p. 357.
9. Derr, Cannon and Beecher, *Women of Covenant,* p. 112.
10. Ibid., p.148.
11. Ibid., p.179.
12. Relief Society General Board Minutes, April 2, 1921, cited in ibid., p. 222, 223.
13. The influential *Dialogue: A Journal of Mormon Thought* published the "pink issue" (vol.6, in the summer of 1971.) Its tenth anniversary edition in 1976 was dedicated entirely issue to women, and women were among the primary contributors. Again, in 1990, *Dialogue* published another issues dedicated to women. Vicky Burgess Olson who wrote *Sister Saints* and Claudia Bushman, author of *Mormon Sisters* opened doors to a little-known past, exploring the relationships and quotidian lives of women in the early Church. A Boston Relief Society published *Exponent II* which was clearly an attempt to revive the powerful chorus of women's voices and experiences called up in the original *Woman's Exponent.* Given Utah's history and the part Mormon women had played in gaining suffrage, these publications and dialogues were every bit as important to modern LDS women as their corollaries had been to their forebears. See Jill Mulvay Derr "Strength in Our Union" in *Sister Saints: Mormon Women in Historical and Cultural Perspective,* pp.194,195.
14. Sonia Johnson, *From Housewife to Heretic,* (Garden City, N.Y.: Doubleday, 1981).
15. Maureen Ursenbach Beecher and Lavina Fielding Anderson, editors, *Sisters in Spirit: Mormon Women in Historical and Cultural Perspective,* (Urbana and Chicago: University of Illinois press, 1987).
16. Merlin B. Brinkerhoff and Marlene MacKie. "Religion and Gender: A Comparison of Canadian and American Student Attitudes." *Journal of Marriage and the Family,* 47 (1985): 415–29, cited in "A Sampling of Latter-day Saint/Utah Demographics and Social Statistics from National Sources," http.adherents.com/largecom/lds_dem.html

17. "A Sampling of Latter-day Saint/Utah Demographics and Social Statistics from National Sources."

18. *Woman's Exponent* 14, (June 15, 1885) cited in Derr, Mulvay, and Beecher, *Women of Covenant*, p. 99.

19. Fifteenth Ward Relief Society Minutes 1868–1873, November 12, 1868, cited in Derr, Mulvay, and Beecher, *Women of Covenant,* p. 99.

20. Sheri L. Dew "Are We All Not Mothers?" LDS Conference Talks, Oct. 2001. http://www.lds.org/conference/talk/display/0,5232,49-1-225-37,00.html.

21. Sharlene Hawkes www.ldsmusicworld.com/artists/sharlene_hawkes.html.

22. A Sampling of Latter-day Saint/Utah Demographics and Social Statistics from National Sources.

23. H. David Burton, Presiding Bishop of the Church, cited in "Humanitarian Efforts" http://www.mormonwiki.com/mormonism/Humanitarian_Efforts.

24. This snippet from the LDS Humanitarian Program Web site describes the worldwide difference made by the LDS Church: "The Church has sent relief to victims of over 150 disasters since 1986 alone. Aid is provided regardless of any consideration, including religion, ethnicity, and nationality, and is valued in the tens of millions of dollars annually. In the last 20 years, 200 million pounds of food, clothing, and medicine were donated in 147 countries, almost all to members of other faiths. Aid is often made to countries where Mormon missionaries are banned by law."

25. "A Sampling of Latter-day Saint/Utah Demographics and Social Statistics from National Sources."

26. Ibid.

27. Terry Tempest Williams, William B. Smart, and Gibbs Smith, eds., *A New Genesis: A Mormon Reader on Land and Community,* (Salt Lake City: Gibbs-Smith Publisher, 1998).

28. Terry Tempest Williams, *Refuge: An Unnatural History of Family and Place,* (New York: Pantheon Books, 1991), pp. 3, 285–286.

29. Terry Tempest Williams works include: *Pieces of White Shell: A Journey to Navajoland* (New York: Charles Scribner's Sons, 1984); *Coyote's Canyon* (Salt Lake City: Gibbs M Smith, 1989); *Desert Quartet: An Erotic Landscape* (New York: Pantheon Books, 1995); *An Unspoken Hunger* (New York: Pantheon Books, 1994); *Leap* (New York: Pantheon Books, 2000); and *Red: Patience and Passion in the Desert* (New York: Pantheon Books, 2001). She also has written two books for children: *The Secret Language of Snow* (New York: Sierra Club/Pantheon, 1984) and *Between Cattails* (Boston: Little Brown, 1985).

Chapter 7

1. Azar Nafisi, *Reading Lolita in Tehran* (New York: Random House, 2003), p. 33.

2. Center for Disease Control, 1998, and Center for Education Reform, "Report Card for Education, 1996, "Sampling of Latter-day Saint/Utah Demographics and Social Statistics from National Sources," pp. 5, 7.

3. Brigham Young, *Journal of Discourses,* 13(July 18, 1869): 61.

4. Julie A. Dockstader, "Limitless Is Your Potential, Magnificent Is Your Future," *Church News,* March 31, 2001.

5. Eliza R. Snow address, "Great Indignation Meeting," *Deseret News Weekly,* January 19, 1870.

6. Valerie Hudson Cassler and Alma Don Sorenson, "Women in Eternity, Women of Zion" (Springville, UT: CFI, 2004), x., cited in Andrea Radke, Ph.D., "The Place of Mormon Women: Perceptions, Prozac, Polygamy, Priesthood, Patriarchy, and Peace." (Redding, CA: FAIR Publications, 2004), p.4.

7. Claudia Bushman, "The Lives of Mormon Women" (Redding, CA: FAIR Publications, 2004), p.2.
8. Jill Mulvay Derr, Janath Russell Cannon, and Maureen Ursenbach Beecher, *Women of Covenant: The Story of Relief Society* (Salt Lake City, Deseret Books, 1992), p. 185.
9. Linda King Newell and Valeen Tippets Avery, *Mormon Enigma: Emma Hale Smith Prophet's Wife, "Elect Lady," Polygamy's Foe* (Garden City, NY: Doubleday, 1984), p. 47.
10. This list is available on the Web site: Voices of Former Mormons.
11. Marie Osmond, *Behind the Smile,*(New York, Warner Books, 2001).
12. "Teen Heroin Use Grows in Utah" KUTV, The Associated Press, July 5, 2005.
13. Kent Ponder, Ph.D. "Mormon Women, Prozac and Therapy" 2003; http://home.tele-port.com/-packham/prozac.htm.
14. "Expert: Mormon Women Less Depressed," USA Today, April 2. 2004. http://www.usato-day.com/news/health accessed December 21,2006.
15. "Sampling of Latter-day Saint/Utah Demographics and Social Statistics from National Sources" p. 2. www.adherents.com/largecom/lds_dem.html. accessed November 28, 2006.
16. Ashley E. Broughton, "Statistics Show Utah is 3rd-Best for Kids," *Salt Lake Tribune*, May 23, 2002. Ibid., p. 2.
17. Radke, "Place of Mormon Women," p. 2
18. Federal Bureau of Investigation, "FBI Ten Most Wanted Fugitives: Unlawful Flight to Avoid Prosecution—Sexual Conduct with a minor, Conspiracy to Commit Sexual Conduct with a minor; rape as an Accomplice." www.fbi.gov.wantedtopten/fugitives/jeff-ws.htm accessed May 16, 2006. "Children Fleeing: States Brace for Trouble in Polygamist Communities" *Arizona Daily Sun,* January 19, 2004. Law Center, "Fugitive Polygamist Sect Leader Caught Near Las Vegas" *CNN.com,* 2006.
19. Gloria Steinem, *Moving Beyond Words* (New York: Simon and Schuster, 1994.)
20. Bushman, "The Lives of Mormon Women," p.4.
21. Maxine Hanks and Courtney Black, "Mormon Women Must Be Heard," *Boston Globe,* October 7, 2000.
22. "Perspective on Mormon Women: A Struggle to Reclaim Authority" *Los Angeles Times,* July 10, 1994.
23. Elizabeth Dionne, "Latter-day Saints' Feminism is Much Stronger Than Many Want to Acknowledge or Believe," *Salt Lake Tribune,* October 22. 2000, AA6, cited in Radke, "The Place of Mormon Women," p. 5.
24. William Fowler, "We Thank Thee, O God, for a Prophet" *Hymns of The Church of Jesus Christ of Latter-day Saints,* (Salt Lake City: The Church of Jesus Christ of Latter-day Saints, 1985), p. 19.
25. Linda Hoffman Kimball, "Being a Mormon Woman or 'Am I Not a Woman and a Sister?' . . .Isn't That Enough?" *Dialogue: A Journal of Mormon Thought* 36 (Fall 2003): p.215.
26. Radke, "The Place of Mormon Women."
27. Elizabeth Dionne, "Latter-day Saints' Feminism is much Strong than Many Want to Acknowledge or Believe," *Salt Lake Tribune,* October 22, 2000.
28. Radke, "The Place of Mormon Women," p.3.
29. "Massacre Novelist May Face LDS Excommunication" Patty Henetz, Associated Press, May 23, 2003.
30. Riane Eisler, *The Chalice and the Blade,* (San Francisco, Harper and Row, 1987) p. 28.

Chapter 8

1. Carol Lynn Pearson, 'Motherless House' in "Healing the Motherless House" *Women and Authority,* ed. Maxine Hanks (Salt Lake City: Signature Books, 1992), p. 2.

2. Carol Lynn Pearson, "Healing the Motherless House" *Women and Authority,* ed. Maxine Hanks (Salt Lake City: Signature Books, 1992), p.4.

3. *Eliza R. Snow: An Immortal* (Salt Lake City: Nicholas G. Morgan, Sr., Foundation, 1957) cited in Carol Lynn Pearson, *Daughters of Light,* (Salt Lake City: Bookcraft, 1973), p. 35.

4. Patty Sessions Diary, typescript, pp. 27–33, in Church Archives, cited in ibid., p. 71.

5. "Sketch of the Labors of Sister Lucy B. Young in the Temples," *Young Woman's Journal,* 4 (April 1893): 299.

6. Andrew Jenson, *Latter-day Saint Biographical Encyclopedia,* 4 vols. (Salt Lake City, Andrew Jenson History Company, 1901), vol.1, p. 695.

7. Mary Bachelor, Anne Wilde, and Mary Ann Thompson, "Best of Friends," *Voices in Harmony* (Salt Lake City: Principle Voices, 2000), p. 101.

8. RaNelle Wallace and Curtis Taylor, *The Burning Within* (Carson City, NV: Gold Leaf Press, 1994).

9. "RaNelle Wallace Near-Death Experience," www.neardeath.com/Wallace.html.

10. Linda Sillitoe, "Song of Creation," in *Dialogue: A Journal of Mormon Thought,* vol. 12 (Winter 1979): 95, cited in Maureen Lisenbach Beecher and Lavina Fielding Anderson, editors, *Sisters in Spirit* (Urbana: University of Illinois Press, 1987), p. 73.

Index

Abravenal Hall, 157
Adam, 4, 41, 43, 70, 144, 216
Age of Accountability, 70, 167
Alger, Fannie, 31
Allred, Benjamin, 75
Anthony, Susan B., 2, 129, 132
"As Sisters in Zion," 1
Avard, Sampson, 41

Benson, Ezra Taft, 148
Big Love, 11
Black, Courtney, 180
Blood Atonement, 13, 41–42
Book of Mormon, 6, 7, 40, 48, 61, 88, 143, 196
Boy Scouts, 57
Bradley, Shawn, 80
Brigham Young University, 73, 139, 173
Brooks, Juanita, 200
Bushman, Claudia
    "Mormon Sisters: Women in Early Utah"
        and, 169, 179

Capitol Theatre, 157
Cannon, Agnus, 64
Cannon, George Q., 143
Cannon, Martha Hughes, 64
Celestial marriage, 17, 18, 19, 29, 34, 35, 43
Chalice and the Blade: Our History, Our Future, The, 190
Civil Rights Act, 166
Cleveland, Sarah, 128
Coray, Martha Jane, 40, 139
Correlation Committee of 1913, 140
Columbine High School, 150–151
Cullom Bill, 33

Deseret Industries, 148

Dew, Sheri
    children's literacy and, 149
    Deseret Book and, 148
    Sharlene Wells and, 148
Dionne, Elizabeth, 181, 183
Doctrine and Covenants, 6, 61,
Draper, Ruth, 156

Edmunds-Tucker Act of 1887, 132
Education, 3, 25–28, 37, 45, 59, 69, 83, 105, 117,
    119, 124–129, 133, 135, 136, 138–143, 145,
    148–151, 156, 158, 160, 164, 175, 177, 187
Education Week, 139
Eisler, Riane, 190
Ensign, The, 116, 152
Environmentalism, 57, 77, 158, 212–213
Equal Rights Amendment, (ERA) 14, 44, 116,
    138, 166
Eve, 2, 4, 12, 15, 21, 40–41, 43, 49, 88, 133, 138,
    144, 148, 164, 216

Father in Heaven, 9, 33, 52, 72, 81, 85, 119, 195
"Family: A Proclamation to the World, The,"
    25, 53, 54, 98
Family Home Evening, 51, 53, 72, 101, 103,
    115–117, 126
Felt, Louise B., 72
Fley, Carol Gerber Allred, 149
For the Strength of the Youth, 60
Freeman, Judith, 188
Friedan, Betty, 134
Fundamentalism, 66
Fundamentalist
    accountability and, 155
    attitude toward abortion and, 68
    birth control and, 66
    birth defects and, 71
    chastity and, 87

child abuse and, 62–63
education and, 142
elite attitudes and, 176
embarrassment and, 93
escaping the community, 177
exploitative leaders and, 84, 144, 153
FLDS, 94
hospitals and, 71
marriage, 39–41
Old Testament law and, 62
underage marriage and, 176
underground, 35
unmet needs and, 154
washing and anointing in, 184

Gifts
    and talents, 52, 56, 78, 80, 139, 148, 157,
        200
    of the spirit, 179, 196, 197, 201, 207,
    of healing, 26, 86, 107, 165, 168, 180, 181,
        184, 186, 196, 197, 197, 199, 209–210,
        214,
    of prophecy, to prophesy, 197, 207, 216
    of speaking in tongues, 197
Grant, Heber J., 133, 197
Great Depression, 134, 147
Great Indignation Meeting, 165

Hancock, Levi, 31
Hanks, Maxine, 180
Hardy, Layla, 109, 116, 189
Hardy, Todd, 76
Hawkes, Sharlene Wells, 148–149
Hinckley, Gordon B., 88, 99, 180 – 181
    comments on birth control, 66
    comments on homosexuality, 91 – 92
    comments on polygamy, 35
    comments on priesthood authority, 82
    comments on women's historical roles, 82
    leadership of LDS church and, 90
    Mountain Meadow Massacre and, 188
    Sheri Dew and, 148
    "The Family: A Proclamation to the
        World" and, 25, 98
    War in Afghanistan and, 90
    women's value and, 59, 82, 165
    9/11 and, 90
Holy Bible, 6, 61, 88, 101, 190,195
Horne, Alice Merrill, 156

Hurricane Katrina, 151
Hurricane Mitch, 151

"I Am a Child of God," 73
International Council of Women, 129

Jacobs, Henry, 32–33
James, Henry
    The Portrait of a Lady and, 168
Jeffs, Warren, 93–94, 176–177
Jesus,
    accountability and, 167
    alignment with, 119
    Apostle of, 197
    Atonement of, 8, 10, 41
    belief in, 10, 182
    "be ye therefore perfect," 5
    by the power of, 79
    children and, 52, 108, 111, 114
    conception and birth of, 138
    democracy and, 164, 178
    dilemmas and, 184, 186, 187, 190
    disciples of, 93
    divine center, 53
    example of, 118,166
    eyes of, 80
    footsteps of, 87,
    Gospel of, 5, 8–10, 64, 86, 89
    head of His Church, 6, 9, 98, 166
    healer and protector, 69, 187
    kingdom of Heaven on earth, 191
    last dispensation and, 136
    martyrs and, 93
    minister and witness for, 58, 80
    portraits of, 99
    Restored Church/ Gospel of, 1, 5, 130, 164,
        167
    sealing power and, 119
    Son of God, Messiah, and Savior of the
        World, 6
    Trinity and, 9
    women and, 43, 44, 96, 141, 161, 166, 190,
        212
Johnson, Lyman, 31
Johnson, Sonia, 137
    From Housewife to Heretic and, 138
    Mormons for ERA Campaign and, 138,
        166
Joseph, Alex, 177

Kapaloski, Gayle, 201
Kimball, Heber C., 13
Kimball, Linda Hoffman, 182
Kimball, Presendia, 13, 33, 43
Kimball, Sarah
    women's equality and, 33
    ZCMI and, 144
King, Larry, 35
Kirby, Robert, 16
Knight, Gladys, 151
Kushner, Rabbi Harold, 73

Laying on of hands, 85, 165, 184
Lion House, 23
Lincoln, Abraham, 34
LDS Hospital, 72
LDS Humanitarian programs, 149, 151–153
LDS Social Services, 103, 109
    adoption services and, 153
    Belle Spafford and, 152
Lee, John D., 188, 200
"Let the Little Children Come," 52
"Love at Home," 99

Magdalene, Mary, 43–44
Manifesto of 1890, 7, 34, 129, 131–132
Mann, S.A., 43, 129, 185
McConkie, Oscar, 15
McGee, Roz, 155
Mexico, 7, 85
Midwives, 65, 71, 139, 184, 186, 187, 197
Missionary Work 7, 55, 58, 73–74, 76, 88, 89,
    199
    Humanitarian, 126, 153
    length of, 73
    proselytizing, 89, 134
    purpose of, 73
    rules, 18, 46, 56, 58, 127
    women's responses to, 88–90
Mitchell, Brian David, 121
Mormon logic, 175
Moroni, 6, 18
Morrison, Toni, *Beloved* and, 208
Mother in Heaven, 9, 33, 81, 85, 166, 195, 217
Motherless House, 193–194
Mountain Meadows massacre, 188, 200

Nafisi, Azar, 163
    Reading Lolita in Tehran and, 14

National Council of Women, 129, 133
National Women Suffrage Association
    (NWSA), 59, 129
New Era, The, 116
Nineteenth Amendment, 71, 132, 133

"O My Father," 14
Organization of The Church of Jesus Christ
    of Latter-day Saints, 6–10
Osmond, Marie, 99
    Behind the Smile and, 173
    maximizing potential and, 157

Partridge, Emily, 31, 131
Partridge, Eliza, 31
Pearl of Great Price: Revelations,
    Translations, and Narrations of
    Joseph Smith, 6, 61, 162, 216
Pearson, Carol Lynn, 81
    Goodbye, I Love You and, 93
    homosexuality and, 93
    Mother Wove the Morning, 195
    Motherless House and, 193–194
Pecking order, 111
Penrose, Romania, B. Pratt, 64
Perpetual Education Fund, 151
Personal revelation, 2, 6, 16, 21, 29, 53, 77, 107,
    171
Perry, Janice Kapp, 157
Pioneer day, 46, 56–57, 131
Pratt, Parley P., 47
    martyrdom of, 92
    persecution and, 92
Priesthood, 95–96
    appropriate use of, 76, 81–84
    authority, 22, 75, 82
    blessings and, 26, 75, 107
    child abuse and, 63, 83
    compared to motherhood, 148
    direction from, 81, 165
    eliminating excessive behaviors and,
        177–178
    honoring, 75, 82–83
    gratitude for, 29, 79
    homosexuality and, 92, 93
    home teachers and, 83, 109
    incest and, 63
    influence of, 169
    laying on of hands and, 85, 207

order and, 21
power of, 26,75, 79, 81
recourse of, 42, 82, 206
Relief Society and, 128, 133, 139–144, 147,
    152, 169
righteous exercise of, 170
responsibilities, 47, 55–56, 75–76,
restoration of, 2, 164
structure of, 58, 83
women and, 9, 96, 100, 134, 166, 168, 179,
    181–182, 184, 209
worthy males and, 44, 118, 137
Primary program, 9, 30, 54–57, 76
Primary Children's Hospital, 72
Principle of Plural Marriage, the,
    abolished, 3, 7, 34, 37, 120, 129, 164, 211
    banned, 13
    Rulon C. Allred and, 86–87, 120, 136, 142
    Brigham Young encourages, 33
    first wives and, 38–39, 131
    hidden, 12
    Warren Jeffs and, 94
    women's rights and, 130–131

Radke, Andrea G. Ph.D., 176, 182
Reed, Clarissa, 31
Reese, Laurie Solomon, 68, 115, 162, 185–186
Relief Society, 67, 71, 145
    and other ladies' societies, 128, 156
    compassionate service, 124
    contemporary leaders, 139
    cooperative efforts with, 72
    commerce and, 144,
    dress, 169
    education and, 140–141
    Employment Bureau, 146
    Family: A Proclamation to the World and,
        25
    financial governing, 81, 147
    Great Depression, 72
    Great Indignation Meeting and, 34, 165
    history of, 2, 127–129
    humanitarian efforts, 152,
    Incorporation of, 145
    leaders set standards for, 169
    lessons, 55, 83, 108, 138–140
    maternal and infant care, 67, 71
    medical education for women and, 64
    Mormon Handicraft, 146
    motto, 128

organization of, 8–9,127–128, 140, 145
partnership with men, 133
priesthood management of, 81, 133
Relief Society Hall, 144
Relief Society Magazine and, 133, 152
response to Cullom Bill, 33, 43
revelation regarding Emma Smith and,
    127
schools and, 139
Social Services Department, 145
socials, 146
suffrage and, 2, 13, 59, 129
tithing and, 147
visiting teachers and, 26, 109, 215
wheat and flour and, 145
women of covenant, 128
Woman's Exponent and, 13, 128
women's organizations, 132
Work and Business Department and,
    145–146
Workdays, 146
Revelation, 44, 100, 106, 133, 198, 199
    defined, 198
    father for his family, 107
    Manifesto of 1890 and, 35
    mother for her children, 107
    of 1978, that worthy males may hold the
        priesthood, 118, 137
    regarding Emma Smith as 'an elect lady,'
        127
    regarding Emma Smith and polygamy, 37
    the Word of Wisdom, 169
Rich, Charles, 32
Richards, Lula Green, 128
Roberts, B.H., 132
Roberts, Margaret Shipp, 64
Romney, Mitt, 99

Salt Lake Arts Center, 157
Salt Lake City, 5, 18, 36, 213
Salt Lake Tribune, 16
Sanchez, Denise, 116, 119–120, 199–200
Sessions, Patty, 197
Shipp, Ellis Reynolds, 3, 64, 139
Sillitoe, Linda, 216–217
Smart, Bill, 158
Smart, Ed, 121
Smart, Elizabeth, 121, 155, 175–176
Smart, Lois, 121
Smith, Bathsheba, 13, 33, 129, 132, 156

Smith, Emma Hale
  Eliza R. Snow and, 32
  Polygamy and, 7, 12, 31–32, 37, 39
  Relief Society and, 127–128
  Word of Wisdom and, 157, 169
Smith, Gibbs, 158
Smith, Hyrum
  martyrdom of, 92, 133
  persecution and, 92
Smith, Joseph Jr., 3, 14, 32, 62, 81, 133, 164,
    198–199
  martyrdom of, 7, 92
  persecution and, 92
  polygamy and, 7, 12, 13, 31, 34, 87, 131
  Relief Society and, 127–128, 145
  restoration of the Gospel and, 6
  Word of Wisdom and, 113, 169
Smith, Joseph F.
  women's appropriate dress and, 169
  women and, 180
  women's suffrage and, 132
Smith, Lucy Mack, 3
Smith, Sally, 15, 208
Snow, Eliza R., 13, 157–158, 188, 196–197
  infertility and, 32
  Joseph Smith and, 198
  polygamy and, 31–32, 37, 129
  Relief Society and, 64, 127, 129
  women's equality and, 33, 34
  ZCMI and, 144
Song of Creation, 216–217
Solomon, Bruce, 55, 77, 136
Solomon, Jeffrey, 75, 88, 89
Solomon, Jennifer Leavitt, 89
Spafford, Belle
  LDS Social Services and, 152
  Relief Society reform and, 152
Stanton, Elizabeth Cady, 2, 129
Stegner, Wallace, 5
Steinem, Gloria, 134, 179
  Moving Beyond Words and, 178
Structure of The Church of Jesus Christ of
    Latter-day Saints, 8, 9, 21
Sundance Film Festival, 157
Swindle, Liz Lemon, 157

Tanner, Sandra, 215
Taylor, John, 161
Thompson, Rhoda, 154
Tracy, Trudy, 69, 104, 149–150

Ulrich, Laurel Thatcher, 188
  *A Midwife's Tale: The Life of Martha
    Ballard, Based on her Diary, 1785–1812*
    and, 187

University of Michigan Medical School,
    139
University of Utah, 136, 143
United Apostolic Brethren, 84
United Nations Commission on the Status of
    Women, 68, 162
United Order, 4, 84, 143–144, 154, 164, 167,
    196
Utah Arts Council, 156
Utah Arts Festival, 157
Utah Children, 154–155
Utah/Arizona Safety Net Committee, 155

Wallace, RaNelle, 214
Wells Emmeline B.
  Eve's redemption and, 133
  gifts of the spirit and, 197
  released from presidency, 133
  suffrage meetings and, 13
  Woman's Exponent editor, 128
  women's equality and, 128, 132, 133
Whitney, Elizabeth Ann, 128
Williams, Clarissa, 71
Williams, Kathleen, 149–150
Williams, Terry Tempest
  A New Genesis, 158
  Refuge, 158
  *Testimony: Writers Speak On Behalf of
    Utah Wilderness*, 159
  The Open Space of Democracy, 159
Wirebaugh, Dee Dee, 209–210
Woman's Exponent, 13, 128, 133, 139, 140
Women and culture, 155–159
Women and education, 138–143
Women and welfare, 150–155
Women and the workplace, 143–150
Woodmansee, Emily H. 1, 52, 157
Woodruff, Phebe, 13, 129
Woodruff, Sister, 132
Woodruff, Wilfred, 129, 132
Word of Wisdom, the, 6, 51, 76, 112, 113, 157,
    169

Young, Brigham 3, 34, 59, 99, 129, 139, 158
  Lion of the Lord, 23

polygamy and, 7, 33, 131
ZCMI and, 144
women's value and, 165
Young Ladies' Mutual Improvement
    Association (YLMIA), 129
Young Ladies Retrenchment Association,
    59–60
Young, Lucy, 197
Young Men's programs, 9, 27, 57, 58,
Young, Steve, 80
Young women
    education and, 45, 164–165
    gifts and talents and, 59
    missionaries and, 18
    missions and, 55
    nannies and au pairs, 146
    potential and, 59, 165
    prayer and, 59

Young Women's Journal, 133
Young Women's programs, 146, 155,
    Beehives, 58
    Laurels, 58–59
    MIA Maids, 58
    motto, 59, 60
    Personal Progress, 58
    presidency, 8, 9, 215
    summer camp, 58
    values, 59
    women's rights and, 129
Young, Women in Excellence, 59
Young, Zina Diantha Huntington Jacobs
    Smith, 33, 145, 158, 197
    polygamy and, 32

Zion's Cooperative Mercantile Institute
    (ZCMI), 144, 148